The Archaeology of the Cold War

The American Experience in Archaeological Perspective

UNIVERSITY PRESS OF FLORIDA

Florida A&M University, Tallahassee
Florida Atlantic University, Boca Raton
Florida Gulf Coast University, Ft. Myers
Florida International University, Miami
Florida State University, Tallahassee
New College of Florida, Sarasota
University of Central Florida, Orlando
University of Florida, Gainesville
University of North Florida, Jacksonville
University of South Florida, Tampa
University of West Florida, Pensacola

The Archaeology of
THE COLD WAR

TODD A. HANSON

Foreword by Michael S. Nassaney, series editor

University Press of Florida
Gainesville · Tallahassee · Tampa · Boca Raton
Pensacola · Orlando · Miami · Jacksonville · Ft. Myers · Sarasota

Copyright 2016 by Todd A. Hanson
All rights reserved
Published in the United States of America

This book may be available in an electronic edition.

First cloth printing, 2016
First paperback printing, 2019

24 23 22 21 20 19   6 5 4 3 2 1

Library of Congress Cataloging-in-Publication Data

Names: Hanson, Todd A., author. | Nassaney, Michael S., author of foreword.
Title: The archaeology of the Cold War / Todd A. Hanson ; foreword by Michael S. Nassaney.
Other titles: American experience in archaeological perspective.
Description: Gainesville : University Press of Florida, [2016] | Series: The American experience in archaeological perspective | Includes bibliographical references and index.
Identifiers: LCCN 2016004178 | ISBN 9780813062839 (cloth : alk. paper) ISBN 9780813068053 (pbk.)
Subjects: LCSH: Historic sites—Conservation and restoration—United States. | Historic sites—Conservation and restoration—Marshall Islands—Bikini Atoll. | Cold War—History. | Excavations (Archaeology)—United States. | Excavations (Archaeology)—Marshall Islands—Bikini Atoll. | Nuclear weapons—Testing—Case studies. | Archaeology and history—Case studies. | United States—History—1945- | United States—Antiquities. | Bikini Atoll (Marshall Islands)—Antiquities.
Classification: LCC E159 .H257 2016 | DDC 973.9—dc23
LC record available at http://lccn.loc.gov/2016004178

The University Press of Florida is the scholarly publishing agency for the State University System of Florida, comprising Florida A&M University, Florida Atlantic University, Florida Gulf Coast University, Florida International University, Florida State University, New College of Florida, University of Central Florida, University of Florida, University of North Florida, University of South Florida, and University of West Florida.

University Press of Florida
2046 NE Waldo Road
Suite 2100
Gainesville, FL 32609
http://upress.ufl.edu

CONTENTS

List of Illustrations   vii

List of Abbreviations   xi

Foreword   xv

Preface and Acknowledgments   xix

1. Introduction   1

2. In Theory and Practice: Archaeological Frameworks   11

3. Matters of Context: Building a Cold War Landscape   28

4. Archaeologies of the Cold War   68

5. Cold War Archaeology: Study and Stewardship Issues   125

6. Conclusion   143

Notes   155

References Cited   157

Index   173

ILLUSTRATIONS

Figures

1.1. Cold War employment boom at Douglas Aircraft Company, California   3

1.2. The Missile Site Control Building at Stanley R. Mickelsen Safeguard Complex, North Dakota   8

3.1. Entrance to the Main Technical Area of Los Alamos Scientific Laboratory, 1951, New Mexico   31

3.2. Gloveboxes at Rocky Flats Nuclear Weapons Plant, 1975, Colorado   38

3.3. Building 1501, Rocky Mountain Arsenal, Colorado   40

3.4. FPS-24 radar antenna at Eufaula AFS, Alabama   42

3.5. BMEWS radome at Clear AFS, 1971, Alaska   43

3.6. Crews of the 770th Antiaircraft Artillery Battalion fire 120 mm guns, 1957, Washington   46

3.7. Nike guided missiles in launch position, 1954, Virginia   47

3.8. A former capsule storage building in the Loring AFB Weapons Storage Area, 1998, Maine   49

3.9. Pillbox at the former Weapons Storage Area, Loring AFB   49

3.10. "Molehole" of the Readiness Crew Building at Whiteman AFB, mid-1990s, Missouri   52

3.11. An Atlas E ICBM arriving at Fairchild AFB, 1961, Washington State 53

3.12. Cheyenne Mountain command and control center, 1960s, Colorado 58

3.13. Home fallout shelter, 1961, Michigan 59

3.14. The PAR building, SRMSC, North Dakota 62

4.1. Column of water rising from the Baker test, 1946, Operation Crossroads, Bikini Atoll, Marshall Islands 71

4.2. Nuclear weapons test bunker on Enyu Island at Bikini Atoll 73

4.3. Soviet graffiti at El Purio missile site in Cuba 77

4.4. Reinforced concrete arches from the Soviet missile hangar at Santa Cruz de los Pinos, Cuba 78

4.5. Rubble of Soviet missile hangers left behind after Cuban locals extracted steel rebar 80

4.6. Aerial view of the Trestle, early 1980s, New Mexico 82

4.7. View of the Trestle from below, 2011, New Mexico 83

4.8. Close-up of the Trestle's wooden bolt system, 2011, New Mexico 84

4.9. Aerial view of Camp Desert Rock, 1955, Nevada 91

4.10. Officers watch the Teapot MET shot from Frenchman Flat, April 1955, Nevada 94

4.11. British and Canadian VIPs during an atomic test, 1955, Frenchman Flat, Nevada 98

4.12. Shadow Children sculpture at the Nevada Test Site Peace Camp 102

4.13. Antinuclear graffiti on a wall of the Nevada Test Site underpass tunnel 103

4.14. Red Lady sculpture, Nevada Test Site Peace Camp 104

4.15. Project Rover control room, 1959, Nevada Test Site 107

4.16. The R-MAD facility at NRDS, 1996, Nevada Test Site 108

4.17. Phoebus engine and rail transport system, Project Rover, 1967, Nevada Test Site 109

4.18. Aerial photograph of the Jupiter AM-23 missile crash crater, 1960, Cape Canaveral, Florida   119

4.19. The reinforced concrete "beehive" blockhouse at LC-31/32, Cape Canaveral AFS   122

4.20. Laser scanning survey of LC-14, 2014, Cape Canaveral, Florida   123

5.1. Members of the DRI archaeology team in anticontamination suits   129

5.2. Reporters witnessing Tumbler-Snapper shot Charlie, 1952, Nevada   134

5.3. Nike Site Summit sentry building before restoration work, Alaska   140

5.4. Nike Site Summit sentry building after restoration work, 2010, Alaska   141

6.1. Heavily eroded former nuclear weapons testing station on Aerokoj Island, Bikini Atoll, 2009   145

6.2. Nike life was not all radar and missiles, 1955, Nike Missile Battalion site, Granite, Maryland   149

Maps

4.1. Soviet MRBM sites in Cuba, 1962   76

4.2. Major areas of the Nevada Test Site   86

4.3. Eastern Missile Test Range   117

Table

3.1. Major North American Cold War peace camps   66

ABBREVIATIONS

ADC	Air Defense Command
AEC	Atomic Energy Commission
AFB	Air Force Base
AFS	Air Force Station
AFWL	Air Force Weapons Laboratory
ALCM	air-launched cruise missile
APT	American Peace Test
ARAACOM	Army Antiaircraft Artillery Command
ATLAS	Transmission Line Aircraft Simulator
BAECP	Burlington Atomic Energy Commission Plant
BMEWS	Ballistic Missile Early Warning System
CAD	Computer-aided drafting
CDR	Camp Desert Rock
CETO	Civil Effects Test Operations
CNSY	Charleston Naval Shipyard
COC	Combat Operations Center
CRM	Cultural Resource Management
CT	computerized tomography
DAC	Danish Agency for Culture
DEW	Distant Early Warning (Line)
DoD	U.S. Department of Defense
DOE	U.S. Department of Energy

DRI	Desert Research Institute
ELF	extremely low frequency
E-MAD	Engine Maintenance and Disassembly facility (at the Nuclear Rocket Development Station)
EMP	electromagnetic pulse
EMTR	Eastern Missile Test Range
EOD	(U.S. Navy's) Explosive Ordnance Demolition
FONSS	Friends of Nike Site Summit
GAMA	ground-launched cruise missile alert and maintenance area
GIUK	Greenland, Iceland, United Kingdom
GLCM	ground-launched cruise missile
GPS	Global Positioning System
GWEN	Ground Wave Emergency Network
H3D	High-Definition Digital Documentation
HAER	Historic American Engineering Record
HEW	Hanford Engineer Works
ICBM	intercontinental ballistic missile
IFC	Integrated Fire Control
LASL	Los Alamos Scientific Laboratory
LBBNM	Little Bighorn Battlefield National Monument
MAD	mutual assured destruction
MET	Military Effects Test
MIRV	multiple independently targetable reentry vehicle
MRBM	medium-range ballistic missile
MRI	magnetic resonance imaging
MSR	Missile Site Radar
NARA	National Archives and Records Administration
NASA	National Aeronautics and Space Administration
NORAD	North American Aerospace Defense Command
NPS	National Park Service
NRDS	Nuclear Rocket Development Station
NRHP	National Register of Historic Places

NTS	Nevada Test Site
OCD	Office of Civil Defense
ORNL	Oak Ridge National Laboratory
OSS	Operational Storage Site
PAR	Perimeter Acquisition Radar
PARCS	Perimeter Acquisition Radar Attack Characterization System
PPG	Pacific Proving Grounds
PSNS	Puget Sound Naval Shipyard
R-MAD	Reactor Maintenance and Disassembly facility (at the Nuclear Rocket Development Station)
RAF	Royal Air Force
RCAT	radio-controlled aerial target
RMA	Rocky Mountain Arsenal
R-MAD	Reactor Maintenance and Disassembly facility (at the Nuclear Rocket Development Station)
SAC	Strategic Air Command
SAM	surface-to-air missile
SCRU	National Park Service Submerged Cultural Resource Unit
SLBM	submarine-launched ballistic missile
SOSUS	Sound Surveillance System
SRMSC	Stanley R. Mickelsen Safeguard Complex
SRP	Savannah River Plant
TAC	Tactical Air Command
TEL	transporter erector launcher
USSR	Union of Soviet Socialist Republics
WMTR	Western Missile Test Range

FOREWORD

I knew surprisingly little about the Cold War before I solicited this contribution to the *American Experience in Archaeological Perspective* series. Sure, I had seen the old black-and-white civil defense films warning the public about the dangers of a thermonuclear attack and teaching schoolchildren to duck and cover under their desks in the event of a nuclear explosion, a precaution I practiced in the 1960s. Who could ignore the palpable tension between the United States and Russia (once the Soviet Union) that lingers to this day? I was no stranger to American xenophobia in its many forms—both subtle and overt—that demonized the Red Menace's political, economic, and social policies antithetical to our own. This hatred was epitomized at home in the false accusations brought against so-called Communist sympathizers by Senator McCarthy, which ruined the lives of countless American screenwriters, actors, directors, musicians, and other entertainment professionals under the guise of patriotism.

In the late 1940s, the United States engaged in a permanent war economy in an effort to keep up with our adversary and simultaneously deter the use of weapons of mass destruction. The Cold War arguably began as a wartime effort, dubbed the Manhattan Project, to design and build the atomic bomb with the help of German scientists. America demonstrated its nuclear capability with the notorious bombings at Hiroshima and Nagasaki that ended World War Two. Luckily, no atomic weapons have been used against humanity since. Yet, for more than four decades after this devastating act, the Cold War raging between the superpowers involved research, development, production, and testing of nuclear armaments in one of the greatest industrial and scientific enterprises of all time, as measured in labor hours and resources. Diverting tremendous amounts of time and money to building bombs added little to the goods and services that citizens produce and consume in their daily lives, prompting some to wonder if the Cold War was an enormous waste of energy. The Cold War is rife with irony, secrecy, and misinformation, driven by patriotism, fear, and paranoia, and contributing to a national obsession in considerable need of study and reflection.

For instance, American leaders claimed to protect the nation through the buildup of their arsenal, yet in doing so they contaminated much of the landscape with unhealthy doses of radioactive fallout. They practiced environmental racism by expropriating land to extract uranium for defense purposes and exposing countless disenfranchised groups to the dangers associated with uranium mining. The testing of weapons of mass destruction often occurred on Native American lands and in Third World countries. Furthermore, the effects of nuclear explosions—despite extensive testing and limited observations on the outcomes of the use of relatively small bombs in Japan—remain generally unknown, with some experts predicting as little as a 20 percent death rate after an attack, provided precautionary measures are taken. In contrast, others suggest that the impact of one (or more) sizeable bombs, with the associated radiation and electromagnetic pulse, and the nuclear winter that would ensue, would lead to massive dislocation, alarming rates of death and illness, and disruption of communication and transportation networks, ending in widespread famine and severe psychological and social trauma among the very few survivors.

Political instability and economic depression on a global scale contributed to the arms and space race that led to the development of nuclear, chemical, and biological weapons with profound material implications for the American landscape. Thousands if not millions of Americans were complicit in portraying the Soviet Union as a specter of unimaginable proportions, prompting rampant public fear and hatred leading to a military standoff in which not a single shot was fired at the enemy. This fearsome heritage is marked by a brutalist aesthetic of concrete facilities, structures, domestic housing, hidden bunkers, observation decks, towers, and associated artifacts. They await the discerning eye of the archaeologist to document, decode, and decipher the detritus of doom and despair. Nuclear sites of one sort or another can be found just about anywhere. As the Cold War emerges as a topic of scholarly interest, it is fitting to offer a synthesis of the materiality of this global struggle and highlight its potential for better understanding the American experience.

In *The Archaeology of the Cold War*, Todd Hanson places the archaeological remains of the military-industrial complex within a historical and cultural framework and issues a convincing plea to involve veterans in the study and stewardship of our Cold War heritage as we interpret this important period in American history. Hanson aptly suggests that Cold War archaeology lies at the intersection of three perspectives: conflict archaeology, archaeology of the recent (or contemporary) past, and archaeology of science. The study of artifacts and places associated with conflict leaves evidence missing from official histories, news reports, and personal recollections. For example, the physical remains at crash sites offer information not available from other sources. In addition, the archaeology of the recent past can focus on the mundane activities of daily life, often exposing the discrepancy between prescribed and actual behaviors. We learn from Cold War veterans that things were not always done according to the book. Finally, the Cold War landscape is littered with the material remains of scientific work, including secrets that were intentionally hidden within the compartmentalized organization of the Department of Defense.

Hanson orders the Cold War landscape into three periods, each with a different material signature that marked the evolution, revolution, and resolution of U.S.–Soviet animosities. The built environment of the Cold War was constructed over four decades (1945–1989) in response to continuous technological innovations. By the 1960s the material evidence of fear and paranoia became deeply entrenched into the Cold War landscape, as public and personal fallout shelters came into vogue. A look at the design and contents of these recognizable but enigmatic subterranean facilities reveals what their prospective occupants would need to ensure survival in the event of nuclear Armageddon.

Hanson discusses various efforts to document and preserve sites associated with the Cold War in order to understand their military, scientific, and political significance. From Bikini Atoll in the South Pacific to Soviet missile sites in Cuba and development and test sites throughout North America, Hanson summarizes some of the more intriguing findings made by terrestrial and underwater archaeologists in their investigations of the remnants of what were frequently clandestine activities. Among the more interesting sites discussed are the peace camps, which were temporary sites of "habitation, refuge, and cooperation among individuals contesting the Cold War and its material effect on local and global environments." Some of these camps, which sprang up around the world, have been subjected to archaeological inquiry. Representing a "symbol of twentieth-century American civil disobedience and creative resistance" to the power of the military-industrial complex, the peace camp at the Nevada Test Site contains graffiti, rock art, campsites, and detention structures. Archaeologists have examined what made the site a distinctive type of settlement and what changes occurred. Peace offerings speak directly to the ways in which protesters expressed to each other their sentiments about nuclear proliferation and their desire for a nuclear-free world. Hanson laments that most Cold War site investigations have been conducted under contract by archaeologists who are not paid to explore the social, psychological, and ideological aspects of Cold War materiality. Thus, studies remain mostly descriptive and seldom explore the broader theoretical implications of their findings, making it incumbent on academic archaeologists to get involved.

This book is an explicit call for protection, interpretation, and increased engagement with the vestiges of the atomic age as these sites begin to attract other stakeholders in Cold War history (that is, atomic tourists) who seek an authentic experience of our fearsome heritage. If all wars end in tourism, then it is no surprise that nuclear sites will have their share of guests. As Hanson notes, visitation, study, and interpretation pose challenges of access, safety, and secrecy. While sites are ubiquitous, many are remote and hazardous due to radiation and chemical contamination. Yet, many of these sites are also rapidly disappearing, decaying, and being ignored in favor of more aesthetically pleasing monuments. These "treasures of the American Cold War landscape" must be studied while they still have integrity. As they become forgotten, their secrets will be lost forever. If liberty, individualism, and perseverance define the American experience, then so do xenophobia, paranoia, and secrecy. If we ignore the dark side of the American experience, we risk losing a full understanding of contemporary American life and our quest to live out positive cultural values.

Michael S. Nassaney
Series editor

PREFACE AND ACKNOWLEDGMENTS

During the time I was writing this book, Russia's annexation of Crimea and the war in eastern Ukraine pushed Russian-American political relations to twenty-first-century lows. As political pundits and the news media began to talk about the situation as the start of a "new Cold War," I shuddered at the casual use of the phrase while wondering if I might need to quickly go back through the book and clarify all my Cold War references as pertaining to the "First Cold War." Giving strange credence to the pundits' talk was a NATO proposal to deploy, or "pre-position," M1-A2 tanks, Bradley fighting vehicles, armored howitzers, and other heavy weapons, along with as many as 5,000 American troops, in the Baltic nations of Lithuania, Latvia, and Estonia. The plan would involve upgrading railways to accommodate the heavy American weaponry and building new warehouses to replace some former Soviet facilities. It was indeed a situation that seemed strongly reminiscent of the Cold War of 1945–1989.

Ultimately, however, any comparison of the two situations is fatuous. Russia is not the Soviet Union; it does not have the vast military force and global ideological power the USSR once had. Russia is also an active participant in the world's economy and unlikely to break these important economic ties. Nonetheless, the situation gave me an opportunity for critical reflection. Given Russia's actions and NATO's proposed response, I began to wonder what, if anything, the world had learned from the political, economic, social, and environmental debacles of the Cold War. Indelibly imprinted on the global psyche and landscape, the Cold War was a long and fearsome element of twentieth-century life that even now seems rife with relevant lessons. Are we still learning from it? If so, I believe that what we can learn from the Cold War depends upon how we study it.

This book advocates the importance of studying the material culture produced as a result of Soviet-American conflict during the Cold War. While material culture studies can range broadly in method and purpose, I espouse a strongly scientific, fieldwork-based approach to the archaeological study of North American Cold War remains. This specificity of method and domain is an essential point, because some of the scholarly work discussed herein will appear at times to be more akin to historic preservation or architectural history studies than traditional archaeology. This emphasis reflects the way the archaeology of the Cold War has been studied over the past several decades, but it is not the only way Cold War archaeology can be, should be, or will be practiced in the future. Where site excavations and scientific analysis have been lacking, this book strongly encourages they be done now and in the future.

Ultimately, this book is about what archaeologists have learned about the Cold War from Cold War sites and artifacts. In it, I present some of the best recent work in the field with the hope that North American historical archaeologists will gain increased interest in the field and begin to develop some synergy with innovative ongoing international research.

I believe there is much to learn about the Cold War that only archaeology seems capable of revealing. As I study Cold War sites, for example, I am inevitably struck by the belief that the world was indeed extremely fortunate to have survived the Cold War. This awareness of having narrowly eluded a global nuclear apocalypse is auspicious, even in the face of the world's seemingly interminable conflicts, but it is nonetheless troubling as I wonder whether humankind's continued existence is simply the result of luck, or if we actually learned something during our time on the brink of extinction. It now seems more important than ever to apply the tools and practices of archaeology to discover how things really were in the Cold War: what we knew, what we did not know, what went right, and what might have just as easily gone terribly wrong had we not been so lucky. With whispers of a new Cold War in the wind, the physical record of the old Cold War surrounds us, waiting to teach us more about our twentieth-century selves.

* * *

Growing up as a Cold War kid faced with such an uncertain future, it seemed natural to me to be more interested in studying the past than thinking about the future. While it was George Bass's 1966 book, *Archaeology under Water,* that initially sparked my interest in archaeology, I will admit that it was the 1980s adventures of a fictional archaeologist that truly lit the flame. Fortunately for me, the first bona fide archaeologist I ever met, Dr. Robert Barth at the University of Wisconsin–Eau Claire, helped me understand that it was much better to pattern my career ambitions after Lewis Binford than Henry Jones, Jr. Bob's formative teachings, guidance, and inspiration put me on the path I follow today. Many years later, another archaeologist would come along to renew and strengthen what had become a flickering commitment to the field. During my graduate studies at New Mexico Highlands University, Robert Mischler taught me, among other important things, how to survive archaeological fieldwork in the New Mexican desert. For his example, wisdom, and counsel, I remain forever grateful.

More immediately responsible for the existence of this book is Michael Nassaney, an accomplished archaeologist, author, and editor for the American Experience in Archaeological Perspective series. It was Michael who first suggested I write this volume. It was a very good suggestion. For giving me the opportunity to write this book in my own way, then helping me make it much better than I ever could on my own, I owe him a proverbial world of thanks.

There are, of course, many others in the archaeology community who have helped me shape the narrative you are now reading. Wayne Cocroft, James Delgado, and Lisa Westwood all provided many excellent suggestions for making this book stronger and better. I am likewise indebted to Colleen Beck, Steve Brown, Mats Burström, Lori Collins, James Delgado, Tomás Diez Acosta, Travis Doering, Harold Drollinger, Susan Edwards, Susan Enscore, Nancy Goldenberg, Estrella González, Anders Gustafsson, Lori Hawthorne-Tagg, Ismael Hernández, Barb Holz, Robaina Jaramillo, William Johnson, Robert Jones, Håkan Karlsson, Daniel Lenihan, Larry Murphy, Patrick Nowlan, Jesús Pajón, Thomas Penders, Jesús Rafael, Rafael Robiana, Michael Brian Schiffer, John Schofield, Martyn Tagg, Karen Van Citters, and Bengt Westergaard for providing excellent archaeological studies on which to report. Photos provided by Darrell Lewis, Ron Van Oers, and Chuck Reuben, and information provided by

Dustin Atkins, Brian Knight, Valerie Renner, Michael Terlep, and Martha Yduarte all helped me tell the story better. To all of these colleagues, and to anyone I might have inadvertently missed naming here, my sincerest thanks.

I also deeply appreciate the editorial assistance of Meredith Babb, Nevil Parker, and all the folks at the University Press of Florida who helped make this book a reality. Kirsteen Anderson, in particular, did a wonderful job of copyediting, adding clarity and consistency where it was most needed. I could not have asked for a finer group of publishing professionals with whom to work.

Finally, I owe my deepest debt of gratitude to my sons, Brady and Parker, who have long endured my seemingly unfashionable anthropological obsession with the occupational narratives, material culture, and built landscapes of science. Their feedback, patience, and love are a blessing to a culture geek like me. Thanks as well to Tanner, my longtime companion, who was patiently at my side as I wrote this book but abruptly left me to finish this journey on my own.

1

INTRODUCTION

The Cold War was unlike any other war in human history. While the world has witnessed many brutal and bloody wars, the Cold War stands unparalleled as the only conflict to have as its anticipated outcome the annihilation of life on Earth. From its beginning in 1945 to its finale in 1989,[1] the Cold War evolved from a simple clash of political ideologies into a global confrontation of unprecedented drama, duration, and complexity. It was a conflict fueled by paranoia and distrust, driven by advances in science and technology, and complicated by a seemingly endless succession of propaganda campaigns, political machinations, and regional proxy wars. Under its shadow, distrust became the watchword of political practice as paranoia and fear materialized in everyday life and political rhetoric was artfully crafted to manipulate the public into sustaining deep and enduring feelings of xenophobia. Suspicion and hatred thrived. New military technologies and political strategies of total destruction were born and normalized during the conflict, many of which would have grave and enduring foreign policy consequences for the superpowers involved. In the end, the Cold War would affect nearly every aspect of twentieth-century life, and its cultural, political, economic, and technological effects remain with us even today. For those who lived through it, no matter where in the world they lived, the Cold War proved to be a war like no other.

Bloodied yet victorious, the United States emerged from World War Two as an unlikely global superpower. While considerably more engaged in twentieth-century political affairs as a consequence of having waged two world wars, the United States initially focused its foreign policy on helping the war-ravaged nations of the world recover and rebuild. In that role, it soon found itself, perhaps unexpectedly, possessing sufficient technical, economic, and military influence to substantially affect the commercial and political affairs of other nations. Emboldened by its ownership of most of the world's gold reserves, buoyed by an industrial economy unscathed and even invigorated by war, and armed with a small but as yet unrivaled atomic arsenal, the United States set out to establish its own ideal of world peace: a so-called Pax Americana (Parchami 2009). Under Pax Americana, the United States would follow an ambitious path of technological discovery, scientific invention, and military construction toward its goal of global peace. And though the intent and rhetoric of Pax Americana may indeed have been peaceful, the actions it engendered appeared anything but. The path to Pax Americana involved sustained technological advances in nuclear weapons; the invention of powerful computers, communications systems, and radar defense systems; and the building of new jet aircraft, missiles, aircraft carriers, and submarines. In particular, the invention, production, and testing of weapons of mass destruction in spaces arrogated from native nations or "Third World" countries, as the latter were then called, bespoke nothing less than imperialism (Gerson 2007).

Meanwhile, the Union of Soviet Socialist Republics (USSR) set out on its own path of invention and construction by building its own nuclear, biological, and chemical weapons; bombers, submarines, missiles, and launch complexes; and weapons research, development, production, and testing sites necessary to compete with the United States. Soon, a Soviet-led military alliance of central and eastern European countries united under the Warsaw Treaty of Friendship, Co-operation, and Mutual Assistance—the Warsaw Pact—would emerge to challenge Pax Americana and create an ideological schism across Europe that would come to be known as the "Iron Curtain." Meanwhile, the rise of socialist and communist governments in other parts of the world sparked American fears of an international Soviet-driven communist agenda that was ominously dubbed the "Red Menace," a term that would become a central element of anti-Soviet rhetoric and American popular culture for decades to come. As fear of the Red Menace collided with hidebound notions of American exceptionalism, life in Cold War America became an obsessive national preoccupation with military might, international political power, cultural dominance, and, ultimately, survival. The Communist threat inspired the search for an ideal American political state that could

Figure 1.1. One of the more profound economic effects of the Cold War was an employment boom for American workers. Workers at the Douglas Aircraft Company in southern California are shown here assembling Nike-Ajax missiles in 1956. By permission of the U.S. Department of the Army.

seemingly be achieved only through the creation of a vast Cold War defense infrastructure.

The consequences of creating this infrastructure were both enduring and inexorable, resulting in physical changes to the built landscape that would profoundly affect the lives and livelihoods of millions of North Americans. Alongside these changes to the land came new economic opportunities. Direct participation in a booming Cold War economy, in jobs such as those pictured in Figure 1.1, would provide employment and drive unprecedented economic growth as the United States and Canada spent more than $19 trillion on national defense in the latter half of the twentieth century (Schwartz 1998).

A War of Science and Technology

Although it is perhaps a truism that all wars are facilitated by science and technology, the Cold War exploited scientific discovery to advance technology in ways that prior wars had not. Cold War scientific research, development, and testing would come to epitomize the notion of technoscience: big scientific projects conducted specifically to advance technology. At the heart of this unprecedented technoscience was the atomic bomb, which had not only hastened the end of World War Two, but whose continued study had ushered in new discoveries in chemistry, physics, and medicine.

A primary result of these technoscientific advancements was the "arms race," a competition between the Soviet Union and United States for military supremacy through the development of ever more formidable and sophisticated weapons of mass destruction. Beginning in earnest in August 1949 when the Soviet Union detonated its first atomic device, the arms race became a rivalry in the development and deployment of a range of conventional, chemical, biological, and of course, nuclear weapons technologies. Emerging as the defining metaphor of the Cold War, the H-bombs (thermonuclear fusion devices) that both the United States and the Soviet Union would build and test were vastly more powerful than the fission bombs used on Japan in World War Two. Complementary advancements in rocket technologies would provide the ultimate platform for nuclear weapons delivery, giving both nations medium-range then long-range (intercontinental) ballistic missile capabilities by the late 1950s. Ultimately, the U.S. and Soviet governments would spend vast sums on increasing the destructive power, size, and accuracy of their respective nuclear arsenals, as well as on maintaining the launch sites, submarines, and aircraft needed to deploy them.

Inasmuch as the Cold War was the stimulus for the nuclear arms race, it was likewise the catalyst for the race into space between the United States and the Soviet Union. While the Space Race can be correlated to the technological capabilities required for unmanned flight into and through outer space (a critical aspect of intercontinental ballistic missiles), it was also a central element of a broader ideological, technological, and scientific competition. By the early 1960s, both sides possessed the technological capabilities required for space flight. Despite a strong early Soviet lead, demonstrated by the launch of the Sputnik satellite and the Luna lunar probe, it was the United States that ultimately triumphed in the Cold War Space Race, culminating with the landing of Americans on the Moon in 1969 and five additional times thereafter. Along the way, the United States developed the knowledge and technologies necessary to launch massive payloads into space, place objects in precise geosynchronous orbits around the Earth, live and navigate in outer space, and land safely on the Moon. Broadly promoted to the American public as a matter more of the "conquest" of space than of national security or ideological superiority, the Space Race required and inspired technological advances in countless fields. Following a common development path from space needs to civilian desires, technologies such as cordless tools (originally created for astronauts' use on space walks), smoke detectors (for space capsule fire protection), portable water filters (for wastewater filtration in flight), and joystick video game controllers (for spacecraft docking maneuvers) would ultimately find ubiquitous uses in American homes.

Taken together, the Cold War space and arms races were responsible for influencing and advancing research and development in many fields, including aeronautical science, chemical engineering, electrical engineering and electronics, nuclear physics, metallurgy, nuclear chemistry, and material science. In the fields of astrophysics, computer science, oceanography, space science, and particle physics they led to nothing less than scientific revolutions. Cold War engineering produced a plethora of new technologies, many of which would ultimately find their way into the material culture of contemporary American life. Technological advancements in satellites, semiconductors, integrated circuits, scientific visualization, image sensors, and nuclear physics spawned developments in wireless communications, computers, video games, digital cameras, magnetic resonance imaging (MRI), computerized tomography (CT) scans, and chemotherapy.

Out of this war of science and technology was born a vast and mostly secret Cold War production landscape encompassing everything from mineral mines and quarries, manufacturing facilities, weapons laboratories, and testing grounds to military bases, intercontinental ballistic missile (ICBM) complexes, airfields, surveillance systems, communications networks, and control and command centers. From Maine to Hawaii, every state in the Union, and much of Canada, had a role in building facilities for the Cold War. As this landscape emerged, so too did a pattern of land use in which sites were developed, used, and abandoned at a whirlwind rate. Driven by the relentless pace of the arms race, the incessant obsolescence of weapons technologies, and the pervasive political paranoia of the period, the pattern began with the construction of a manifestly permanent concrete-and-steel structure or facility. Once completed, the premises were often occupied for only a short period before being vacated in favor of another better or bigger site. While a rare few sites, such as the Minuteman ICBM sites, were used for relatively long periods, most Cold War facilities and structures were impermanent, sometimes being shuttered only months after being put into service. As the conflict progressed, this pattern of land use continued unabated with sites being occupied, closed, and abandoned almost as quickly as new ones could be designed, built, and occupied. Over the course of 40 years, the result was a massive Cold War footprint that dominated the North American landscape.

Attempting to build both a North American continental defense system and a global military presence sufficient to constrain the Soviet Union, the United States also began exporting military technologies and facilities to allied nations in the 1960s. This was not a traditional combat basing strategy in which the United States was rapidly erecting temporary bases on foreign soil for immediate tactical advantage, but a calculated construction of permanent or semipermanent structures intended for long-term occupation and use, often under formal land-lease contracts with foreign governments. Built by the U.S. military—typically using American designs, materials, and contractors—the technologies and facilities included military bases, long-range radar installations, communications and intelligence-gathering facilities, and missile complexes.

Under this practice, Jupiter medium-range ballistic missiles armed with nuclear warheads were deployed in Italy and Turkey, while permanent Nike Hercules missile sites were built in Denmark, West Germany, Greece, Italy, Korea, Norway, Okinawa, Taiwan, and Turkey (Cagle 1973). Large intelligence-gathering antennae known as Circularly Disposed Antenna Arrays (*Wullenwebers*, or "Elephant Cages") were erected in Canada, West Germany, Italy, Japan, the Philippines, Thailand, Turkey, and the United Kingdom (Reed 2010), while massive Ballistic Missile Early Warning System (BMEWS) radar sets were constructed at Thule, Greenland, and at the Royal Air Force (RAF) Station Flyingdales in the United Kingdom (Fletcher 1989).

This practice was frequently controversial. For example, the 1981 deployment of American cruise missiles to the RAF Greenham Common airbase in the United Kingdom led to large, multiyear antinuclear protests. The Jupiter missiles deployed in Turkey were withdrawn as a condition for resolving the Cuban Missile Crisis. Ironically, it was the Soviet Union's use of the selfsame military strategy in deploying missiles to Cuba that helped provoke that crisis.

Roots of Cold War Archaeological Scholarship

Throughout the late twentieth century, the Cold War remained a central, even defining, element in the U.S. identity as a global superpower. Chilling for many, and yet perhaps comforting for others, that nuclear superpower identity was deeply rooted in creating and sustaining, both physically and metaphorically, a global landscape of culturally and politically powerful artifacts, places, and spaces. When the Cold War abruptly ended in 1989 and the world began to move ever so slowly, yet never quite completely, away from the apocalyptic future that had once seemed inevitable, the massive Cold War landscape that had taken decades to build was suddenly inapposite, even superfluous. Its sheer size dictated that it be reduced, yet as the process of demobilization and demolition began, politicians and scholars realized that preserving certain aspects of the landscape could be critical to understanding and preserving the Cold War history and heritage of North America. Complicating matters, however, was the fact that relatively little was known about many of those spaces, places, and artifacts in terms of their true military, scientific, or political significance. Because Cold War facilities were typically built in secret and operated in silence, their operational histories are both untold and at growing risk of being forever lost.

Ultimately, the Cold War was a conflict fought on land, in the skies, on and below the sea, and even in space. It is under this multi-terrain paradigm that historical archaeologists, maritime archaeologists, architectural historians, and historic preservationists around the world have set out to understand and capture the material pasts of many once-secret spaces and places. Developing and employing specific theoretical frameworks and archaeological research methods used for the study of earlier periods and places, these scholars have produced an impressive body of scholarly work.

Like the Cold War itself, the archaeology of the Cold War is different from other types of archaeology. Schofield and Cocroft (2007) have characterized the archaeological study of the Cold War as the study of a "fearsome heritage." This is an apt description, as there seems to be little within the realm of the Cold War built landscape that is not capable of evoking at least some level of subconscious fear or nonspecific dread. In this postulation there also lies a deeper truth: that within our shared cultural heritage some materialities are more capable than others of evoking the darker

8 · The Archaeology of the Cold War

Figure 1.2. The monumental Brutalist aesthetic of the arms race. The Missile Site Control Building was part of the Stanley R. Mickelsen Safeguard Complex at Nekoma, North Dakota. It was declared fully operational on October 1, 1975, but the very next day the U.S. House of Representatives voted overwhelmingly to adopt a federal budget that closed the site. By permission of the U.S. Air Force.

aspects of human history. Studies of these dark and fearsome heritages are frequently explorations into the memories, places, and events that societies strive to collectively forget, perhaps because of the horrifying chord they strike in the human song.

Chief among the material remains of the Cold War are concrete monuments of the American defense landscape such as the modern pyramid in Figure 1.2. Lending its stone-like attributes to hundreds of North American structures and sites, concrete proved to be the very embodiment of Cold War strength, solidity, and indestructibility. Its widespread use in construction ushered in what ultimately would be known in twentieth-century architecture as the Brutalist aesthetic (Hampton 2012). Massively built, Cold War structures were often monumental in nature and scale. Yet with deeper awareness comes the knowledge that some of the most remarkable concrete structures of the Cold War were created for the singular, fearsome purpose of facilitating the deaths of millions of other humans. Indeed, the relatively bloodless history of the Cold War is overshadowed by the notion that if certain political or military events had gone differently, millions if not billions of human lives might have been lost in a nuclear apocalypse.

This book presents some of the most notable scholarly work that has developed in the pursuit of an archaeological understanding of this fearsome heritage. Looking specifically at the approaches, discoveries, challenges, accomplishments, and potential future directions of the archaeological study of the Cold War in North America, I cover mostly continental sites, but also explore important international sites where U.S. Cold War political or military actions had consequential material effect.

I begin in Chapter 2 with a review of the principal analytical constructs and theoretical orientations supporting the archaeological study of the Cold War. Predominantly processual in nature, the best of this research falls into three main theoretical frameworks: conflict archaeology, the archaeology of the contemporary or recent past, and the archaeology of science. While much of the most prolific work in the archaeology of the Cold War has focused specifically on the materiality of conflict, both the archaeology of the contemporary past and the archaeology of science hold strong potential for producing meaningful archaeological studies of the Cold War.

Providing context for the archaeological site studies that are discussed in Chapter 4, and background for understanding the sheer magnitude and complexity of the Cold War environment, Chapter 3 summarizes the creation of the Cold War built landscape in North America. Taking a temporal-thematic approach, I examine the development of the landscape during three discrete periods: 1945–1957, 1958–1975, and 1976–1989.

In the fourth chapter, the narrative focuses on a collection of innovative and substantive research contributions made by historical archaeologists, architectural historians, and historic preservationists. While I focus on studies of North American sites, I look as well at Cuba and the Republic of the Marshall Islands, where U.S. Cold War scientific, military, and political activities had significant and profound effects upon the built landscape.

In Chapter 5 I examine some of the issues related to the archaeological study and stewardship of Cold War cultural heritage. Specifically, I address the physical, psychological, and political challenges facing researchers; the various and sometimes conflicting audiences for Cold War historic preservation efforts, and the role of Cold War veterans in understanding and preserving the Cold War past.

Chapter 6 concludes the volume with a discussion of some of the issues inspiring and complicating Cold War archaeological research efforts, as well as some recommendations for potential future research directions for the field.

2

IN THEORY AND PRACTICE

Archaeological Frameworks

Three theoretical frameworks are commonly employed in the study of Cold War materiality: conflict archaeology, archaeology of the contemporary or recent past, and archaeology of science. While all three provide relevant and useful constructs for studying the Cold War material record, they are markedly different in their methods and objectives. My purposes here are to acquaint readers with the basic contexts, concepts, and uses for each construct as a way of providing contextual background for later chapters.

Taking an archaeological approach to the study of Cold War North America is a profoundly useful method of providing material perspective on the formative role the Cold War had in the making of modern America. The archaeology of the Cold War offers opportunities to study the tangible aspects of a war that was fought for the most part through secrecy, intimidation, and strategic deterrence during what was arguably the most prolific period of scientific and technological advancement in American history. Although archaeologists have historically approached the study of the Cold War almost exclusively as an archaeology of conflict, it is increasingly evident that the Cold War was too much a part of late twentieth-century everyday life to be viewed only through the prescriptive lens of conflict. Aspects of Cold War material culture not directly connected to conflict might, for example, be more constructively studied as the archaeology of the contemporary past. And because the Cold War was heavily dependent upon scientific advancements for its existence, the archaeology of science also cannot be excluded as a legitimate theoretical approach. Ultimately, the archaeology of the Cold War is an intellectual endeavor best pursued using a variety of inferential approaches, and eventually the archaeology of the Cold War may see a more robust mix of multiple philosophical and theoretical approaches. For now, however, these three domains, each itself an emergent field of archaeological inquiry, have made the strongest claims to the field.

Conflict Archaeology

Accounting for what is certainly the largest body of scholarly work on the archaeology of the Cold War, conflict archaeology is itself a relatively new field of archaeological inquiry. Seeking to redefine, revitalize, and broaden what was already the well-established field of battlefield archaeology, conflict archaeology emerged in the 1990s as an inquiry focused on the tangible material aftermaths of violent social interactions across a wide range of spaces. Over time, conflict archaeology grew to encompass battlefield archaeology, which had traditionally focused on individual historical battle sites or discrete spaces of large-scale military actions between nations. Now neither restricted to the study of singular battlefields nor exclusively focused on the study of large-scale wars between nations, the theories and practices of conflict archaeology are used to study the materiality of violent human conflict across the broad temporal and spatial ranges of human existence. Rooted in the notion that participants in any conflict, large or small, brief or enduring, leave behind sites and even entire landscapes littered with the artifacts of aggression, conflict archaeology is the close study of the artifacts and landscapes that intergroup and intragroup conflict creates and leaves behind. Aimed at understanding the broad range of cultural, social, psychological, spiritual, technical, and historical aspects of conflict, this type of archaeology, when broadly practiced, recognizes that extreme economic, political, religious, and nationalistic motivations often drive human conflict. Moreover, these motivations are neither trivial nor ephemeral.

In North America, the field of conflict archaeology has explored a broad range of material culture associated with human conflict. The range of recent research in the field extends from the anthropological archaeology of prehistoric conflict sites (Arkush and Allen 2006; Lambert 2002; Potter and Chuipka 2010; Rice and LeBlanc 2001) to historical archaeology studies of famous American battlefields (Conlin and Russell 2006;

Geier et al. 2010; Scott 2013), and from studies of defensive fortifications and technologies (Broadwater 2012; Starbuck 2011) to archaeological investigations into the materiality of rebellions, riots, and acts of civil disobedience (Saitta 2007; Saitta et al. 2005).

Among North American conflict archaeology studies, the archaeological investigations at Little Bighorn Battlefield National Monument (LBBNM) are particularly notable for having developed and influenced many of the analytical and methodological constructs used in conflict archaeology studies worldwide. As such, these investigations are worthy of a brief discussion.

Infamous in American military history as the site of Lieutenant Colonel George Custer's proverbial Last Stand, Little Bighorn was the site of a two-day battle in June 1876 that pitted Lakota and Cheyenne warriors against soldiers from the U.S. Seventh Cavalry. In the late twentieth century, scholars of the site recognized its larger historical implications as a battleground between two cultures and, facilitated in no small measure by conflict archaeology, began its reinterpretation as a complex historic site of violent cross-cultural conflict.

Beginning in 1958 and continuing to the present day, investigations at LBBNM have increasingly stretched archaeological frameworks. Incorporating innovations in archaeological science, theory, and method, LBBNM archaeological investigations advanced conflict archaeology in the United States as a whole through their early adoption of advanced scientific tools and technologies, use of amateur/professional research partnerships, and engagement with what might be described as "outside the trench" thinking involving new and novel interpretations of existing data, using innovative methods and analytical constructs to generate new data, and sharing widely knowledge gained from that research. Making use of advancements in metal detecting technology, LBBNM investigators in 1956 began the earliest published use of metal detectors in American battlefield archaeology, combining this technology with an existing history of well-documented surface collecting of firearm cartridge casings and bullets. From these finds, a renowned research program in firearm cartridge forensics would emerge (Scott 2013). Starting in the late 1980s LBBNM investigators began extensively using forensic pathology to study human remains either accidentally or intentionally disinterred, giving each discovery the attention of a modern crime scene and, in the process, gathering detailed information about every unearthed battle casualty.

Osteological studies of Little Big Horn combatants generated a wealth of data relative to the victims' ages, social statuses, diets, lifestyles, health, and probable cause of death (Scott 2010). LBBNM researchers shared data and knowledge on these and other topics widely among both professional and avocational archaeologists and historians, often leading to compelling international research collaborations. Ultimately, the impacts of the LBBNM archaeological investigations on the field of conflict archaeology were far-reaching. Patterning their work after that done at Little Bighorn, conflict archaeologists now regularly make new and novel use of data in collaborative research efforts, employ more critical analytical constructs, and work to foster engagement with amateurs and the interested public. This approach is yielding new insights in the archaeological study not just of older conflict sites, but of more recent sites as well, which often fall under the scope of what has become known as modern conflict archaeology.

Modern Conflict Archaeology

Whereas conflict archaeology in general focuses on conflict in all eras and of all magnitudes and durations, the archaeology of modern conflict looks exclusively at the material culture remains of twentieth-century and later conflicts. Dubbed modern conflict archaeology by its most prolific and proficient practitioners (Carman 1997; Saunders 2004, 2012; Schofield 2005, 2009; Schofield, Klausmeier, and Purbrick 2006), the approach blends traditional archaeological methods and perspectives with the analytical constructs and theoretical frameworks of fields such as cultural studies to produce research that is distinct, both temporally and philosophically, from conflict archaeology. While conflict archaeology has struggled to shake its battlefield archaeology origins, connotations, and traditions, the field of modern conflict archaeology emerging in the late twentieth century focuses explicitly on conflict as a multidimensional social phenomenon capable of producing a materiality and range of physical traces that are specifically ascribed to conflict. Possessing multiple meanings that may change over time, artifacts of conflict can also incorporate notions of identity, ethnicity, class, and nationality (Saunders 2012). A prime example of this is the Avtomat Kalashnikova, or AK-47, assault rifle, a well-known artifact of the Cold War that was recognized worldwide as a symbol of the Soviet Union, and by association, of communism. Since the end of the Cold War, however, it has taken on new meaning to become a metaphor for violent revolution, class struggle, and even terrorism (Graves-Brown 2007).

In the analytical constructs of modern conflict archaeology we witness the influences of postmodern/post-processual archaeological theory and its strong corollaries to research in the archaeology of the contemporary past. Within these constructs, modern conflict archaeologists have studied the materiality of recent conflict using theories that intersect with issues of agency, hegemony, gender, class, nationalism, ethnicity, identity, and exclusion, among others. The critical study of modern conflict and its material legacies typically employs an interdisciplinary approach, centered on the application of theories, practices, and analytical methods drawn from a strong range of academic disciplines, including anthropology, architecture, chemistry, earth science, engineering, geography, heritage studies, history, marine studies, metallurgy, psychology, sociology, and others. And while modern conflict archaeology still derives its core field research methods, practices, and theory from historical archaeology, it possesses characteristics that make it a distinct subfield of conflict archaeology.

One particularly elemental characteristic of the archaeology of modern conflict has been its focus on the material aspects of mechanized conflict and industrialized warfare. Beginning in the late nineteenth century and continuing today, nations have armed their militaries with increasingly advanced weapons and technologies manufactured using mass production processes. Whereas in the pre-industrial era muzzle loading rifles and cannons, and wooden warships, had limited the pace and mortality of even the largest and longest conflicts, by the turn of the twentieth century mechanization had created industrialized warfare. Mass production supplied huge conscripted armies with new and deadly armaments, including long-range artillery, high-velocity ammunition, high explosives, armored vehicles, and rapid-fire small arms. Beginning in World War One and continuing throughout the twentieth century, the increasing sophistication of weapons technologies led to higher casualty rates, culminating with the atomic weapons used on Japan and the threat of even greater losses in future wars due to the use of biological and nuclear weapons. Industrialized warfare created an unprecedented material legacy whose cultural correlates, social consequences, and aftermaths are today the purview of modern conflict archaeologists.

A defining characteristic of the archaeology of modern conflict is the notion that investigations need not be limited to the tangible effects of conflict. While the study of materiality is elemental to exploring the cultural, social, or political dynamics of any conflict, whatever its scale, scope, or form, there are intangible aspects of the material culture of modern conflict that can offer valuable insights. Studies of such intangibles of modern conflict as creativity among combatants (Buchinger and Metzler 2006; Cocroft and Wilson 2006), fear (Grguric 2008; Jacobson 2009; Wilson 2011), paranoia (Hanson 2010), and memory (Moshenka 2010; Myers 2008; Trigg 2007) have all made valuable contributions to the post-processual aspirations of the field.

Although the archaeology of the Cold War is deeply rooted in the study of modern conflict, this does not preclude future studies that might explore the substantial and enduring materiality of the Cold War from other relevant analytical, social, or temporal perspectives. In fact, one of the most promising of these other perspectives is the archaeology of the contemporary past.

Archaeology of the Contemporary Past

For nearly a century, historical archaeology in the United States has focused on understanding conditions of life for literate, historical-period people in periods and places where archival documents were either limited or absent, or for which the excavation of buried remains was the best or only method for obtaining new information. Over roughly the past decade, however, an archaeology of the contemporary past, or "contemporary archaeology" as it is often known, has emerged to study the material culture of the very recent past. This is a past for which archival documents may be abundant and the excavation of remains may be a supplemental method of obtaining historical information. Using the tools, methods, and even theories of traditional historical archaeology, contemporary archaeology is characterized by efforts to apply traditional archaeological methods and practices for new data collection uses at twentieth- and twenty-first-century sites.

Archaeologies of the contemporary past are concerned with studying the cultural artifacts, systems, places, spaces, and events found within the realm of late-modern industrial societies, in so-called living memory. In this context, living memory is considered to be the collective, remembered events of a human social generation extending back roughly 80 years into the past (Assmann 2011:37). Contextually, this notion of living memory roughly equates to a human life span. At the time of this writing in 2015, archaeologists of the contemporary past are studying the material aspects of events and places broadly remembered by a living public back to around the 1930s. While this notion of living memory may appear to cause overlap between the work of archaeologists of the contemporary past and historical archaeologists studying the material aspects of the early twentieth century, in reality archaeologists of the contemporary past tend to concentrate on much more recent periods. Harrison and Schofield (2010) define the archaeology of the contemporary past as encompassing the people, places, spaces, and objects from 1950 to the present. In contrast, Burström posits that the emergence of contemporary archaeology means that archaeology as a field of inquiry can no longer be defined in terms of traditional chronological criteria, noting, "Archaeology of the present crosses disciplinary boundaries and calls into question modernity's categorical distinction between the past and the present. Under the gaze of archaeology, familiar everyday objects are transformed into archaeological artefacts" (2011:126).

However one defines the contemporary past, archaeologies of the contemporary past apply the same analytical practices, data-recovery methods, and theoretical frameworks once reserved for the study of the ancient and prehistoric pasts, but with a focus on material culture of recent origin. It was in this framework that Pearson and Mullins (1999) explored the material culture and domestic ideologies of Barbie dolls using what they described as "the standard archaeological understanding of structured material description, identification of materials patterns, and anthropological analysis of the relationship between those patterns and their cultural and historical context" (226). By and large, however, archaeologies of the contemporary past tend to distinguish themselves from the larger field of historical archaeology in several ways.

First, practitioners of the archaeology of the contemporary past typically regard it as the intentional study of the quotidian: the places, spaces, and objects that make up everyday life. Whereas the emphasis of historical archaeology, in North America at least, has long been on sites of significant historical importance, the emerging archaeologies of the contemporary past are more interested in the materiality of the unremarkable, the unexceptional, and the mundane. As Harrison and Schofield (2010) observe, the study of the mundane deserves intellectual equality with the great and important, because "if we overlook the everyday, we overlook what it means to be 'us,' and we run the risk of remembering only the noteworthy or the unusual" (11). International contributions to the archaeology of the contemporary past range from an investigation of everyday life in British public housing (Buchli and Lucas 2001) to an archaeological study of a 1991 Ford Econoline van (Bailey et al. 2009).

A second distinguishing aspect of archaeologies of the contemporary past is that they have increasingly brought attention to the past life experiences of the subaltern and marginalized, especially individuals in ethnic, racial, gender, and socioeconomic groups that have been politically, socially, or geographically excluded from the hegemonic state. These are classes of people that Elizabeth Scott (1994) described as "those of little note." From studies of the archaeology of "de-industrialization" in Cornwall's tin- and copper-mining industries in postwar England (Orange 2012) to the materiality of homelessness in Bristol, UK (Kiddey and Schofield 2011), archaeologies of the contemporary past have shown potential to contribute to broader social scientific understandings of the contemporary world by bringing to light aspects of history that hegemony seeks to suppress or that modern memory simply fails to remember.

In this regard, the field appeals to scholars for its potential role in what Harrison and Schofield (2010) call "archaeology as a form of material witness." This use implicates archaeologists of the contemporary past in the politics of modern life where the archaeological act is more than a creative intellectual engagement with modern material culture and with the individuals and groups that produced that material culture. Instead it becomes a performance of social activism or arbitration of social justice that works by unearthing histories that have been kept hidden, either intentionally or unintentionally, from the present state of knowledge. Examples of this work include excavations of mass graves of Republican sympathizers from the Spanish Civil War (Renshaw 2010) and victims of Argentinian juntas (Doretti and Fondebrider 2001). Just as archaeologists employing conflict archaeology methods and theoretical frameworks might produce studies exploring such post-processual themes as aggression, subordination, and resistance, archaeologies of the contemporary past have the potential to engender studies exploring the material aspects of Cold War power, ideology, gender, symbolic meaning, structuration, and reification. This notion of archaeology as activism seems particularly useful in Cold War archaeological studies concerned with understanding sites that have entailed the control or active concealment of historical information; that is, secrecy.

Yet another defining aspect of the field is its search for parts of human experience that can only be accessed through archaeology. Lucas (2004) calls these the parts of our world that are not fully constituted in historical accounting, where "there are gaps, shadows, silences, and absences which are not simply outside discourse, but are often structurally excluded by discourse" (117). Relying on the notions that materiality is a requisite element of much if not all human experience, and that the unremarkable, unexceptional, and mundane are often intrinsic to that materiality, the archaeology of the contemporary past is the search for material evidence of those gaps, shadows, silences, and absences in recent everyday discourse that lie buried in the archaeological record. Perhaps more importantly, the archaeological search for these "missing pieces" of recent human experience can be tied to post-processual archaeology, where we recognize that considerations of gender, race, and class are increasingly fundamental to archaeological understandings of the recent past (Shackel and Little 1992).

Finally, the aspect of living memory in archaeologies of the contemporary past pushes archaeology to make direct connections between the material past and the living present. That is, connections between the artifacts and their makers or users, or perhaps the descendants of either, are unmuted by the passing of time, making legitimate artifact interpretations potentially less conjectural. Unlike the occasionally tenuous connections that archaeologists of deeper time must make between an artifact and its user or maker, these connections in living memory are often incontrovertible.

This aspect of the work is not, however, without both risk and challenges. Even as artifacts are more easily identified by their former users, the archaeology of the contemporary past requires heightened sensitivity to the potential legal, emotional, and psychological investments and interests of various stakeholders, including governments, landowners, and the living persons, or their descendants, being studied. Discretion, empathy, and respect are essential elements of field investigations and subsequent uses of data, especially when it comes to the publication of data or public exhibition of any recovered artifacts that may reflect negatively upon the communities or individuals whose pasts are being unearthed.

Situated as they are within the living memory of early twenty-first-century society, materialities of the Cold War are optimal subjects for the archaeology of the contemporary past, particularly in light of both their substantial physical presence and their continuing relevance to everyday life. Among the archaeological investigations of the Cold War conducted within theoretical frameworks consistent with the archaeology of the contemporary past are investigations of dissent and opposition: studies of antinuclear protest sites, peace camps, and civil resistance movements. Among such studies are the Nevada Test Site Peace Camp fieldwork described in Chapter 4 and archaeologies of the protest camps at RAF Station Greenham Common in the United Kingdom (Marshall et al. 2009; Schofield and Anderton 2000). Cold War studies with strong attributes of contemporary archaeology include Buchinger and Metzler's (2009) survey of the Soviet murals at Forst Zinna near Juterborg, Germany; Petrauskas's (2011) report on the excavation of a former bunker belonging to the Union of Lithuanian Freedom Fighters, an anti-Soviet resistance group, and McWilliams's (2013) explorations of Iron Curtain materiality. Even as the aforementioned contemporary archaeology studies share research methods with conflict archaeology, they likewise share practices with the archaeology of science, yet another inferential approach laying claim to archaeologies of the Cold War.

Archaeology of Science

The centrality of science and technology to the Cold War is virtually undisputable. Significant scientific and technical advances occurred in literally every field of physical science and engineering, most notably in the fields of physics, computer science, aerospace engineering, and space science. In this omnipresent context, the archaeological study of Cold War science is concerned principally with the material aspects and practices of scientific work.

Among the three frameworks that provide theoretical underpinnings for the archaeology of the Cold War, the archaeology of science is certainly the newest and least fully formed subfield. This fact is perhaps obvious in the relatively few reports or peer-reviewed papers reporting archaeology of science results; Schiffer (2013) was the first to provide an overview of the field. Yet these few papers and reports reveal a field with strong future potential, one with archaeological work that ranges from studies of Isaac

Newton's experiment waste (Spargo 2005) to the excavation of Australia's first optical observatory (Bickford et al. 2011).

Certainly one of the first questions that might come to mind when considering the archaeology of science is, What do archaeologists consider science? Seeking to avoid some of the more problematic aspects of defining science exclusively as Western nations' knowledge-producing activities that employ the scientific method, archaeologist Michael Schiffer (2013) more broadly characterizes science as any activity geared toward the creation of useful knowledge. Specifically, he refers to the kind of useful, predictive knowledge for which scientific effort is historically known and that facilitates successful human interactions with living and nonliving phenomena. Put more simply, knowledge activities qualify as scientific by virtue of their coherent, replicable approach and predictive utility in understanding or dealing with people, places, and things. This kind of science may start with an observation, hypothesis, question, theory, anomaly, enigma, or problem, and reach its result by inductive, deductive, or abductive reasoning.

Schiffer likewise provides a functional definition of the archaeology of science as "archaeological research into the processes and products of science, which includes the scientific activities of any person, organization, or society as well as the comparative study of such activities" (2013:13). Not only does this definition provide a suitable contextual framing of the work, but the somewhat ambiguous "processes and products" element nicely leaves sufficient latitude for investigating the broad range of tangible and intangible features and artifacts associated with science, including the landscapes, places, spaces, tools, and other objects of scientific work. Tied to the behavioral archaeology school of thought, Schiffer's main interest is archaeologically exploring the processes of science and its material products through the remains of scientific activities left by individuals, organizations, or societies in prehistoric, historic, or modern times, and therefore he tends to frame research questions in terms of people-artifact interactions (2013:13).

Several characteristics not necessarily exclusive to science but common in scientific endeavors help frame archaeological investigations of science or scientific work. First, scientific work typically occurs as discrete projects; that is, large, organized endeavors aimed at a specific goal or set of goals. The Manhattan Project effort to develop the first atomic bomb is an excellent example of this. As Schiffer (2013) notes, scientific projects consistently require a range of natural, human, economic, ideological, informational, and technological resources, which supply raw material, support, and even context for the performance of scientific activities both large and small. Most importantly for the archaeologist of science, the production, use, and disposal of these resources generally leave tangible and intangible remains in the spaces, places, and landscapes of scientific work, which might then become the purview of archaeology. Second, the archaeology of science is currently evolving as an intensely cross-disciplinary pursuit. Schiffer (2013) argues that just as archaeology traditionally reaches across subject matter and disciplinary boundaries, so too does the archaeology of science. Borrowing constructs and theoretical frameworks from numerous social scientific and humanities disciplines, some of which have been studying science and scientific practices for decades, an archaeological study of science might begin by excavating the remains of an astronomical observatory but end up in a chemistry laboratory studying the materiality of telescope optics.

While archaeologies of American science are not abundant in the historical archaeology literature, the studies are often notable. One example is an archaeological investigation of the scientific workplace of Thomas Edison. Archaeologists at Monmouth University conducted fieldwork in 2002 at Thomas Edison's Menlo Park Laboratory in New Jersey (Gall et al. 2007). After being notified of a small but growing sinkhole on the property, investigating archaeologists discovered a secret subterranean vault they believed Edison used to protect documents relating to his research and development facility during the late nineteenth century. After excavating the upper portion of a doorway sufficiently to gain access to the vault, archaeologists took measurements and photographs of its interior before the vault was reburied for safety and security reasons. Research revealed a 7 by 12 foot vault of mortared brick with a brick-arched ceiling, built entirely below grade with a complex double-door system that provided both security and fire protection for the storage of office records, patent drawings, laboratory notebooks, and other business records. A rather innovative aspect of the vault was a heating pipe running through it, which helped maintain a relatively constant temperature even during the frigid New Jersey winters. After reviewing thousands of documents and company records generated by laboratory staff and finding only two veiled passing references to the vault in Edison's assistant's documents

(Gall 2004), archaeologists postulate that it was likely kept secret from the laboratory workforce to protect the intellectual property it held.

The excavation of Edison's vault is a noteworthy example of the archaeology of science. Similarly, the scientific practices of the Cold War provide a material record for archaeological study. The principal challenge for Cold War archaeology is to develop a research design that focuses on matters of science outside the purview of the more widely practiced conflict archaeology. Two studies summarized in this volume have achieved notable success in this regard. Delgado (1996) explores the material aspects of Cold War nuclear weapons science metrology as exhibited in the remains of test instrumentation at Bikini Atoll. Influenced by nuclear weapons anthropologist Hugh Gusterson, he interprets the rudimentary pressure test gauges and instrumentation found on the wrecks at Bikini as technological adaptations designed to help nuclear weapons scientists comprehend the nuclear bomb's incredible nature by quantifying some of the most elementary physical characteristics of nuclear blasts (Delgado 1996:170). Delgado draws on ethnographic studies by Gusterson (1992) to provide a more nuanced psychological context to the testing artifacts recovered from the wrecked *Saratoga*, including peak pressure gauges constructed of steel plate sets drilled with holes of various diameters and sandwiched with tinfoil which ruptured at various pressures, and lead plates that recorded blast overpressures through indentations created by small steel balls pressed against the plate during the explosion.

In her studies at the Nevada Test Site (NTS), Colleen Beck similarly frames the remains of nuclear tests as being more scientific experiment than military effects testing. As Beck notes, "A focus has been placed on the structures that most resemble similar structures in everyday life, such as a train trestle, a bank vault and a house. While these types of structures survive and were integral to testing experiments, they represent only a few of the remains and are not the common ones. Yet, they are the constructions that most people relate to easily, and, therefore, will continue to dominate the representation of Nevada Test Site remains" (Beck 2002:68). In other words, for the general public the most obvious and interesting artifacts of Cold War nuclear weapons testing at NTS are not the far more numerous blocks of concrete, which were used for experiments such as neutron line-of-sight studies, but rather the familiar objects of everyday life that were the focus of the more infrequent military tests. Independent of public interest, future archaeologies of science at NTS might well focus on these relatively mundane artifacts of scientific inquiry.

Although I discuss both Delgado's and Beck's work more deeply in Chapter 4, a point worth making here is that when framed as archaeology of science these investigations can be novel approaches to understanding the practices of nuclear testing. The characterization of Bikini Atoll measurement devices as instruments for comprehending the incomprehensible and the understanding of NTS remains as the products of scientific, rather than military, experiments are just two possible approaches to the study of the material culture of Cold War science. Studies such as these help make the archaeology of science a viable and substantive framework for conducting archaeologies of the Cold War.

Archaeology of the Cold War

Regardless of which theoretical framework archaeologists choose to apply to the material culture study of the Cold War, the nature of the conflict itself has had a profound impact on the ways in which the field is approached in academia and accepted by the general public. While some readers may view the notion of the Cold War as a fearsome heritage as disproportionately subjective or dramatic, it is nevertheless useful in confronting the powerful mythologies and nationalistic metanarratives that have arisen out of the Cold War memory to tell the story from heroic, hegemonic perspectives and in simplistic, binary terms of communism versus capitalism, East versus West, or good versus evil. The waging of the Cold War was in reality far more complex and multifaceted than popular history would lead us to believe. This reality begs for scholarly studies that bring more than simply memories and propaganda to the table, even though archaeological studies of the Cold War are neglected by much of American academia. As I write this, not a single academic program or university course is being taught in the United States on the archaeology of the Cold War, despite the inspiring archaeological work being done and the tens of thousands (literally) of North American Cold War sites in need of deeper, broader, and more theoretically challenging interpretations.

Because no particular school of thought is claiming academic ownership of Cold War scholarship, the dominant theoretical approach to the archaeological study of this period in the United States has been decidedly processual, which has served a demand for accurate and relatively objective information about military heritage sites gathered via historical archaeology methods. This approach predominates because the majority of archaeological studies of U.S. Cold War sites are aimed at meeting the government's cultural resource management needs.

In the United States the archaeology of the Cold War was initiated, and remains substantially driven, by federal government mandate. The Department of Defense Appropriations Act, 1991 created the Department of Defense (DoD) Legacy Resource Management Program, an effort intended to manage natural and cultural resources on lands controlled by the DoD. In particular, the act ordered the DoD to "establish and coordinate by fiscal year 1993 with other Federal departments, agencies and entities a project to inventory, protect and conserve the physical and literary property and relics of the Department of Defense, in the United States and overseas, connected with the origins and development of the Cold War, which are not already being carried out by other capable institutions or programs" (U.S. Congress 1990). By 1994 the DoD had published *Coming in from the Cold—Military Heritage in the Cold War* (Cameron 1994), a report describing how the Legacy Program would fulfill its federal mandate by (1) creating thematic and contextual studies related to American military activities during the Cold War, (2) conducting surveys of Cold War historic resources controlled or operated by the DoD, and (3) establishing fundamental guidelines for the management and preservation of DoD Cold War cultural assets. *Coming in from the Cold* was followed by other publications by DoD scholars, most notably Lavin (1998) and Salmon (2011), who developed and refined methods for surveying Cold War historic resources, records management, and museum collection curation, while also contributing to international scholarly activities in Cold War archaeology and architectural history.

This last activity proved essential to international researchers because it provided information about U.S.-leased facilities that might not be readily available from foreign government sources. The information included unclassified or declassified information about U.S. military missions, intelligence activities, weapons testing, force training, and scientific research and development. The gesture accompanied various international accomplishments in the archaeology of the Cold War. For example, the Royal Commission on the Historical Monuments of England (later to become English Heritage) undertook a comprehensive study in the 1990s documenting sites and collecting data on all of the United Kingdom's Cold

War historic resources (Cocroft and Thomas 2003). In addition, several British universities (including the University of Bristol and the University of York) made the archaeological study of the Cold War part of their archaeology curricula, typically taught under the domain of conflict archaeology or archaeology of the contemporary past.[2] In a similar vein, the Danish Agency for Culture (DAC) coordinated the Cold War Installations Project, a project undertaken in 2012 to identify Cold War installations in Denmark, Greenland, and the Faroe Islands and to promote their study and conservation. Employing archival records and lists of state and government installations from the Danish Defense Construction and Infrastructure Service and the Danish Maritime Safety Administration as a basis, the DAC created a list of roughly 1,350 Cold War installations and sites ranging from airfields and radar installations to Continuity of Government bunkers (Hansen et al. 2013; Stenak et al. 2014).

In the United States, historians and historic archaeologists conducting archaeological studies of Cold War sites for the National Park Service (NPS) and the DoD would likewise produce a wealth of historic building reports and National Historic Landmark designations. Because a large number of early Cold War properties had already passed the 50-year threshold for National Register of Historic Places (NRHP) evaluations by the mid-1990s, evaluations of the Cold War properties, mostly under the DoD, could no longer be delayed unless they were "exceptionally important" and clearly required special consideration. This 50-year threshold was critical as it also meant that the number of evaluation-eligible Cold War properties would continue to grow with each passing year. By 2006, some 115,000 properties, out of an estimated 345,000 total facilities in the DoD property inventory, were already past the 50-year threshold, and by 2025 the number will reach 230,000 properties (Gregory and Tagg 2008). Making conservative estimates, Gregory and Tagg calculate a cost of $2,000 per building evaluation, and assuming only half of the facilities are ever inventoried, predict that it could cost the DoD more than $230 million and many decades of work to conduct just the initial historical documentation and NRHP eligibility determinations for those Cold War properties that were eligible in 2006. The burden of properties awaiting review will continue to grow until 2039, when the last Cold War building—built in 1989—will require eligibility evaluation.

Given the tremendous cost and intellectual effort required simply to conduct NRHP eligibility determinations, it is not surprising that investigations of Cold War military sites in the United States have rarely gone beyond the field survey stage to initiate field excavations. Nonetheless, studies of Cold War sites have been conducted across most of the principal areas of Cold War military-industrial activity from air defense to the design, development, manufacturing, testing, transport, and deployment of nuclear weapons and related defensive technologies (Schofield et al. 2002). With only a few exceptions, these archaeological studies of the Cold War in the United States have focused on the earliest decades of the conflict, principally because the 50-year threshold for NRHP evaluation has driven much of the funding and legitimacy of the work. Conspicuously absent from archaeological study of Cold War North America are North American academic archaeologists. That is, archaeologists teaching and working at colleges and universities, rather than employed as Cultural Resource Management (CRM) archaeologists, have provided little in the way of research contributions. The result of this pattern has been a plethora of very well-recorded sites with a general lack of theoretical discussions about the findings. Missing from what has proven to be an extensive geographical and topical mix of Cold War site studies are philosophical explorations of the underlying social, psychological, and ideological aspects of Cold War materiality that CRM archaeologists simply are not paid by their sponsors to develop. This situation leaves open the door to independent or collaborative scholarly research between academic archaeologists and the CRM archaeologists who are typically experts on the facilities and sites under their study and stewardship.

Summary

The archaeology of the Cold War draws on a range of methods and theoretical frameworks, from conflict archaeology to the archaeology of the contemporary or recent past to the archaeology of science. Each of these approaches provides relevant and useful constructs for studying the Cold War material record. Yet, in order to understand how the confluence of Cold War social, scientific, and political material life has become the topic of serious archaeological study, we must also understand a bit about the ways in which the North American Cold War built landscape emerged. That landscape and its creation is the focus of the next chapter.

3

MATTERS OF CONTEXT

Building a Cold War Landscape

Few events of the twentieth century shaped the North American built landscape as substantially as the Cold War. Across the continent, a Cold War landscape emerged with a purpose driven substantially by technological responses to the conflict. Strategic air bases, radar stations, and missile launch sites were built to detect and repel Soviet air strikes. Research laboratories, weapons factories, and testing sites occupied vast tracts of land to build better bombs. Underground bunkers were constructed to assure continuity of government as Canada and the United States assembled a landscape premised exclusively upon ersatz attacks. This preparation even crept into North American civilian life as private and public fallout shelters, transportation systems, and communications infrastructures were built.

Dividing the Cold War into three discrete historical periods, which may not necessarily correspond to any temporal divisions used by either historians or political scientists, I trace the building of this expansive and expensive Cold War landscape across twentieth-century time and space as the result of evolution, revolution, and resolution. In the first period (1945–1957), a built landscape evolved out of preexisting World War Two military-industrial capabilities. These were primarily research and development, production, and continental defense sites. During this period, the United States would not only maintain a robust conventional weapons capability but would expand the capabilities of the former Manhattan Project sites, transforming them from what had been small-scale scientific or experimental facilities into larger-scale industrial production sites.

In addition to artillery, tank, airplane, and ship manufactories, there were various arsenals, high-explosives works, and ammunition depots, including 21 Army ammunition plants in 15 states (Shiman 1997).

By the middle period (1958–1975), the U.S. military-industrial complex was involved in a technological revolution driven by six core technology areas regarded as essential to winning the Cold War conflict. I examine these as advances to continental defense, production, command and control, and civil defense sites. During this period, the United States also worked to extend and expand its global influence and military presence. Even before all of the U.S. Nike Ajax sites were fully operational, they began being replaced by Nike Hercules, a surface-to-air missile with even greater speed, range, and accuracy. These Nike Hercules missiles were also deployed throughout the 1960s to Denmark, West Germany, Greece, Italy, Korea, Norway, Okinawa, Taiwan, and Turkey with U.S. Army troops (Cagle 1973). Built internationally in configurations identical to their North American counterparts, Nike missiles and their production facilities are prime examples of how U.S. defense technologies and physical infrastructures were widely exported during this era to allied nations.

By the third period (1976–1989), North America was experiencing a marked decrease in Cold War construction as domestic and global opposition to the conflict grew. Types of sites discussed in this last period include continental defense, production, and unique to the Cold War landscape, sites of antiwar and antinuclear protest.

This virtual journey through the Cold War built landscape is, by necessity, neither a comprehensive chronology of the war nor a complete catalogue of all its sites. Rather, it is a survey of some of the most important and abundant historic properties of the landscape grouped according to a typology originally suggested by Salmon (2011).

Evolution: Early Cold War (1945–1957)

I begin where few other Cold War histories start, with the atomic bombings of Hiroshima and Nagasaki. From a political perspective, the Cold War had not yet begun in 1945, as the United States had generally yet to engage the Soviet Union with the strong rhetoric that would characterize later interactions. Relations between the two future superpowers were more or less friendly. From a technological perspective, however, by late 1945 the postwar military landscape in the United States was already evolving to respond to a potential Soviet threat. Running counter to the post–World War Two demobilization was the creation of a defense industry, with Manhattan Project facilities at its core, that was capable of producing and deploying more atomic weapons. With the passage in 1946 of the Atomic Energy Act and creation of the Atomic Energy Commission (AEC), nuclear weapons development and production in the United States fell wholly under civilian control. The AEC became a driving force in the building of the U.S. nuclear weapons complex. By 1951, nearly three-quarters of the AEC's $2 billion annual budget would go to construction projects (Gerber 1992).

While the AEC was coming into its own, significant organizational changes were affecting the U.S. military: the National Security Act of 1947 created the Department of the Air Force, along with the Department of the Navy and the Department of the Army (formerly called the Department of War), as branches of a new Department of Defense (DoD). Three combat commands comprised the new U.S. Air Force: the Strategic Air Command (SAC), which had command and control of land-based strategic bombers and ICBMs; the Tactical Air Command (TAC), which provided support for ground forces operations using tactical air, air defense, and air reserve forces; and the Air Defense Command (ADC), which provided for the air defense of the continental United States using early warning radar defenses, the Ground Observer Corps, antiaircraft missiles, and interceptor air defense forces (Wolf 1987). All three of these commands would ultimately have strong roles in shaping North America's Cold War defense. Together, the AEC and DoD would bring about broad changes to the twentieth-century built landscape, beginning with facilities and sites for scientific research and development.

Research and Development Sites

Exemplifying the role scientific research and development played in advancing and sustaining the Cold War were America's science laboratories. Chief among these were the nuclear weapons laboratories, which conducted the design, development, and experimental testing of nuclear fission, and later nuclear fusion, weapons. Manhattan Project Site Y, later to become known as Los Alamos Scientific Laboratory (LASL), evolved from a scattering of hastily constructed World War Two–era wooden buildings into a complex of roughly 2,000 permanent structures spread

Figure 3.1. The entrance to the Main Technical Area at Los Alamos Scientific Laboratory in New Mexico, in 1951. Five years into the Cold War, facilities at LASL were non-hardened, much as they had been under the Manhattan Project. In the next decade, successful creation of a hydrogen bomb led to funding for dozens of new scientific facilities. By permission of Los Alamos National Laboratory.

across 43 square miles of high desert mesas. High explosives formulated at LASL were tested in surrounding remote canyons, while experimental nuclear devices designed, built, and assembled at LASL were shipped to "proving grounds" in the central Pacific Ocean and Nevada. Although LASL's Cold War mission encompassed a broad range of basic scientific research in physical and biological sciences, the laboratory's core research focused on nuclear weapons physics theory and experimentation.

Prioritizing function over form, the early LASL structures were simple and pragmatic. Most early buildings were wooden (Figure 3.1), but as the permanence of the site grew, later structures were made of reinforced concrete. Unlike most Cold War military structures, however, LASL structures were generally neither buried nor hardened against potential Soviet nuclear attack, in order to create and sustain a more campus-like atmosphere.

By April 1948 the nuclear weapons ordnance and engineering functions had been completely transferred from LASL to Sandia Base in

Albuquerque, creating what was thereafter known as Sandia Laboratory. By 1951, Sandia Laboratory had expanded to 14 permanent wooden buildings distributed across two technical areas. Over the early decades of the Cold War, Sandia expanded into five technical areas with hundreds of buildings, mostly wooden, distributed across nearly 9,000 acres and evolving into what would ultimately become Sandia National Laboratories (Furman 1990; Johnson 1997; Ulrich 1998).

In 1952, the University of California Radiation Laboratory at Livermore (later Lawrence Livermore National Laboratory) joined Los Alamos as the nation's second nuclear weapons design facility. Built to provide competition with and peer review for Los Alamos nuclear weapon designs, Livermore was smaller, encompassing only a single square mile. Nonetheless, it would contribute significantly to the development of the U.S. nuclear weapons arsenal. Ultimately, LASL, Livermore, and Sandia would constitute the core scientific and engineering laboratories for America's nuclear weapons complex throughout the Cold War and beyond.

Critical to Cold War research and development were facilities and sites for testing all types of weapons and defensive technologies. Although the first American atomic tests conducted in the Pacific occurred under Operation Crossroads in 1946, it was not until 1951 that the United States established permanent testing facilities at what would come to be known as the Pacific Proving Grounds (PPG). Consisting of Enewetak and Bikini Atolls in what is now the Republic of the Marshall Islands, the PPG would be the site of eight major nuclear weapons test series, or operations, as they were more often called. Although tests at the PPG constituted less than 15 percent of the total number of U.S. nuclear tests, it bore the brunt of 80 percent of the total U.S. nuclear explosion yields, a combined explosive yield of more than 200 megatons released in little more than a decade of testing.[3] With relatively large, shallow lagoons and land areas totaling just two and three square miles, respectively, Enewetak and Bikini Atolls teemed with military and scientific encampments, laboratory facilities, and firing sites from 1947 through 1958.

Established in 1951 as a continental nuclear weapons test site, the Nevada Proving Grounds, later called the Nevada Test Site (NTS), was intended to supplement PPG testing operations by providing a site closer to home for testing less powerful atomic devices. The Nevada Proving Grounds site is described further in Chapter 4.

Beyond these nuclear weapons testing spaces, other "proving grounds" also emerged. Consisting of more than 3,000 square miles of restricted access rangeland, White Sands Proving Ground was a place to test the Cold War's most dangerous, and often unpredictable, non-nuclear weapon technologies. It developed into a plethora of specialized technical facilities and structures, including missile launch sites, rocket sled tracks, rocket engine test stands, and radar tracking stations. Between 1946 and 1952, more than 60 V-2 rockets confiscated from Germany at the end of the war in Europe were launched from White Sands, requiring the construction of a large rocket assembly building, launch platforms, a gantry crane, a blockhouse, and an observation tower (Quinn 1986). A military cantonment built in 1948 allowed the Proving Ground to become a permanent facility for the testing of Corporal, Talos, Nike, Athena, Hawk, Sprint, Patriot, and other Cold War missile systems.

Supplementing the White Sands test facilities were launch facilities at Vandenberg Air Force Base (AFB) in California and Cape Canaveral Air Force Station (AFS) in Florida. Vandenberg and Cape Canaveral served as the principal launch points for the Eastern and Western Missile Test Ranges, respectively. The Eastern Missile Test Range (EMTR) extended southeastward across the Atlantic Ocean, while the Western Missile Test Range (WMTR) extended west from its Vandenberg AFB launch point across the Pacific Ocean as far as Kwajalein Atoll in the Republic of the Marshall Islands at its western end. The two ranges constituted the most extensive missile testing spaces appropriated in the Cold War; combined, they restricting commercial air and sea traffic through corridors covering more than a million square miles of ocean. The WMTR was used both to launch missiles and to train and test the launch crews. Advanced missileer training often involved launching unarmed ICBMs across the Pacific to land in Kwajalein Atoll lagoon as part of live-fire missile exercises known as "glory trips." At Kwajalein, 11 of the atoll's 97 islands host radar installations, optics instruments, satellite telemetry, and communications equipment used for a wide range of missile-related tests.

Built on 42 miles of California coastline, Vandenberg AFB was established in 1956 at the site of Cooke AFB. This former Army training camp has unique geospatial characteristics that not only allow test missiles to be launched across the ocean without flying over populated areas, but enable satellite-bearing rockets to be launched directly toward the South Pole to achieve polar orbits around the Earth. Polar orbits were critical to Cold War reconnaissance and Earth-mapping satellites, as on each of their polar-crossing orbits they would also pass over the equator at a different longitude, allowing the satellites to monitor or photograph every part of the planet as the Earth rotates beneath them every 90 minutes. Vandenberg AFB has played a role in the development and testing of every historically significant American ballistic missile system, including Thor, Atlas, Titan, Minuteman, and Peacekeeper (Corbett 1994; Nowlan et al. 1996). The archaeologies of Cape Canaveral and the EMTR are discussed more extensively in Chapter 4.

Production Sites

One of the first atomic weapon production facilities to evolve from a Manhattan Project role into a larger, long-term Cold War manufacturing plant was Mound Laboratory. Originating in 1943 as the Dayton Project, and composed of three Dayton, Ohio, operations for extracting and purifying polonium for use in the initiators of early atomic weapons, in 1949 the operations moved to a 182-acre site near Miamisburg, Ohio. Named for the Miamisburg Mound, a nearby Woodland Period (Adena Culture) Native American burial mound, Mound Laboratory was the first new AEC facility constructed after World War Two. Seventeen large buildings, constructed mostly of reinforced concrete, were interconnected by 6 miles of paved roads and enclosed within an 8-foot-high chain-link fence. Among these structures was the two-story Technical Building for polonium research and production. Built 50 feet underground on an 8-foot-thick slab with 16-foot-thick reinforced-concrete walls and a 15-foot-thick roof, it was perhaps the most hardened facility of the Cold War. In 1956, high explosives work replaced polonium production after initiators became obsolete. For the remainder of the Cold War, Mound produced detonators, cable assemblies, timers, firing sets, and other non-nuclear components of nuclear weapons (Buchanan and Auxier 2000).

Beginning its existence as the Clinton Engineer Works, Oak Ridge Reservation was another former Manhattan Project site. Built on 59,000 acres in the Clinch River valley near Oak Ridge, Tennessee, the facility was both a research-and-development and a production site. The production areas consisted of the K-25, Y-12, and X-10 facilities. A massive U-shaped building encompassing more than 44 acres, the K-25 facility used a gaseous diffusion process to separate uranium-235 from uranium-238. The smaller Y-12 plant contained massive electromagnetic coils for separating uranium-235 from natural uranium ores. The X-10 facility, which evolved into the current Oak Ridge National Laboratory (ORNL), initially used neutrons emitted from the fission of uranium-235 to convert uranium-238 into plutonium-239 for use in nuclear weapons, but after the war shifted from weapons work to military and commercial nuclear reactor, nuclear physics, and health physics research, and production of medical isotopes.

Occupying roughly 640 square miles in Washington State's Columbia River valley, the Hanford Engineer Works (HEW) was the largest of the original three Manhattan Project sites, producing plutonium for use by other nuclear weapons production facilities. Divided into three main material production areas, Hanford had a vast footprint in order to keep the production buildings—in this case, nuclear reactors—safely separated by at least a mile, and the production areas themselves separated by at least four miles.

Three massive expansion programs at HEW in 1947 made it the largest peacetime construction project in American history up to that time (Gerber 1992). By 1949, the Plutonium Finishing Plant was complete, enabling conversion of the plutonium nitrate paste, which Hanford had been making using precipitation and solvent extraction processes, into plutonium metal buttons for shipment to Los Alamos, and later to the Rocky Flats Nuclear Weapons Plant in Colorado. HEW continued to grow throughout the Cold War, at its peak encompassing more than 500 structures. Many of these structures, with the notable exception of the B Reactor facility, which was designated a National Historic Landmark in 2008, have since been decommissioned and razed.

During World War Two the uranium for America's first atomic bombs came from the Shinkolobwe Mine in the Katanga Province of what is now the Democratic Republic of the Congo in Africa (Nichols 1987). In 1950 a Navajo shepherd set in motion what would become one of the most profitable—and toxic—transformations of the American Cold War landscape when he discovered uranium ore on Haystack Mesa near Grants, New Mexico. The discovery of domestic uranium ore would cause a surge in uranium exploration and mining across the American West in general, and on Navajo sovereign lands in particular. Miners in the 1950s opened more than 1,000 uranium mines on Navajo Nation lands alone. Soon, the American Southwest was teeming with uranium mines, processing mills, and ore-shipping facilities, both large and small (Brugge et al. 2006). As the Cold War progressed, the Grants District of New Mexico and Gas

Hills area of Riverton, Wyoming, emerged as the nation's two largest uranium producers (U.S. Environmental Protection Agency 2008). From these sites, ore for the U.S. nuclear arsenal would flow into an extensive nationwide refining process.

By October 1950, in light of growing concern over increased Soviet military strength and a successful 1949 atomic bomb test, President Truman ordered the AEC to expand its uranium production capabilities. By 1951, the first buildings of the Fernald Feed Materials Production Plant had been built on 1,050 acres of farmland near Cincinnati for converting and refining uranium-bearing pitchblende ore, initially from the African Congo and later from the American Southwest, into high-purity uranium compounds and metals. Fully operational by 1954, Fernald's 10 production buildings covered 136 acres of the 1,000-acre site. Fernald produced uranium trioxide for enrichment at the Paducah Gaseous Diffusion Plant in Kentucky, as well as uranium fuel core elements for the Hanford Site in Washington and the Savannah River Plant in South Carolina. The five production buildings of the Paducah plant had been built on a 3,500-acre site, only 74 acres of which was covered with actual floor space. By 1954 the facility was producing low-grade enriched uranium from uranium hexafluoride shipped from the Weldon Spring Uranium Feed Materials Plant in Missouri for refinement at the Oak Ridge gaseous diffusion plant.

In 1952, the first enrichment cells of the Portsmouth Gaseous Diffusion Plant near Columbus, Ohio, also began producing highly enriched uranium-235, on 640 acres of a 3,800-acre former farmstead. More than 190 buildings comprised the Portsmouth site, including Building X-333, which alone covered 65 square acres and, when completed in 1955, was among the largest single structures of the American Cold War production landscape (Makhijani et al. 1995).

By June 1957, operations of the former Mallinckrodt Chemical Works had moved to a 200-acre site near Weldon Spring, Missouri. Mallinckrodt had begun purifying uranium from high-grade African pitchblende ore at its Destrehan Street Refinery and Metal Plant in St. Louis in 1942, and by 1956 this plant had processed more than 50,000 tons of uranium ore. The new plant at Weldon Spring consisted of 44 buildings built on what had once been part of the 17,000-acre Weldon Spring Ordnance Works. Mallinckrodt Chemical Works's transformation into the Weldon Spring Uranium Feed Materials Plant significantly increased the facility's uranium production capacity, expanding its operations for assaying ore concentrate, called yellowcake, and converting it to uranium hexafluoride, uranium trioxide, and uranium metal for use at Cold War nuclear weapons sites.

The AEC broke ground in July 1951 on what would become the first of four buildings on a remote plateau northwest of Denver, Colorado, known as Rocky Flats. Completed in 1952, the first structure of the Rocky Flats Plant was Building 991, the final assembly, inspection, and shipping point for nuclear weapon trigger components fabricated on-site and at Hanford and Oak Ridge. By 1957, Rocky Flats had grown to 27 buildings. Until its closure in 1989, Rocky Flats produced the triggers, or "pits," for every nuclear weapon in the U.S. arsenal (Ackland 1999).

Eventually comprising more than 6,500 acres in total, Rocky Flats consisted of a core area of 436 structures spread across 384 acres surrounded in turn by a 6,116-acre buffer zone. Production at Rocky Flats took place in four geographically separated facilities, each designed for a different type of work. Workers cast and machined parts out of uranium produced at the Paducah and Fernald plants, recovered highly enriched uranium from "buttons" produced at the Oak Ridge Y-12 plant and, beginning in 1953, processed plutonium. Plutonium processing involved refining plutonium and fabricating weapons component parts from them in gloveboxes such as those shown in Figure 3.2 (Aaron and Berryman 1997).

The Savannah River Plant (SRP) began operations in 1954 as the largest atomic bomb component production site east of the Mississippi River. Situated near Aiken, South Carolina, the SRP specialized in the extraction, purification, and processing of tritium gas, a critical component for boosting the explosive energy of nuclear weapons. The 310 square miles of land required for the SRP was acquired under the authority of eminent domain, seizing a large portion of farmland occupied primarily by African American sharecroppers, as well as by the former small towns of Dunbarton, Ellenton, Hawthorne, Meyers Mill, Leigh, and Robbins. The SRP site was partitioned into seven separate areas. At its core were five tritium production reactors aligned in a massive arc, each purposely separated from the others by 2½ miles. A second area at SRP had two large tritium gas-separation-process facilities. Both four stories tall, these 850-foot-long reinforced-concrete structures had two interior rooms dubbed "canyons" that stretched the length of the building. At the end of each canyon was a railroad tunnel with a large shielded door for receiving and shipping tritium containers (Gillett et al. 2007; Reed et al. 2003).

Figure 3.2. Workers at Rocky Flats, near Denver, Colorado, using gloveboxes in a plutonium analysis area in 1975. Production work at Rocky Flats typically required the use of such gloveboxes, equipped with lead-lined gloves for handling the radioactive plutonium and its compounds. By permission of the U.S. Department of Energy.

Built in 1941 on 19,000 acres outside Burlington, the Iowa Ordnance Plant was initially constructed to load, assemble, and pack artillery shells and bombs for World War Two. At war's end, ordnance production ceased and the plant sat idle until the AEC appropriated 16,000 acres of the site in 1947 for high explosives production and machining facilities. By 1949, non-nuclear weapon-component assembly operations at Sandia and nuclear-weapon assembly operations at Los Alamos had been moved to what would become known as the Burlington Atomic Energy Commission Plant (BAECP)(Norris 1992; Poole and Harrison 1954). At its peak, BAECP contained roughly 50 structures and sites, including facilities for high explosives casting, machining, and inspection; high explosives storage igloos (magazines) and vaults; bays for the final assembly of nuclear weapons, firing sites for explosives testing, and so-called burn grounds, for disposing of excess explosives by burning. Some of the most unusual facilities at BAECP were its nuclear weapon assembly bays. Circular reinforced-concrete structures constructed below grade supported roofs made of wire mesh and steel bridge cable. Loaded onto this wire mesh was a mound of rubberized asbestos meant to fall into and fill the workspace below in the event of a catastrophic non-nuclear explosion, thereby containing any potential radiation release (Poole and Harrison 1954). Similar structures for nuclear weapons assembly and disassembly were later built using gravel as fill at Pantex in Texas, at the NTS, and in the United Kingdom. These were dubbed "gravel gerties" after the Dick Tracy comic strip character of that name.

On the high plains of the Texas Panhandle northeast of Amarillo is the Pantex Plant. Drawing its name from its Pan[handle] of Tex[as] location, the plant was once one of 14 Army ordnance facilities built in World War Two to produce artillery shells and bombs. Immediately after the war the 16,000-acre facility was closed, but the AEC reopened it in 1951 for non-nuclear component assembly operations. Over the course of the Cold War Pantex evolved into a heavily fortified site for high explosives development, testing, and manufacturing, and nuclear weapons assembly and disassembly, with site-specific structures such as gravel gerties, earthen bunkers for weapons storage, and burn grounds for the disposal of waste explosives. To this day Pantex continues to provide sites for the testing, disposal, and destruction of high explosives with minimal disturbance to neighbors, and to serve as an isolated site for handling nuclear weapons (History Associates 1987; Makhijani et al. 1995).

Throughout the early years of the Cold War, the Soviet Union and the United States created and stockpiled thousands of tons of chemical agents and chemical munitions. The principal U.S. facility for these purposes was the Rocky Mountain Arsenal (RMA). Built on 20,000 acres west of Denver, Colorado, the RMA was a high-security enclave of roughly 300 structures, including the infamous Building 1501 (see Figure 3.3), for the production of sarin (nerve gas), mustard gas, and lewisite, a skin-blistering agent (Hess 1984). Until 1969 chemical agents were produced at RMA on an industrial scale, injected into munitions ranging from artillery shells to cluster bombs, and held in secure storage for the military (Tucker 2007).

Recognizing that the Cold War would likely be a conflict fought not just on land and in the air, but also at sea, the production landscape of the early Cold War includes shipyards where military and civilian workers produced one of the most important Cold War naval technologies to emerge in this era: the nuclear-powered submarine. In January 1955, America's first nuclear submarine, the USS *Nautilus*, traveled more than 1,300 miles underwater from the New London Naval Submarine Base in

Figure 3.3. Built between 1951 and 1953 in Commerce City, Colorado, Rocky Mountain Arsenal's Building 1501 was a windowless, five-story concrete blockhouse that served as the nation's principal sarin gas manufacturing facility until 1957. By permission of the U.S. Department of the Army.

Connecticut to Puerto Rico propelled exclusively by nuclear power. Submerged for 90 hours, *Nautilus* achieved the longest submerged cruise by a submarine to that time. This journey would usher in an era in which submarines would be capable of operating underwater for long periods without surfacing. By 1957, the USS *Skate* and other so-called *Skate*-class submarines were being launched from the General Dynamics Electric Boat facility at Groton Shipyard in Connecticut, Mare Island Naval Shipyard in California, and Portsmouth Naval Shipyard in New Hampshire.

The U.S. Navy's oldest continuously operating shipyard, Portsmouth Naval Shipyard built more than 19 submarines during the Cold War, including several of the Navy's nuclear fast attack and nuclear ballistic missile submarines. Mare Island Naval Shipyard, covering more than 2,625 acres of dry land and 1,900 acres of tideland, was one of only a few U.S. naval facilities that both built and overhauled submarines. During the Cold War, Mare Island workers would build 21 submarines (electric-diesel, nuclear fast attack, and nuclear ballistic missile) and overhaul dozens more. Registered in 1960 as a California Historical Landmark and with parts designated a National Historical Landmark District in 1975, Mare Island was decommissioned in 1996 (Adams 1974). Beginning in this first period and continuing throughout the Cold War, nuclear-powered submarines would become a key element in North America's continental defense (Polmar and Moore 2003).

After 25 years of silent service, the *Nautilus* was designated a National Historic Landmark in 1982, as was the USS *Albacore* in 1989, for innovation in Cold War submarine design. In 1990 and 1991, respectively, the destroyer USS *Edson* and aircraft carrier USS *Hornet* also joined the list of National Historic Landmarks, each for its unique role in Cold War naval service

Continental Defense Sites

In March 1948 the ADC began operating radar installations at Portland, Oregon; and at Arlington, Spokane, Neah Bay, and Hanford, Washington, 24 hours a day in order to protect the HEW from Soviet bomber attacks. Over the course of 1948, the ADC deployed additional World War Two–era radar antennae to sites at Twin Lights and Palermo, New Jersey; Montauk, New York; Albuquerque, New Mexico; and 13 other sites across the northeastern U.S. stretching from Maine to Michigan (Schaffel 1991). Because these makeshift radar systems were intended as an interim air defense measure, the radar antennas were simply lashed to the top of elevated wooden platforms in what was known as the "Lashup" system, with equipment and radar operators housed below in temporary wooden structures and Quonset huts. The temporary antennas were incorporated with other permanent radar installations in 1949, giving the Lashup radar network system a total of 44 operational sites by June 1950 (Winkler and Webster 1997).

The ADC constructed 23 new permanent radar stations in 1950, and renovated five former Lashup installations, in the first phase of creating a nationwide early warning radar network called the Permanent System. Operational in May 1952, the Permanent System would eventually consist of 75 primary radar stations supplemented by a number of small, unmanned "gap-filler" radar stations along with other mobile or semi-mobile installations (Grant 1954:41). By 1957, the Permanent System had grown to well more than 100 stations across the United States, most with steel towers of varying configurations accompanied by a small complex

Figure 3.4. As part of the Permanent System, the giant FPS-24 radar antenna of the 609th Radar Squadron at Eufaula AFS in Alabama searched the skies for distant incoming objects while the smaller antenna (*right*) measured their height above the terrain. The radar was part of the North American Aerospace Defense Command (NORAD) system. By permission of the U.S. Air Force.

of support buildings such as those at Eufaula AFS (Figure 3.4). These radar antennae, some weighing as much as 80 tons, were also mounted on 85-foot-high concrete towers and covered when necessary with domes, or radomes, to protect them against the elements.

The addition to the Permanent System of the Pinetree Line—a series of 39 pulsed-mode radar stations along the fiftieth parallel—and the Mid-Canada Line—a string of 90 unmanned Doppler radar sites along the fifty-fifth parallel—added still more radar sites to the North American Cold War landscape in the early 1950s. Before long, however, Soviet bomber advancements rendered the Pinetree and Mid-Canada Lines unable to provide adequate advance warning, due to the fact they were too far south in latitude. In response the U.S. and Canadian governments began construction in 1955 of one of the most ambitious, expensive, and logistically difficult projects of the Cold War, the Distant Early Warning (DEW) Line.

Composed of 63 interconnected radar stations, the DEW line crossed the northern reaches of the continent deep inside the Arctic Circle at roughly the sixty-ninth parallel, more than 800 miles closer to the Soviet Union than the Mid-Canada Line. Construction of DEW Line radar stations continued until 1957; the building of antennae, communication towers, and support buildings in highly remote regions required millions of work hours and hundreds of tons of construction materials and equipment, all delivered by cargo planes in the winter and ships to the closest port in summer.

Supplementing the DEW Line in later years was the BMEWS, long-range radar, computer, and communications systems built between 1960 and 1963 at Thule, Greenland; Clear, Alaska; and RAF Base Flyingdales in the United Kingdom. Thule and Clear consisted of three and four "billboard" detection radar antennae 165 feet high by 400 feet wide, along with rotating dish-type tracking radar (Figure 3.5). Together, the three radar systems covered a range of 3,000 nautical miles (Fletcher 1989).

Advanced warning for continental defense did not end at the continent's edge however. In 1952, the U.S. and UK navies secretly began deploying underwater listening arrays in the North Atlantic basin under the code name SOSUS (Sound Surveillance System). Consisting of hydrophones distributed at intervals of 5 to 15 miles along a cable connected to

Figure 3.5. The BMEWS radome at Clear AFS in Alaska in 1971. By permission of the U.S. Air Force.

a shore station, SOSUS became a fundamental method for detecting the presence of Soviet ballistic missile submarines crossing the GIUK gap; that is, the areas between Greenland, Iceland, and the United Kingdom in the North Atlantic Ocean through which Soviet Northern Fleet submarines would pass en route to the Atlantic from their Barents Sea ports. SOSUS used the ocean's "deep sound channel," a horizontal layer of water where the cumulative effects of pressure and temperature slow the speed of sound, allowing underwater acoustic signals to be detected by hydrophones over distances of hundreds, even thousands, of miles. Multiple SOSUS listening arrays deployed along the edge of the U.S. continental shelf allowed the Navy to detect Soviet submarine locations using principles of triangulation. Used extensively throughout the Cold War, the SOSUS system consisted of 20 monitoring arrays deployed in both the Atlantic and Pacific Oceans by the mid-1970s, but it was gradually deactivated in the waning years of the twentieth century. The United States currently maintains SOSUS arrays on standby status in shore facilities at Dam Neck, Virginia; Whidbey Island, Washington; and St. Mawgan in Cornwall (Whitman 2005).

Starting in 1956, a trio of three-legged ADC facilities in the Atlantic Ocean extended America's radar surveillance coverage eastward. Dubbed "Texas Towers" after the offshore oil drilling platforms used off the Texas coast, these towers were located 110 miles off the New York, Massachusetts, and New Hampshire coastlines, providing an additional half-hour advance warning of any Soviet bomber attack. Each tower consisted of a triangular steel platform, 200 feet wide on each side, standing on steel caisson legs anchored to the ocean floor. On decks roughly 80 feet above the water sat three radome-covered radar systems. Belowdecks were the radar equipment and control rooms, mess hall, and crew quarters. Three Texas Towers were operational by 1959, but four years after entering service, they were all gone. In 1961, the tower off Long Island, New York, collapsed into the sea during a winter storm, killing its entire crew of servicemen and civilian maintenance workers. The two remaining towers were decommissioned in 1963 after improved Soviet ICBMs eliminated any significant advantage to their standoff distance (Ray 1965).

Military housing emerged as an aspect of U.S. continental defense during the first decade of the Cold War. During World War Two, military housing had consisted principally of barracks on military bases for enlisted troops in training for overseas duty or for military personnel assigned to stateside duty. Whereas in previous wars soldiers had returned to their homes after service, the continuing nature of Cold War service necessitated that the military provide family housing on-base (Twiss and Martin 1998). In order to retain technologically trained service personnel, the military needed to create long-term housing not only for unmarried personnel, but for families as well. In light of substandard and inadequate housing at most military bases, Nebraska Senator Kenneth S. Wherry introduced legislation in 1949 to allow the construction of family housing by private developers at critical U.S. military installations. By 1950, the first Cold War military family housing project of 250 homes was completed at Maxwell AFB in Montgomery, Alabama (Baldwin 1996; Temme 1998). Under Wherry's bill, real estate developers built rental housing on leased government lands, with military families having rental priority for the first 50 years, after which the land and improvements would revert to the government.

Nearly 84,000 houses were built in the first five years after passage of the Wherry Act, until a financial fraud scandal hobbled it. By 1955 Indiana Senator Homer E. Capehart had introduced new legislation to replace the floundering Wherry program. Capehart Act homes were similarly built on or near military bases, but the housing was under military ownership. By the time the Capehart program ended in 1964, nearly 200,000 homes had been built, substantially changing the face of American military housing (Kuranda 2003).

Among the U.S. military's earliest responses to the first Soviet atomic test in 1949 was the development of antiaircraft defenses employing the Army's antiaircraft artillery battalions. From 1951 to 1959, the Army Antiaircraft Artillery Command (ARAACOM) defense network placed radar-guided 90 mm and 120 mm antiaircraft artillery batteries in a series of defensive arcs around major American cities and other critical defense areas (Figure 3.6). At the core of the ARAACOM defense was Skysweeper, an automated antiaircraft defense system with a built-in computer and radar system that could locate and track approaching aircraft while simultaneously firing its gun. Self-contained and initially intended as permanent defense resources, only seventeen 90 mm and five 120 mm antiaircraft artillery battalions were deployed in defensive positions across the United States by July 1950. Completion of the ARAACOM network would prove difficult, as most sites lacked permanent housing for troops. In fact, ARAACOM units deployed near Detroit, Brooklyn, and Chicago

Figure 3.6. Crews of the 770th Antiaircraft Artillery Battalion fire 120 mm guns during training at the Yakima Firing Center in Washington State in 1957. By permission of the U.S. Department of the Army.

were still living in tents in the winter of 1953 (Elliott 1953). By mid-1954, antiaircraft guns were being replaced by surface-to-air guided missiles, as faster, higher-flying Soviet airplanes presented greater nuclear attack risk.

By May 1954 the first Army Antiaircraft Artillery battalion was replaced by a Nike Ajax surface-to-air missile (SAM) battery south of Baltimore at Fort George G. Meade Radar Station. Over the next eight years, 265 more Nike Ajax sites would be built across the country, making Nike SAM batteries one of the most visible and pervasive elements of the early Cold War built landscape. Deployed in circular arrays called defense areas around important strategic sites—including major metropolitan areas, important defense factories, and military bases—Nike sites were considered the last line of defense against Soviet aircraft attacks.

Fully operational in 1963, the defense area system numbered 40 sites, with 4 to 19 Nike missiles per area, depending upon its size and the perceived strategic value of the potential targets. A typical Nike Ajax missile site consisted of at least two discrete tracts of land. One six-acre site contained the Integrated Fire Control (IFC), encompassing the radar and computer systems used for detecting, tracking, and targeting enemy aircraft and often serving as an administrative area with offices, barracks, and dining and recreation halls. The Launcher Area, a second tract of roughly 40 acres, was separated from the IFC by a distance of 1,000 yards. This area had underground missile storage magazines with a large elevator that brought the missiles to the surface as needed. The missiles then had to be manually pushed along rails into one of four separate launch positions as shown in Figure 3.7 (Lonnquest and Winkler 1996).

With Cold War weapons production increasing, the AEC soon required high-security storage sites for its growing stockpile of nuclear weapons. Creation of these sites, however, required a compromise in the longstanding rivalry between the AEC, which designed and built the weapons, and the DoD, which used them. The solution was to construct National Stockpile Sites where nuclear weapons components could be stored, protected, and prepared for deployment to the military as needed. Stockpile sites were built within the boundaries of existing military facilities but were under AEC control. The first three National Stockpile Sites were built at Kirtland AFB in New Mexico, Fort Hood in Texas, and Fort Campbell in Kentucky in 1948, and designated the Manzano, Killeen, and Clarksville

Figure 3.7. Nike guided missiles raised into firing positions at a battery in Lorton, Virginia, in 1954. By permission of the U.S. Department of the Army.

Bases, respectively. Additional Stockpile Sites (dubbed Bossier Base, Lake Mead Base, and Medina Base) were built during the 1951–1955 period at Barksdale AFB, Louisiana; Nellis AFB, Nevada; and Lackland AFB, Texas, respectively.

As the SAC continued to locate bomber bases closer to the nation's periphery throughout the 1950s, a demand for greater combat readiness necessitated the construction of smaller Operational Storage Sites (OSSs) at the Loring (Maine), Ellsworth (South Dakota), Fairchild (Washington), Travis (California), and Stony Brook (Massachusetts) SAC bases, as well as at the Seneca Army Depot (New York). The OSS decreased combat response times by placing nuclear weapons in close proximity to bomber alert crews. Prior to building of the OSS, U.S. bombers flying attack missions would need to be diverted to one of the National Stockpile Sites to load nuclear weapons before engaging the enemy, a trip that would have substantially increased response times. A B-36 bomber deployed out of Loring would have spent eight hours on a round-trip flight to obtain its nuclear payload from the nearest National Stockpile Site at Clarksville Base in Kentucky, prior to starting its attack.[4]

Access to the OSSs was restricted to Armed Forces Special Weapons Project personnel with Q-level, top-secret AEC security clearances. The heart of every OSS was its so-called Q Area, a collection of structures used for stockpiling, safeguarding, surveillance, maintenance, and final assembly of nuclear weapons. Surrounding the Q Areas and separating them from their encompassing military facilities were three concentric lines of chain-link security fencing topped with razor wire. Inside these fences were conventional military structures for administrative, security, and fire protection functions, as well as a collection of architecturally unique structures. These structures included rest houses (buildings for the temporary storage of explosives), igloos (earth-covered magazines for long-term explosives and ammunition storage), and reinforced-concrete capsule storage buildings (for nuclear warhead storage), along with their associated, strategically placed concrete pillboxes (Figures 3.8 and 3.9), where heavily armed security forces stood guard whenever personnel were handling warheads inside the capsule storage buildings (Weitze 1999). Although most SAC bases have been decommissioned and razed, leaving little or no significant architectural remains, examples of Q areas still exist, most notably at Clarksville Base, Kentucky; the former Stony Brook AFS, Massachusetts; and the former Loring SAC base, Maine.

Above: Figure 3.8. A former capsule storage building in the Loring AFB Weapons Storage Area, Limestone, Maine, in 1998. These windowless, reinforced-concrete structures were disguised with false fenestrations on the exterior to make them look like conventional buildings from a distance, but inside they had 10-foot-thick walls and interior bank vault doors for the high-security storage of nuclear weapons components. By permission of the U.S. Air Force.

Left: Figure 3.9. Guarding the entrance to each capsule storage building were pillboxes, like this one at the former Weapons Storage Area, Loring AFB. Security personnel armed with Thompson submachine guns entered the pillbox via a trapdoor on the roof. Once inside, the guards provided a formidable security presence during capsule building operations and nuclear weapons transfers. By permission of the U.S. Air Force.

Equally essential to mounting an effective Cold War continental defense were communications, energy, and transportation infrastructures. One of the most enduring and visible features of this type was North America's system of interstate and interprovincial highways. In Canada, the Trans-Canada Highway Act of 1949 authorized the Trans-Canada Highway, while the United States created a national interstate highway network colloquially known as "the Interstate."

Originally authorized but not built under the Federal-Aid Highway Act of 1944, the interstate highway system was reauthorized under the Federal-Aid Highway Act of 1956 (Public Law 84-627) with increased funding and a new name as the National System of Interstate and Defense Highways. Fearing a possible Soviet invasion, President Dwight D. Eisenhower signed the act into law and pushed for rapid completion of the system in order to increase the U.S. military's ability to transport troops and equipment quickly and efficiently across the country and from airports, seaports, and rail terminals to military bases. The act created 40,000 miles of uniformly constructed, reinforced-concrete, two-lane superhighways stretching across the United States, using 423 million tons of concrete and 7 million tons of steel (Sullivan 2006).

By the end of the first period of the Cold War, North America's research and development laboratories, production facilities, testing sites, and civil infrastructure were well established. A revolution was coming, however. The crisis erupted in 1957 when the Soviet Union launched the Sputnik satellite into orbit around Earth. Sputnik's tacit message to the West was that the Soviets possessed the technological capabilities to fly rockets over long distances carrying heavy payloads, which could include nuclear warheads. While Sputnik was a significant achievement, it was also mostly symbolic, as the USSR had already successfully conducted its first ICBM test flight two months earlier. Known as 8K71 No.8, that missile flight exploded the long-held belief that a Soviet nuclear attack against the United States could only come on the wings of Soviet bombers (Podvig 2001). Lacking substantial ICBM research effort of its own, and having created an extensive continental attack warning system premised solely on defense against relatively slow-moving (as compared to missiles) bombers, the United States suddenly needed to shift its technological development work toward the creation of long-range ballistic missiles and missile defense warning systems. That shift would bring about a technological revolution in North America.

Revolution: Middle Cold War (1958–1975)

The middle period is characterized by changes to the North American landscape tied to an industrial base that was rapidly expanding around six core technology areas deemed essential to the Cold War. Requiring increasingly intimate cooperation between a burgeoning military establishment and a growing defense industry, technological growth in the areas of civil defense, command and control, communications, infrastructure, intelligence gathering, and weapons development would create what President Dwight Eisenhower would dub the "military-industrial complex." The production of new weapons systems, including nuclear weapons, jet aircraft, ballistic missiles, and nuclear-powered submarines and aircraft carriers, increased substantially during this period, requiring new production facilities. Improvements in early warning defense radar, needed to counter the new Soviet missile threat, required the deployment of radar systems to some of North America's most remote regions. The Soviet missile threat also set in motion the construction of elaborate command and control bunkers of unprecedented size and complexity.

Perhaps the most profound changes to the continental defense landscape, however, came with the construction of more than 1,000 Minuteman missile silos among the farm fields of the northern Great Plains, turning that region of rural America into a primary Soviet first strike target (Heefner 2012). At the same time, construction of private and public fallout shelters surged. Built in unknown numbers throughout the war as refuges in the aftermath of a nuclear attack, they became recognizable yet enigmatic features of the American Cold War landscape as paranoia and fear became ever more deeply etched into North American daily life.

Continental Defense Sites

Although the SAC headquarters had been established at Offutt AFB in Omaha, Nebraska, in 1948, it was not until 1957 that SAC moved into Building 501, the fortress facility on the base that would become emblematic in American culture of SAC's Cold War mission. From the Command Post, the SAC commander oversaw the readiness and deployment of nuclear-armed bombers at 22 Air Force bases, as well as of all of America's ICBMs after 1962. Built three stories below the surface with two-foot-thick concrete walls and a 42-inch-thick roof of reinforced concrete buried beneath several yards of earth, the SAC Command Post maintained enough food, water, and power-generating capacity to sustain 800 personnel underground for two weeks. Designed to survive anything less than a direct hit from a high-yield thermonuclear weapon, the Command Post was notable for a 264-foot-long status board that ran along the main wall showing the constant operational status of U.S. military forces worldwide (Weitze 1999).

From 1956 to 1960, 66 SAC bomber alert facilities were constructed across North America with structures standardized to facilitate a rapid attack response. B-52 Stratofortress bombers and crews were kept in a constant state of nuclear combat readiness with "alert crews" on 24-hour alert in seven-day duty rotations and able to take off at a moment's notice in response to an enemy threat. SAC Bomber Alert Facilities, or Readiness Crew Buildings (see Figure 3.10) housed alert crews of 100 or more airmen, who were quartered in the reinforced-concrete structures built partially belowground on the edge of the airfield. These buildings were often referred to as "moleholes" for the way flight crews moved up to the airfield surface through corrugated steel tunnels. Meanwhile, SAC airfield runways were designed for rapid takeoff, with bombers parked in clusters

Figure 3.10. The moleholes of the Readiness Crew Building at Whiteman AFB in Missouri, circa 1996. Three exit tunnels lead from the building's lower levels to the runway surface. Rapid egress through the tunnels enabled the alert crews to be airborne in 15 minutes or less. By permission of the U.S. Air Force.

Figure 3.11. An Atlas E ICBM arrives at its launch complex outside Fairchild AFB in Washington State in 1961. By permission of the U.S. Air Force.

of eight on concrete aprons built in herringbone, or "Christmas tree," patterns (Spires 2012).

Despite being virtually synonymous with the Cold War, ICBMs did not appear on the North American defense landscape until 1959, when Atlas missiles, the first of four systems (Atlas, Titan, Minuteman, and Peacekeeper) were developed and deployed in the United States. Following testing at Cape Canaveral, Atlas Ds were deployed in October 1959 at Vandenberg AFB. Deployments at F. E. Warren AFB in Wyoming and Offutt AFB in Nebraska followed, bringing the total number of operational launch sites to 24 by 1961. Stored horizontally in a shallow aboveground concrete launch complex called a "coffin," the Atlas D was raised to a vertical position just prior to launch (Neufeld 1990). The next-generation Atlas E ICBMs possessed greater range and more advanced inertial guidance systems, but were otherwise similar to their predecessors in design and launch method, except that their coffins were buried below grade. Nine Atlas E missile squadrons, with a total of 30 launch sites, were deployed by early 1961, beginning with sites at Fairchild AFB in Washington (Figure 3.11) and followed by deployments at Forbes AFB in Kansas and F. E. Warren AFB in Wyoming. The Atlas F, the final generation of missiles, was deployed during 1961 at Walker AFB in New Mexico, Altus AFB in Oklahoma, Dyess AFB in Texas, and Schilling AFB in Kansas. The Atlas F differed from its predecessors in that the entire missile launch complex was buried underground and the missiles were raised (albeit relatively slowly) out of their vertical protective silos to be launched. The deployment of Atlas F missiles at Lincoln AFB in Nebraska and Plattsburg AFB in New York in 1964 created a force of 72 operational sites (Lonnquest and Winkler 1996).

Even as the Atlas F missiles were being deployed, a more powerful ICBM called Titan was being put into service in 1962 at Beale AFB in California, Ellsworth AFB in South Dakota, Larson AFB in Washington State, Lowry AFB in Colorado, and Mountain Home AFB in Idaho. Capable of traveling more than 6,000 miles at speeds of 16,000 miles per hour, a Titan could leave its silo in less than a minute to deliver a single nine-megaton warhead that would lay waste to 900 square miles. Titan complexes were large subterranean facilities, consisting of separate modules for personnel quarters and operations support equipment, all connected by tunnels to the missile silo (Penson 2008).

By 1965, Atlas and Titan missiles were being supplanted by yet another missile as America's primary ICBM force. Radically different from its predecessors in both launch method and deployment strategies, the Minuteman missile would be the centerpiece of America's strategic nuclear attack capabilities for the ensuing five decades. The first Minuteman entered service in October 1962 at Malmstrom AFB in Montana at the height of the Cuban Missile Crisis, in what Kennedy would call his "ace in the hole." Deployments across North and South Dakota and Missouri followed in 1963. Minuteman was America's first operational solid-fueled ICBM capable of being launched remotely from centralized underground launch control facilities located miles from silos. The silos themselves were built of prefabricated steel, rather than concrete, which allowed for cheaper and faster construction of sites (Spires 2012).

At the same time the United States was expanding its land-based ICBMs, it was deploying submarine-launched ballistic missiles (SLBMs) at sea. SLBMs became the third component of America's nuclear triad, a strategic defense system composed of ICBMs, SLBMs, and long-range bombers and structured to eliminate the possibility of an enemy destroying the U.S. nuclear capability in a first-strike attack.

The U.S. Navy developed and deployed three generations of SLBMs (Polaris, Poseidon, and Trident) during the Cold War. The first Polaris missiles, Polaris A-1, went into service in 1961 aboard the nuclear submarine USS *George Washington*. This two-stage solid-fuel rocket had a range of 1,000 nautical miles and carried a 600-kiloton nuclear warhead. The *George Washington* carried 16 Polaris A-1s standing vertically in its center section, as did the 40 other U.S. Navy Fleet Ballistic Missile submarines, bringing the total number of SLBMs deployed by the United States in 1967 to 656. Poseidon SLBMs were introduced in 1971 as replacements for the Polaris. Equivalent to the Polaris A-3 in range (2,500 nautical miles) and speed (8,000 miles per hour) the Poseidon had multiple independently targetable reentry vehicle (MIRV) capability, which allowed one missile to deliver up to 14 thermonuclear warheads. Trident SLBMs were placed in service to replace the Poseidon in 1992. Capable of reaching 20,000 miles per hour over distances of 4,000 nautical miles, Trident forms the basis of the current U.S. naval nuclear deterrent, with 24 SLBMs deployed on each of America's 14 active Ohio-class submarines (Polmar and Moore 2003).

Supporting the deployment of U.S. Navy Fleet Ballistic Missile submarines and their SLBMs were two submarine bases: Naval Submarine Base Bangor (now Naval Base Kitsap) on Washington's Kitsap Peninsula, for Pacific Fleet operations, and Kings Bay Submarine Base in Georgia on the Atlantic coast. Kings Bay base—originally developed by the Army in 1958 as a military munitions shipping terminal and storage facility, with a 2,000-foot-long concrete wharf and more than 47 miles of connecting railroad tracks—began providing operational support for Atlantic Fleet submarines in the 1970s (CLUI 2015).

Production Sites

After the USS *George Washington* successfully launched the first Polaris missile in 1960, the ballistic missile submarine quickly became a key element in America's strategic nuclear deterrence. Like America's first nuclear-powered submarine, the first nuclear-powered ballistic missile submarine was built at General Dynamics Corporation's Electric Boat Division in Groton, Connecticut. Ultimately joining General Dynamics in building Fleet Ballistic Missile submarines were production facilities at Charleston Naval Shipyard (CNSY)in South Carolina, Mare Island

Naval Shipyard in California, Newport News Shipbuilding in Virginia, and Puget Sound Naval Shipyard in Bremerton, Washington (Polmar and Moore 2003).

Although CNSY served as home port to numerous cruisers, destroyers, submarines, and submarine tenders of the Atlantic Fleet throughout the Cold War, of particular significance were CNSY's nuclear submarine overhaul capabilities. A submarine overhaul yard since 1948, the shipyard completed the first nuclear reactor refueling of the submarine USS *Skipjack* in 1966. CNSY closed in 1996, but was listed on the National Register in 2006 (Cannan et al. 1995).

Still in operation today, Newport News Shipbuilding remains the largest privately owned U.S. Cold War shipyard. Newport was responsible for building the world's first nuclear-powered aircraft carrier, as well as 10 other Nimitz-class nuclear-powered aircraft carriers and numerous ballistic missile submarines.

Across the country, Puget Sound Naval Shipyard (PSNS) covers 1,347 acres and contains nearly 1,000 facilities for the maintenance and repair of conventional and nuclear-powered submarines, aircraft carriers, and ships. In 1992, 187 acres of PSNS was granted National Historic Landmark status as a historic district that includes 22 contributing buildings and 42 drydocks, piers, and other contributing structures (Thompson 1990).

Command and Control Sites

In 1953, Raven Rock Mountain Complex, a vast underground bunker, was built in the Pennsylvania countryside to provide "continuity of government" operations in the event of a nuclear attack. Funded and built during Harry Truman's presidency, and known officially as the Alternate Joint Communications Center, Site R, or more informally as "the underground Pentagon," Raven Rock was designed to provide shelter for the president and top-level government officials in the event of a national emergency. Consisting of 5 three-story buildings constructed in tunnels inside Raven Rock Mountain, the 650-acre site located near the Camp David presidential retreat had enough shelter space for 3,000 people. In addition to 700,000 square feet of conference rooms, communications services, sleeping accommodations, dining services, and medical facilities, Raven Rock even had its own underground water reservoir (Bamford 2004).

Raven Rock proved to be only the first of several civilian government underground command and control bunkers to be built in the United States and Canada. Other facilities included Mount Weather, built in 1959; the Greenbriar Hotel bunker (1962); and Mount Pony (1969). In Canada, the Canadian Forces Station Carp (colloquially dubbed the Diefenbunker), and the North American Aerospace Defense Command (NORAD) Underground Complex at North Bay were built in Ontario in 1962 and 1963, respectively. Constructed in an abandoned gravel pit outside the rural farming community of Carp, Ontario, Canadian Forces Station Carp contained 100,000 square feet of emergency shelter space. Canada's largest command and control bunker, it could accommodate 500 government officials for up to a month. Decommissioned in 1994, the Diefenbunker was designated a National Historic Site of Canada and reopened as a museum in 1998.

Buried 600 feet below the surface inside a cavern carved out of bedrock, the NORAD Underground Complex at North Bay housed a three-story building that was capable of supporting 400 NORAD staff members for a month without support from the outside world. Yet as impressive as these two command and control facilities were, neither could compare in the world's popular imagination to the most legendary of all North American command and control bunkers—Cheyenne Mountain Complex.

Nestled deep within a 10,000-foot granite peak near Colorado Springs, Cheyenne Mountain Complex opened in 1967 after six years of difficult excavation and construction. Constructed to withstand the effects of a nuclear attack from weapons as large as 30 megatons, the facility initially served as the operational center for NORAD and later for the U.S. Strategic Command. NORAD personnel, jointly deployed from U.S. and Canadian air forces, were tasked with monitoring the North American skies for potential Soviet air attacks and coordinating a defensive response. Cheyenne Mountain was connected to the outside by a mile-long tunnel with two entrances on opposite sides of the mountain (see Figure 3.12). Inside the 100-foot-high main cavern NORAD built its Combat Operations Center (COC), a collection of 11 interconnected, multistory steel buildings enclosing almost 170,000 square feet of space. The buildings were mounted on 937 steel springs, which allowed them to sway up to several inches in any direction to cushion a nuclear blast shockwave.

The COC had all the amenities of a small town: offices and workspaces, sleeping quarters, cafeteria, barbershop, and pharmacy, was well as medical, dental, and fitness facilities, enabling personnel inside to live for a

Figure 3.12. The north portal of Cheyenne Mountain bunker southwest of Colorado Springs, Colorado, is shown around 1960. Perhaps the most renowned of all American Cold War bunkers, Cheyenne Mountain holds a singular place in popular imagination as the world's most impenetrable command and control center. By permission of the U.S. Air Force.

month without access to the outside. In tunnels adjacent to the main cavern were redundant electrical power generators, a four-million-gallon water reservoir, and air filtration and radioactive decontamination systems. The cavern and tunnels could be sealed off from the entrance tunnel by two massive 30-ton vault doors (Schaffel 1991).

Civil Defense Sites

Few features of the twentieth-century American landscape evoke the Cold War zeitgeist like fallout shelters. Bomb shelters intended as protection against atomic attacks emerged shortly after the USSR tested its first atomic weapon in 1949. Constructed in relatively few numbers, these shelters were rendered obsolete by the increased destructive capabilities of Soviet nuclear weapons. Only in the middle of the Cold War did the fallout shelter emerge, and it offered only limited protection against nuclear explosions but promised to provide protection against the radioactive debris—that is, fallout—from nuclear warfare.

Construction of fallout shelters, both private and public, began in earnest in 1961, yet surprisingly little is known about the total number of private fallout shelters built. Shelters in basements (see Figure 3.13) were often built clandestinely, and some individuals who built shelters in their backyards worked only at night in an attempt to keep the shelter's existence concealed from neighbors, whom they felt might expect or demand access to the shelter in a nuclear attack (Rose 2001). Roy (2011) posits that

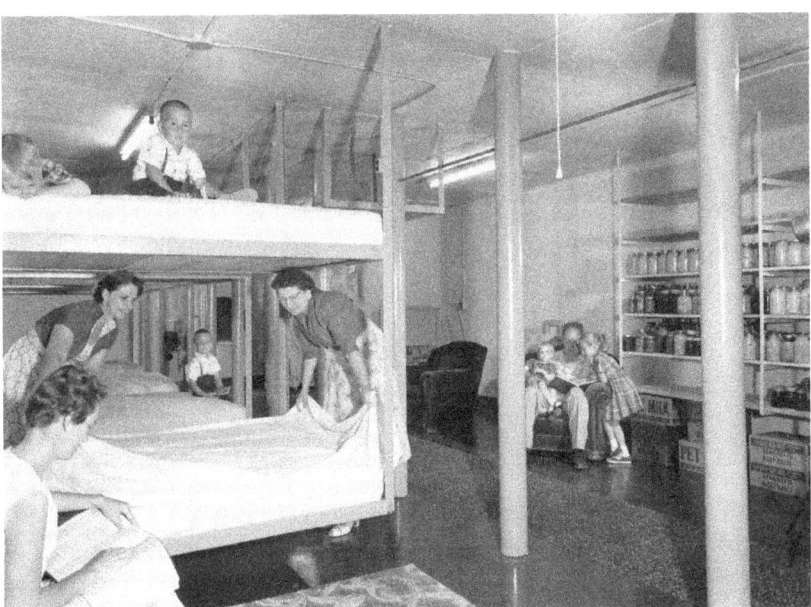

Figure 3.13. This is the Reichert family of Battle Creek, Michigan, in their $10,000 home fallout shelter in 1961. By permission of the Federal Civil Defense Administration.

perhaps tens or even hundreds of thousands of Cold War home shelters were built, but the actual number remains unknown and may only be determined by Cold War archaeologists of the future.

Faced with the challenge of creating broad support for private fallout shelters and not knowing exactly how many private shelters existed, the federal government focused its plans on public sheltering. In the National Fallout Shelter Survey, the Office of Civil Defense (OCD) employed architects and civil engineers trained in fallout shelter analysis to identify as many shelter spaces as possible in government office buildings, hospitals, schools, churches, and police stations. Buildings with concrete or masonry basements, or high-rises where the upper stories offered distance from fallout on the ground, were considered promising if they had space for a minimum of 50 people at 10 square feet per person, had adequate ventilation, and were publicly available 24 hours a day (Monteyne 2011). Once identified, shelters were marked with the familiar fluorescent yellow-and-black triple-triangle shelter sign and stocked with water, canned food, and other supplies. By the mid-1960s, millions of potential public shelter spaces had been identified across the country, but there were never nearly enough to shelter all North Americans had there actually been an attack.

The end of the middle period found the world as deeply embroiled in the Cold War as it could ever be. Mutual assured destruction (MAD) remained the prevailing nuclear politics doctrine, and there seemed to be no end to Cold War madness as the United States and Soviet Union relentlessly replaced their missile and warhead fleets with newer, more powerful versions. By 1976, the harsh realities of a prolonged Cold War were deeply etched into both the American psyche and the landscape.

Resolution: Late Cold War (1976–1989)

The final 15 years of the Cold War proved to be a rough descent into peace for the builders and keepers of North America's Cold War landscape. Though some new construction took place in the late 1970s, by the 1980s Cold War military construction across the globe would be in steep decline as public opposition to the conflict grew stronger. Ultimately, there would be more military site closures than additions to the landscape during this period. The BAECP, for example, closed during this period after consolidating its nuclear weapon assembly work with Pantex (Norris 1992). RMA was decommissioned and razed during the 1980s, leaving behind no significant architectural remains.

In a strange irony, antiwar protest groups would contribute to the Cold War built landscape by building and occupying makeshift encampments called peace camps to support their protest actions at military bases and production sites. During this final period, continental defense, production, and antiwar protest sites dominated the changes to the Cold War built landscape.

Continental Defense Sites

No Cold War construction project better epitomizes the challenges of the Resolution period than the Stanley R. Mickelsen Safeguard Complex (SRMSC). Built as part of a massive defense project dubbed the Safeguard System, the SRMSC was the last big U.S. Cold War defense construction project. Construction on the antiballistic missile defense system began in 1970 on 430 acres of grassland northwest of Grand Forks, North Dakota. Completed five years later, the SRMSC contained three sites. The central site consisted of the Missile Site Radar (MSR) building, an 80-foot-high truncated concrete pyramid (pictured in Figure 1.2) housing phased-array radar and computers for tracking and targeting enemy ICBMs as well as more than 100 support buildings. These included administrative offices, family housing, and quarters capable of housing 800 enlisted personnel. The MSR Complex also had a chapel, commissary, medical dispensary, heliport, and community center complete with bowling alley. Ten to 20 miles from the MSR were underground missile silos housing 30 long-range Spartan and 16 short-range Sprint antiballistic missiles. At a third site, roughly 20 miles away, the Perimeter Acquisition Radar (PAR) (Figure 3.14) provided early long-range surveillance, detection, and trajectory data on incoming targets, which would be confirmed by the MSR before the Spartan or Sprint missiles were launched to destroy the target. Supporting the PAR facility were administrative buildings and housing for several dozen personnel (Hubbs 1992).

The SRMSC complex was deactivated in 1976 after being in full operation for a little more than four months. While the PAR site continues to be used for military purposes refitted as the Perimeter Acquisition Radar

Figure 3.14. Hardened against nuclear blast and electromagnetic pulse (EMP) effects and using more than 58,000 cubic yards of concrete and 17 million pounds of steel reinforcing rods, the 120-foot-high PAR building housed a phased-array radar system that could spot an object the size of a basketball at a distance of 2,000 miles. Part of the SRMSC in North Dakota. By permission of the U.S. Air Force.

Attack Characterization System (PARCS) at Cavalier AFS, the larger SRMSC MSR complex was sold at public auction to the Spring Creek Hutterite Colony in 2013 (Bonham 2013).

In a decade that would come to be dominated by military force reductions and base closures, one of the few U.S. Navy construction projects funded was Project ELF, an advanced radio antenna system for communicating with deeply submerged submarines. Construction on ELF began in 1982 but was not completed until 1989 due to years of protest from antiwar groups. Together, the two transmitter facilities near Republic, Michigan, and Clam Lake, Wisconsin, consisted of a total of 84 miles of electrical cable strung on wooden utility poles, much like conventional electrical transmission lines, which at that time transmitted extremely low frequency (hence ELF) radio waves directly through the Earth. Synchronized to operate as a single antenna for greater range, the two ELF sites could also operate independently. The operational history of ELF is notable for the sustained protest actions it witnessed, often as site intrusions with attempts to fell the antennas' wooden poles.

Like the Navy architects of Project ELF, Air Force defense planners in the 1980s were similarly interested in creating an advanced military-only communications system. Called the Ground Wave Emergency Network (GWEN), the Air Force system was a nationwide network of radio transmitters and receivers designed to ensure uninterrupted radio communications between land-based nuclear forces and military authorities after a nuclear attack. GWEN was immune to disruptions in the electrical power grid and radio communications caused by electromagnetic pulses (EMPs). Originally planned to consist of 300 nodes across the United States, the system was designed to send messages using low-frequency ground waves that traveled out from a ground-level transmitter along the Earth's surface, so as not to be affected by EMPs. Construction of the GWEN system began in 1982 and continued, with frequent delays and interruptions, until 1994, when Congress added wording to the Defense Appropriations Bill for fiscal year 1995 prohibiting the Air Force from using any additional funds on the system. By then, however, the system was already obsolete due to the 1994 launch of the first Milstar communications satellite.

Occupying 11 acres apiece, GWEN sites were sparse, consisting of a guyed 300-foot steel tower at the center, which served as a low-frequency radio antenna, along with two smaller metal radio towers and three small equipment enclosures. Belowground lay a radial grid composed of 100 lengths of buried copper wire extending out 300 feet from the tower base, much like the spokes of a bicycle wheel (National Research Council 1993). After quietly constructing nine GWEN pilot sites in Arkansas, Colorado, Kansas, Nebraska, Oklahoma, and South Dakota, the Air Force encountered heavy public opposition as it sought to build more sites. Public criticism often incited protests that forced the Air Force to delay construction on a tower, or to repeat the lengthy site selection process several times over before a location was found. Ultimately, only 58 GWEN sites were built in 31 states before the 1994 ban. Operational until 2000, many GWEN sites have since been dismantled, while others remain under federal government ownership for nondefense communication and navigation uses.

Production Sites

While production of nuclear and conventional weapons and munitions continued during the Resolution period, the work was conducted discreetly. Nuclear testing, having been forced underground in 1962 by worldwide protest, still continued at the NTS, with 815 underground shots conducted over the remainder of the Cold War in shafts and tunnels (Fehner and Gosling 2000).

Cruise missiles also found a larger defense role in this last period. Able to deliver nuclear warheads quickly to distant ground targets while flying close enough to the ground that they could evade radar detection, air-launched cruise missiles (ALCMs) were designed to be launched from aircraft in flight. Stored, handled, and deployed more like bombs than missiles, they required none of the substantial concrete-and-steel infrastructure normally associated with SAM or ICBM sites. Ground-launched cruise missiles (GLCMs) required some of the infrastructure associated with ICBM sites, including hardened concrete storage facilities called GLCM Alert and Maintenance Areas (GAMAs), which were used for the storage of mobile transporter erector launchers (TELs). Carrying four cruise missiles, a camouflaged TEL could be deployed from a GAMA to a discrete launch site during a conflict. Beginning in 1982, GLCMs were deployed internationally to six locations in Europe. These deployments sparked severe protests, most notably in the women's peace camps established outside RAF Greenham Common in Berkshire, England, and at Seneca Army Depot in New York (Schofield and Anderton 2000).

Protest Sites

Largely overlooked in most accounts of the Cold War, peace camp histories are essential to any comprehensive understanding of the Cold War landscape. Juxtaposed against the military spaces and actions their occupants protested against, peace camps were sites of temporary habitation, refuge, and cooperation among individuals contesting the Cold War and its material effect on local and global environments. Typically but not always transient in nature, peace camps were casual, sometimes chaotic tent encampments that served both as economical alternatives to commercial lodging and as critical components of antinuclear or antiwar protest rituals. Beyond simply providing shelter, the camps served as operational bases for planning and organizing demonstrations, media interactions, protest walks, and acts of civil disobedience.

Inspired by the successes of an increasingly permanent Greenham Common peace camp, camps sprang up in the summer of 1983 at various sites across the United States and Canada. Populated almost exclusively by women, as Greenham Common was, the American peace camps provided support for antiwar and antinuclear protest, but in several cases focused protest efforts on opposition to the manufacture and deployment of air-launched cruise missiles. The Seneca Women's Encampment for a Future of Peace and Justice formed outside the Seneca Army Depot in Romulus, New York, as several thousand women made camp to protest against the existence of nuclear weapons in general, but more specifically to prevent the anticipated deployment of American cruise missiles from the depot to Europe later that year. The Seneca Encampment was occupied, mostly during the summer months, for more than a decade (Krasniewicz 1992). In Kent, Washington, the Puget Sound Women's Peace Camp was occupied for 18 months to protest Boeing Aerospace's manufacture of cruise missiles (Lederman 1989). In 1983, the Minnesota Women's Camp for Peace and Justice assembled in St. Paul on the property of Sperry Univac, a company that manufactured missile guidance systems. After being ejected from company grounds, the camp was reestablished on adjacent public land and occupied for a year. Unique among the peace camps was the Peace Farm, which was created in 1986 after activists purchased 20 acres of land adjacent to the Pantex Plant near Amarillo, Texas, for use in staging protests outside the plant (Pasternak 2002). Major North American peace camps of the period are shown in Table 3.1.

Summary

This chapter has traced the development of the North American Cold War built landscape over the course of 40 years. Widely dispersed, complex, and heavily reliant on the use of concrete as a construction material, this landscape consisted principally of research and development, production, command and control, civil defense, and continental defense sites and was constructed both to protect and endure.

Since the Cold War's end, much has happened to diminish that landscape. Rocky Flats was closed in 1989 for violations of federal anti-pollution laws, and by 1999 its facilities had been decommissioned and

Table 3.1. Major North American Cold War peace camps

Camp Name	Location	In Opposition To
Ann Arbor Women's Peace Encampment	Ann Arbor, MI	Manufacture of cruise missile engines by Williams International (Funk 1983; Kirk 1985)
Little Peace Camp on the Prairie	Shelby, MT	Presence of Minuteman ICBMs (Heefner 2012)
Livermore Women's Peace Camp	Livermore, CA	Nuclear weapons research at Lawrence Livermore National Laboratory (Haber 1984)
Minnesota Women's Camp for Peace and Justice	St. Paul, MN	Manufacture of missile guidance systems at Sperry Univac plant (Diaz 1984)
Nanoose Peace Camp (Nanoose Conversion Campaign)	Vancouver Island, Canada	Canadian Forces Maritime Experimental Test Range (MacBride 1985, 1986)
Nevada Test Site Peace Camp	Entrance to Nevada Test Site, NV	Nuclear weapons testing (Beck et al. 2007)
Peace Farm–Red River Peace Network	Amarillo, TX	Nuclear weapons work at the Pantex Plant (Pasternak 2002)
Puget Sound Women's Peace Camp	Kent, WA	Manufacture of cruise missiles at Boeing Aerospace (Lederman 1989)
Seneca Women's Encampment for a Future of Peace and Justice	Romulus, NY	Deployment of cruise missiles from Seneca Army Depot (Krasniewicz 1992)
Silence One Silo Peace Camp	Conrad, MT	Minuteman ICBMs, specifically the Romeo-29 silo (Heefner 2012)
Tucson Peace Encampment	Tucson, AZ	Cruise missile crew training at Davis-Monthan AFB (Hess 1983; Kirk 1985)
Women's Peace Encampment	Aiken, SC	Tritium production at Savannah River Plant (Terp 2005)
Women's Peace Presence/Stop Project ELF	Clam Lake, WI	Construction and use of Project ELF antenna (Kirk 1985; Terp 2005)

razed, leaving no significant architectural remains. The Paducah, Weldon Spring, Fernald, and Portsmouth uranium processing plants likewise have all been decommissioned and razed, also leaving no significant architectural remains to study.

Both the Cheyenne Mountain Complex and Canada's North Bay facility are today in "warm standby," meaning unused and unoccupied, but heated and maintained for possible future use. BMEWS radar sites are still in use, but most elements of the Permanent System have been decommissioned and razed. And while much of the Wherry-Capehart housing was demolished in the latter decades of the twentieth century as Cold War military bases were closed or repurposed, examples of the housing have been preserved at several Army bases. Although the North American Cold War landscape has been intentionally diminished, it nonetheless remains a formidable collection of sites. In the next chapter, I look at how archaeological investigations are aiding understanding and preservation of the history of some of these sites.

ARCHAEOLOGIES OF THE COLD WAR

For nearly three decades, historical archaeologists have investigated the materiality of the North American Cold War under a diverse range of theoretical constructs. Driven substantially, but never entirely, by the federal government's cultural resource management needs, these studies form the basis for a respectable canon of archaeological literature regarding the Cold War. In this chapter, I draw from that canon to examine 10 notable Cold War archaeology studies. Following a range of research motivations, from intellectual curiosity to salvage archaeology of sites facing imminent decommissioning and demolition, the diverse examples presented here share similar field practices and theoretical constructs, but also have in common a particular regard for how archaeology can better inform our understandings of the Cold War. In general, the research featured here focuses on continental North American sites, but for two international sites (in Cuba and the Republic of the Marshall Islands) the archaeology is so compelling, and the sites so intrinsic to the Cold War story, that their research accounts are required reading in the archaeological study of the Cold War. The first exemplary study takes us to the Central Pacific and the early days of American atomic testing.

Bikini Atoll, Republic of the Marshall Islands

In the summer of 1989, just as the Cold War was winding down, a small group of American underwater archaeologists from the NPS were beginning a study of one of the most iconic archaeological sites of the early Cold War era: Bikini Atoll. Invited by the governing Bikini Council to assess the historical significance of the atoll's sunken fleet, the researchers had a secondary goal of assessing the feasibility of developing the lagoon as a marine park.

Located in the Republic of the Marshall Islands, Bikini Atoll was the center of U.S. nuclear weapons testing in the Pacific with 23 tests, including the first hydrogen (fusion) device in 1952 and the most powerful U.S. nuclear weapon test ever exploded in 1954. Bikini is a roughly oval-shaped ring of 23 low-lying islands surrounding a 230-square-mile lagoon. The atoll's original 167 inhabitants agreed to evacuate to a neighboring atoll during U.S. nuclear testing activities, but with the exception of an aborted resettlement attempt in the 1970s, they have remained in exile ever since because of potential radiological exposure on the islands. From 1946 to 1957 the AEC built on the atoll numerous bunkers, several test and photography towers, and hundreds of other structures and buildings to support nuclear experiments, both temporary and permanent, but the 1989 research team's principal interest was the "ghost fleet," a collection of 21 ships sunk in the lagoon in July 1946 as part of the Able and Baker atomic weapons tests of Operation Crossroads.

Led by members of the NPS Submerged Cultural Resource Unit (SCRU), the research team included a dive team from the Bikini Council, members of the U.S. Navy's Explosive Ordnance Demolition (EOD) Unit One, and an oceanographer from Holmes and Narver, Inc., which was then the Department of Energy's principal contractor in the Pacific and operator of the Bikini Field Station (Delgado et al. 1991). During two fieldwork seasons in July–August 1989 and April–May 1990, the SCRU team surveyed 11 of the 21 ships sunk at Bikini, as well as the wreck of the former German warship *Prinz Eugen*, which had survived the Bikini tests, but subsequently sank at Kwajalein Atoll after being towed there for decontamination. The ships in Bikini Atoll lagoon are the sunken remains of an original array of 95 target vessels, large and small, anchored in the lagoon for the test. Consisting of captured World War Two German and Japanese ships, as well as several retired U.S. naval vessels, the target ships were positioned around the detonation points for the Able and Baker atomic weapons tests, and 75 percent of them survived the blasts intact. In the months following the Crossroads tests, those undamaged ships were towed out of Bikini Atoll lagoon. The ships that were sunk at

Bikini were the most significantly damaged ones and, like many of the ships that survived, were irreversibly irradiated by the nuclear explosions. Although many ships were damaged to various extents, the only ship to be completely destroyed in the tests was the USS *LSM-60*, a World War Two–era medium amphibious assault landing ship, from which Baker atomic device had been suspended in a watertight steel casing 90 feet below the lagoon surface.

Perhaps not surprisingly, the SCRU team concluded that the "ghost fleet" did have substantial historical significance. Sunk by a nuclear test, and unseen by the public since the Crossroads tests, the ships of Bikini Atoll presented an unparalleled atomic history site. Among the many noteworthy features of the submerged site was the USS *Saratoga* (CV-3) aircraft carrier, which had survived the Crossroads sinking virtually intact and, with its nearly 1,000-foot-long deck still holding armament and airplanes, and was easily accessible for tourism at standard sport scuba diving depths (Delgado et al. 1991).

The archaeological investigations of the Bikini wreck sites were constrained somewhat by relatively short fieldwork periods and deep-water diving requirements. Diving to depths of 180 feet, where most of the Bikini wrecks lay, required decompression dives, which necessitated slow, controlled descents and ascents. Nonetheless, at a rate of two dives per day, in a fieldwork period that cumulatively totaled only four weeks, the team performed 50 dives. The underwater work was also complicated by the hazardous nature of the archaeological site. The target ships at Bikini had been fully loaded with live munitions in order to simulate actual war conditions. Many of these munitions were not exploded in the tests, but instead sank along with the ships. In response, the U.S. Navy EOD Mobile Unit One assisted the NPS by assessing and rendering safe any potentially hazardous live ordnance found in, on, or around the sunken Bikini ships. EOD Mobile Unit One successfully mitigated the dive site's explosive hazards and fieldwork was conducted safely (Delgado et al. 1991). Although the researchers collected some sediment samples for radiological testing, there was no excavation due to radiation hazards. Using photography, as well as video footage taken during the dives, the team would produce technical sketches and narrative site descriptions for 11 of the site's wrecks.

The Bikini work challenges a long-standing crossroads mystery in which the USS *Arkansas* battleship was believed to have been lifted completely out of the water and drawn up into the stem of the mushroom

Figure 4.1. Column of water rising from the Baker atomic weapons test of Operation Crossroads at Bikini Atoll in the Marshall Islands, July 1946. By permission of the U.S. Department of the Navy.

cloud during the Baker test (pictured in Figure 4.1). Eyewitness assertions were supported by historical photographs purporting to show the 26,000-ton *Arkansas* standing upright in the water column rising from the blast. Archaeological evidence gathered during the survey suggests, however, that the *Arkansas* may have sunk within seconds of the detonation, virtually hammered to the lagoon bottom by the explosive force of the blast, well before the water and debris rose to form the mushroom cloud (Delgado 1996). The case of the *Arkansas* demonstrates how archaeological methods can contribute to our understanding of the Cold War in ways that archival or oral history data alone cannot.

One more unexpected conclusion from the Bikini research was that the residual radiation intrinsic to nuclear weapons testing locations did not present a serious hazard at the site. Consequently, under normal conditions, sport divers diving in the lagoon would not be exposed to radiation levels any higher than elsewhere on Earth. This fact was significant to Bikini's potential as a heritage site, since radiation exposure was then and still is a broadly held fear among tourists visiting nuclear-related sites.

The notion of Bikini Atoll lagoon becoming an atomic tourism site was innovative at a time when the world was still technically waging the Cold War. Yet even despite any potential hazards associated with diving around shipwrecks, the grace and grandeur of Bikini's sunken ships retain strong tourism potential. And, as Delgado and colleagues (1991) note, the socioeconomic implications of a marine park at Bikini Atoll are considerable. The concept that a displaced group might use the occupation and pollution of its environment as the means of its reoccupation and revitalization provides a heritage preservation model with potential implications and applications far beyond Bikini Atoll.

Despite the SCRU's pioneering underwater work, archaeological investigations of Bikini Atoll's terrestrial Cold War sites have been slower in coming. Steve Brown (2010) was the first to conduct field surveys on the remains of buildings, bunkers, test and photography towers, and other experimentation structures built at Bikini during the course of the 12-year (1946–1958) U.S. occupation of the atoll. Brown identified and documented 11 large reinforced concrete complexes (bunkers), each consisting of 2 to 5 separate structures or interconnected rooms. Locating 4 bunkers on Eneu Island; 2 on Bikini Island; and 1 each on Aerkoj, Aoemen, Bakor, Jabej, and Nam Islands, he reported they were well preserved, although typically enveloped in dense vegetation, with some being partially buried in sand mounds and their massive steel exterior doors rusted open by time (Figure 4.2).

Identifying what he calls both landscape and seascape modifications at Bikini, Brown (2013a) documented extensive landscape modifications consisting not only of the bunkers but of roads, causeways, jetties, and patterns of occupation that substantially altered native vegetation. Seascape modifications to the atoll took the form of the aforementioned "ghost fleet," as well as of underwater blast craters marking vaporized islets, miles of massive submarine communications cables, and reef cuttings to facilitate boat landings. Brown points to an abundance of artifacts and features that he calls the "technological ensemble of nuclear testing," including the remains of work camps, tower anchors, cables, and machinery, as well as the deposited radioactive materials (fallout), which qualifies as part of both landscape and seascape modifications. Of particular promise to future archaeological studies of Bikini is Brown's assertion that, "The extent of [Bikini] landscape modification and construction suggests that there is

Figure 4.2. The remains of an American nuclear weapons test bunker on Enyu Island at Bikini Atoll. By permission of Rom Van Oers.

likely to be substantial surviving buried (archaeological) evidence of [the nuclear] test period" (2010:13).

In his post-survey analysis, Brown (2013b) identifies a number of social and environmental factors having the potential to adversely affect Bikini Atoll's nuclear heritage sites. Sea level rise due to climate change poses an immediate threat of increased storm surges and generally higher tides. Because the average elevation of the islands is roughly 7 feet above low tide level, as sea levels rise, Bikini's low-lying atoll may be among the first in the world to be inundated. Even minimal sea level increases could produce wave actions and storm surges that increase erosion and groundwater salinization, leading to increased devegetation and deforestation, decreased island biodiversity, and threatened freshwater supplies, all of which would ultimately make the atoll inhabitable. While the natural weathering and deterioration of the concrete bunkers may be exacerbated and accelerated by storm surges, of equal immediate impact is the rapid growth of vegetation whose intrusive actions are causing structural damage to bunker ceilings, walls, and foundations. Similarly, human-caused threats to the material remains of nuclear testing include the salvage of metals, at either small or industrial scales, from both the land and sea sites. Although Bikini Atoll was designated a UNESCO World Heritage site in 2011, making salvage illegal there, the reclamation of copper, lead, and brass from communications and electrical cables used during nuclear testing had once been considered as a potential income source for the Marshallese, making looting of the atoll's tangible heritage an ongoing risk.

Based on the intrinsic heritage value of its historic land and marine remains, Bikini Atoll became the first Cold War site inscribed on the UNESCO World Heritage List. Both the underwater and terrestrial archaeologies of the Cold War at Bikini played a role in helping secure the designation. In particular, Brown's archaeology of Bikini Atoll was decidedly post-processual; he critically explored aspects of the materiality of nuclear testing at Bikini in terms of the relationship that exists between local and global forces working toward the recognition, protection, and management of Bikini's nuclear heritage landscape/seascape. Brown (2013b) asserts that while the World Heritage Listing initially establishes protection for the site's historical resources through a mutually beneficial political equilibrium between UNESCO and the Bikini community, the potential implications of any future resettlement of the atoll, which remains an open and enduring goal of the Bikini people, has significant potential to destabilize the relationship. Unwittingly, the Bikinians appear to have enmeshed UNESCO World Heritage in the politics of indigenous people's rights, while potentially co-opting the global heritage protection system as a powerful political tool for exposing the persistent and lasting consequences of nuclear weapons testing. Hence, archaeology of the Cold War and heritage preservation work at Bikini Atoll merits continued scrutiny.

Soviet Missile Sites, Cuba

For more than a decade, a multinational research team has worked to unearth history at another of the Cold War's most iconic sites. The story begins in late 1962 with the Soviet deployment of R-12 Dvina medium-range ballistic missiles (MRBMs) at locations in the Republic of Cuba. Acting on intelligence reports of Soviet troop buildups in Cuba, the United States conducted aerial surveillance and on October 14 an Air Force U-2 spy plane provided evidence of the missile deployment. Declaring the placement of these MRBMs a clear and present danger to the United States, President John F. Kennedy established an air and sea blockade of Cuba and demanded the Soviets dismantle the missile sites. The global politics of nuclear brinksmanship that ensued became the Cuban Missile Crisis, or to the Cubans, the Crisis de Octubre (the October Crisis).

Archaeological study of the Crisis de Octubre missile sites in Cuba was premised upon a 1991 field survey of the missile sites conducted by Cuban historians and military engineers (Diez Acosta 1991). In 2002, archaeologists, historians, and anthropologists from Cuba's Instituto de Historia de Cuba, Instituto Cubano de Antropología, and Instituto de Información Científica y Tecnológica joined archaeologists of the contemporary past from Stockholm and Gothenburg Universities in Sweden and from Sweden's National Heritage Board, creating a multinational team to conduct field surveys, remote sensing, excavations, and oral history collection (Burström et al. 2009). Benefiting from the team's distinguished Cuban contingent, the collaboration gained unprecedented access to the research sites to study not only the physical remains of the crisis, but to explore issues of memory and, in particular, how archaeological excavations might help local Cubans remember and share personal insights about a pivotal moment in world history that had been locally silenced (Burström and Karlsson 2008). This emphasis on discovering and decoding the social contexts of the sites and artifacts associated with the crisis lent the research a theoretical framework lying clearly within the purview of the archaeology of the contemporary past.[5]

The Soviet MRBM sites in Cuba shown in Map 4.1 are part of a larger Cold War assemblage of features and artifacts spread across that country. These sites were occupied from midsummer until October, when the Soviets decided to withdraw. The MRBM and SAM missile launch sites were interspersed with other Soviet military support features and missile-related infrastructure modifications, such as construction of new bridges in and around some villages, or strengthening of existing bridge spans by Soviet construction crews, to support heavy vehicle loads (Diez Acosta 1991).

Field surveys were conducted at the Sitiecito and El Purio missile sites, dubbed Sagua La Grande 1 and Sagua La Grande 2, respectively, in U.S. intelligence documents, near the town of Santa Clara in central Cuba. Erected but never completely finished due to the developing global political crisis and a severe mosquito infestation at the site, the Sitiecito missile

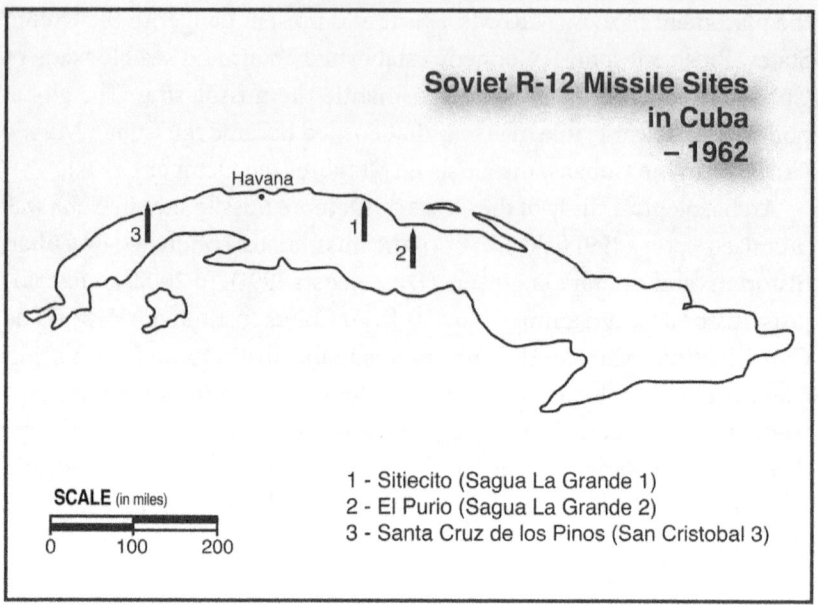

Map 4.1. Soviet MRBM sites in Cuba that precipitated the Crisis de Octubre. Map by the author.

hangar site is one of the few standing structures remaining from the crisis. According to Diez Acosta (1991), all of the hangers were supposed to have been destroyed as part of the withdrawal agreement between the Soviet Union and United States, but the Sitiecito hangar, along with others located at El Cacho and Bartolomé, survived. Survey findings at El Purio included some demolished hangars, as well as Soviet graffiti (Figure 4.3) left in a small cave near the missile launch site (Burström et al. 2009).

Located roughly 60 miles west of Havana, the missile site at Santa Cruz de los Pinos, dubbed San Cristobal 3 in U.S. intelligence documents, was the principal site of the archaeological study. Among the first Soviet missile sites to be identified, San Cristobal 3 was extensively photographed by U.S. reconnaissance planes in 1962. The San Cristobal 3 site showed relatively little change in vegetation coverage when compared to the surveillance photos, despite the fact that 40 years had passed. The San Cristobal 3 surveillance photos proved particularly useful in collecting oral histories, as many of the residents who had lived in the area in 1962 had never before seen the images. Researchers found that discussing the surveillance photos' origins and soliciting help in locating some of the objects pictured

Figure 4.3. Soviet troops working at El Purio missile site inscribed their names on the walls of the cave while they sought relief, as locals often did, from Cuba's oppressive midday heat and humidity. By permission of Håkan Karlsson, University of Gothenburg.

in them on the present landscape helped engage interviewees and often made for useful starting points in conversations about their personal memories of the crisis (Burström et al. 2009). Through conversations with the locals the team was able to locate some of the most enduring evidence of the Soviet presence at Santa Cruz de los Pinos: the remains of a destroyed missile hangar. A structure in which to covertly join and store nuclear warheads with missiles, the hangar consisted of reinforced concrete arches that had been transported to Cuba by ship from the Soviet Union during the summer of 1962 (Figure 4.4), as much of the site's construction materials had been.

Figure 4.4. Giant reinforced concrete arches that were once a Soviet missile hangar lie amid the dense Cuban underbrush in Santa Cruz de los Pinos. By permission of Mats Burström, Stockholm University.

Remote sensing at Santa Cruz de los Pinos began in 2005 with metal-detecting sweeps at the site of a former farmhouse occupied by Soviet officers during the period, in an attempt to locate possible rubbish pits and lost objects. A trial excavation of a small manmade earthen mound was later made near the missile hangar. With the exception of some pieces of Soviet-type barbed wire, the finds from the mound, which consisted of bottles, batteries, and fragments of aluminum, could not clearly be attributed to the Soviet presence. In 2007, the team conducted several metal detector surveys and excavated 130 meters of trench at a location known as the "open storage area" adjacent to a Soviet enlisted men's tent encampment. The site, where the investigators presumed that considerable activity would have taken place, yielded a similar scarcity of finds (Pajón et al. 2006). Notable among the finds at this location, however, were a great number of bottle shards bearing measure marks in the glass indicative of a type of bottle used to dispense a variety of extra strong rum sold only at Cuban pharmacies. According to the researchers' informants, the locals considered this rum too strong to drink, but the Soviets seem to have greatly enjoyed it (Burström et al. 2009). By the end of the excavations, researchers were puzzled at the meager amount of artifacts they found, as archival and anecdotal evidence had promised stronger results. Given that more than 1,000 Soviet soldiers had been living and working at Santa Cruz de los Pinos over the course of several months, investigators had expected to find significant evidence of that occupation. The anomaly was ultimately resolved through the oral histories gathered.

The team discovered in interviews that shortly after the Soviet sites were abandoned in October 1962, local residents scavenged them in search of useful materials, salvaging and reusing such articles as spoons, tin cans, boots and other clothing, shovels, lumber, and empty wooden ammunition boxes. The local farmers also told investigators they had periodically cleared the sites of cans, bottles, and scrap metal in the late 1960s and 1970s to prevent injuries to cattle grazing in the area. This helped explain why metal-detecting surveys and excavations had yielded so few artifact finds. Oral interviews about the missing artifacts also yielded information on the removal and reuse of perforated steel planking known as Marston (or Marsden) matting, which Soviet forces had laid on the ground in order to move vehicles across muddy tropical soil, and then left behind during the withdrawal.[6] Once Marston matting was identified as part of the material culture of the crisis, investigators observed the planks being used ubiquitously across the local landscape: as a footbridge to a house, as part of a barn wall, as a bottle holder, and even to construct a pigsty (Burström et al. 2013). Also salvaged for use as building materials, but requiring significantly more physical effort to acquire, were stones the Cubans removed from floors of Soviet army barracks and concrete arches they took from the partially demolished missile hangars. Also often appropriated were the steel reinforcement bars, or rebar, that had been used within the structural concrete. To extract the rebar, the Cubans often broke the concrete arches of Soviet missile hangars into pieces in situ, leaving chunks of concrete littering the ground (Figure 4.5).

The team's oral histories also gathered substantial information on the local Cubans' interactions with the Soviet soldiers. Forbidden from entering the Soviet military sites without special permission, all Cubans, civilians and military personnel alike, could interact with the soldiers only outside the bases. The Soviet soldiers were likewise not supposed to travel outside their bases, but apparently were still able to do so. Researchers learned that when Soviet soldiers were on leave, or traveling to or from their bases, they often traded soap, wristwatches, knives, boots, and

Figure 4.5. The concrete arches of Soviet missile hangars were often broken into pieces in situ by local Cubans in search of steel rebar. By permission of Mats Burström, Stockholm University.

clothes for local commodities, including rum—thus explaining the rum bottle finds. Strangely, while numerous stories were told about watches in particular being received through exchange or as gifts, no informant had any material evidence to substantiate the claim. Such evidence would have supported the anecdotal claims that Cubans interacted with the Soviet soldiers on individual levels, despite the language barriers (Burström et al. 2009). The search for such materiality would seem to be a potential objective of future Cold War archaeological studies in Cuba, especially through excavations of household or village middens.

Ultimately, the archaeological investigations at Santa Cruz de los Pinos can claim some compelling victories. Information was learned about locations and conditions of various features and structures associated with the Cuban Missile Crisis, as well as about the reuse of various Cold War material remains. The archaeological fieldwork at Santa Cruz de los Pinos and elsewhere provided a venue for conversations with local residents, prompting memories and stories about how the crisis was experienced and lived locally. The team's attention to the sites also helped increase their visibility locally, nationally and internationally as sites of historical importance to Cuba and the world (Burström et al. 2009).

The Trestle, New Mexico

One of the best examples of the lengths to which American Cold War scientists and engineers were willing to go to ensure the nation's security stands in Albuquerque, New Mexico. Colloquially known as the Trestle, but officially designated the Air Force Weapons Laboratory (AFWL) Transmission Line Aircraft Simulator, or ATLAS, the Trestle was a structure secretly built to test aircraft response to the sort of EMP that would occur in the upper atmosphere after a nuclear detonation. Archaeologists, architectural historians, and historical architects working for Van Citters: Historic Preservation conducted archival research, did field surveys, and gathered oral histories from former Trestle scientists and technicians to produce site reports and Historic American Engineering Record (HAER) documentation of the Trestle's once highly secret life.

Located deep within the 51,000 acres of Kirtland Air Force Base, the ATLAS Trestle was a structural engineering masterwork. Constructed of more than 6 million board feet of lumber, which at the time would have been enough to build 4,000 single-family homes, the Trestle is built in a canyon on the edge of a mesa, roughly one-half mile east of the Kirtland airport (Figure 4.6). Twelve stories high and 1,000 feet long, the Trestle is the largest horizontal EMP simulator ever created and, at the time of its construction in 1980, was the largest all-wood structure in the world (Van Citters and Bisson 2003).

The origins of the Trestle lie in the discovery of EMP effects during nuclear weapons testing. During the 1962 Operation Dominic tests at Johnston Island in the Pacific, an EMP produced by the Starfish Prime nuclear test caused radios and televisions to malfunction, electrical power

Figure 4.6. Aerial view of the Trestle, with a B-52 Stratofortress under testing, Albuquerque, New Mexico, circa 1982. By permission of the U.S. Air Force.

lines to fuse, and streetlights to fail in Hawaii, more than 800 miles away from the detonation (Hanson 2009). Defined as short, strong bursts of electromagnetic energy caused by the release of gamma rays during a nuclear explosion, EMPs ionize the atmosphere to produce massive electrical fields through which flow strong current and voltage surges. Moving at the speed of light, these transient electromagnetic disturbances are powerful enough to damage or destroy electronics. Because of the orientation of the earth's magnetic field, a megaton-range nuclear explosion over the northern United States or Canada could cause EMP effects to spread across much of North America, incapacitating both military and civilian electronic devices. After Operation Dominic EMPs became of great concern, since some of the most potentially devastating effects of nuclear warfare could occur to military aircraft avionics, literally causing planes to fall out of the sky (Van Citters 2003).

The halt of atmospheric nuclear testing in the early 1960s ended opportunities to study EMPs resulting from nuclear explosions. The Trestle and its accompanying EMP pulse generator (dubbed "the Wedge") were constructed to remedy that predicament, allowing scientists to perform free space simulations of EMPs that were similar to what would result from a high-altitude nuclear burst. Planes parked on top of the Trestle were exposed to EMPs produced by the Wedge, and the wooden structure of the Trestle prevented any signal interference. The Trestle was used to verify that the technologies designed to harden electronics against EMPs performed as desired. The aircraft tested on the Trestle were the largest of the North American air defense response fleet, including B-52 and B-1 bombers, along with C-5 cargo planes and Marine One, the president's helicopter.

The heart of the structure is the test stand (shown in Figure 4.7), composed of a 200 × 200 foot framework topped by a platform lying 115 feet above the canyon floor and built to support aircraft weighing 200 tons. Constructed entirely of 12-inch-square laminated Southern yellow pine and Douglas fir structural timbers, some more than 120 feet in length, the Trestle is held together with 150,000 phenolic resin-impregnated beechwood bolts, shown in Figure 4.8. The dielectric, or nonconductive, nature of the wood ensured that the test stand would neither interfere with nor distort the EMP test results. The topography of the Kirtland site allowed test planes arriving at the airfield to be towed from the runway down a

Figure 4.7. View of the Trestle in 2011, looking up from below. By permission of Charles Reuben.

Figure 4.8. Close-up of the Trestle's wooden bolt system. By permission of Charles Reuben.

gentle slope and across a 400-foot-long bridge to the test stand (Van Citters 2003).

The study of the Trestle represents a project deeply rooted in the archaeology of science. As the only EMP simulator capable of testing large aircraft under simulated yet realistic flight conditions, the Trestle served its unique scientific mission as an outdoor laboratory.

The Trestle studies are also part of a broader Air Force effort to digitally document important, historically significant aspects of scientific structures and, in this case, a highly secret scientific mission. To document the Trestle, researchers used lidar laser scanning technology to develop a three-dimensional computer model of the structure. Over the course of eight days, field technicians conducted 800 scans to produce 37 million data points, which then served as the basis for creating the 3-D model and 2-D HAER drawings. Completing the 3-D model of the structure took roughly 10 weeks and included both a digital fly-through and an animation of the electromagnetic pulse (Witt 2004). Taken together, this digital data can be used for historic preservation and stewardship efforts, as well as for heritage studies, museum displays, and 3-D virtual tourism, which may someday allow people to explore historic environments without having to travel to them.

The Van Citters team also worked with Avista Video Histories of Albuquerque to create a 44-minute documentary video entitled *TRESTLE: The Landmark of the Cold War*, which tells the structure's history through interviews with engineers and scientists involved in its design, construction, and use.

The Trestle is a case study in the ways American military tacticians and scientists tasked with predicting, understanding, and defending the United States against every imaginable, and some unimaginable, forms of Soviet attack approached their job. The pursuit of scientific knowledge during the Cold War often required innovative thinking and unchecked spending, but the knowledge gained was generally considered priceless.

Unfortunately, scientifically unique and historically significant structures such as the Trestle can pose difficult preservation challenges. As a wooden structure weathered and dried by decades in the New Mexican desert, the Trestle demands ongoing maintenance costs and poses fire protection challenges. Deemed unnecessary and unsafe for continued scientific use, the Trestle was taken out of service in 1991 and is currently not being maintained. Since it has no potential contemporary scientific or military uses and is located in the middle of an active military base, where tourism options are limited, it will be allowed to go to ruin. Only comprehensive historic preservation studies adding to those already made will ensure that the Trestle will never be lost to American history, even when it is finally gone.

Nevada Test Site (NTS), Nevada

Some of the most ambitious and innovative archaeological investigations into the material culture of nuclear weapons development have been conducted in and around what was arguably the epicenter of Cold War nuclear testing in North America: the NTS. Originally known as the Nevada Proving Grounds, but renamed the Nevada Test Site in 1955, this location provided an isolated environment for dropping nuclear devices from planes, suspending them from balloons, or most commonly, exploding them on steel towers. Situated on 1,360 square miles of rugged desert and mountain terrain in the southeastern corner of Nevada, NTS was the

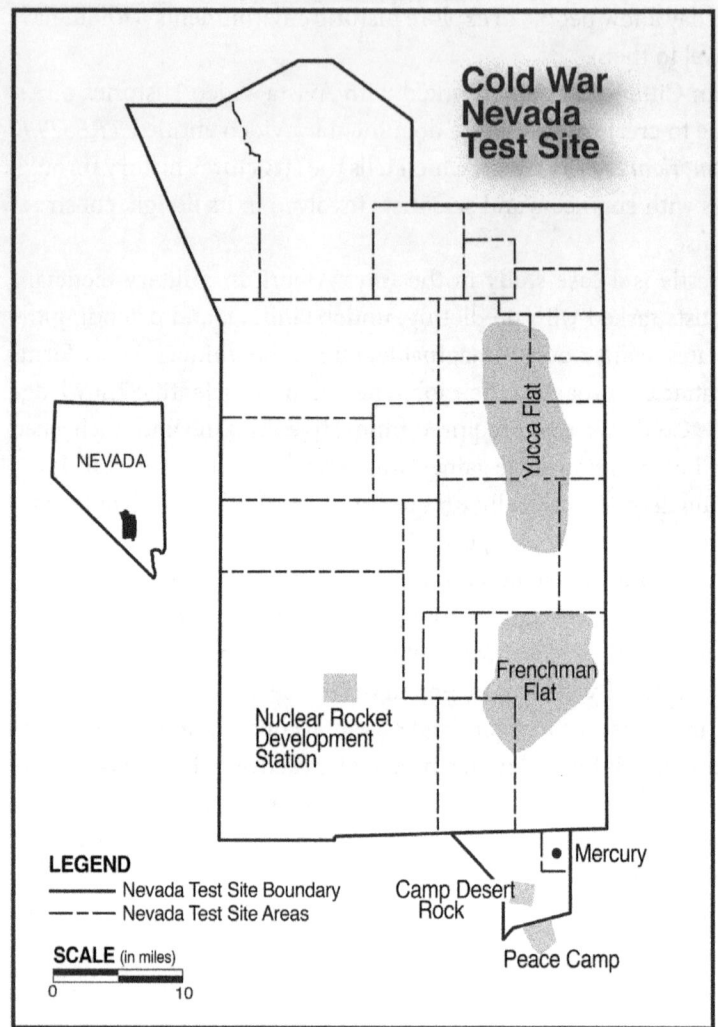

Map 4.2. Principal areas of the Nevada Test Site during the Cold War. Map by the author.

site of 100 aboveground nuclear tests and hundreds more underground tests during its 41-year nuclear testing history.

The archaeological study of the NTS, now known as the Nevada National Security Site, has for the past three decades been the nearly exclusive purview of historians and archaeologists from the Desert Research Institute (DRI) in Las Vegas. In this section, I describe archaeological work that DRI researchers are doing at four separate yet culturally interconnected sites. These sites are Camp Desert Rock, an abandoned military cantonment used by U.S. Army forces observing atomic tests from 1951 to 1957; Frenchman Flat, the site of America's earliest continental atomic testing activities; the NTS Peace Camp, the world's longest-standing Cold War peace camp; and the Nuclear Rocket Development Station, which was home to the world's first thermal nuclear rocket engine test facilities (see Map 4.2).

Camp Desert Rock, Nevada Test Site

While the invention of the atomic bomb had clearly given the United States a strategic military advantage in post–World War II geopolitics, and although a significant portion of America's Cold War infrastructure had been built solely to meet the testing, manufacturing, security, and deployment needs of nuclear weaponry, not all branches of the U.S. military found equivalent utility in the bomb. Accustomed to a world where marching armies had been the central element of warfare for the previous 3,000 years, the U.S. Army, in particular, questioned the potential tactical uses for nuclear weapons in combat. Though the weapon was certainly appealing for its destructive power to demolish enemy strongholds and annihilate large numbers of land forces with a single blast, the immense and ostensibly uncontrollable explosive energy it released tended to limit its uses to large-scale, strategic operations rather than battlefields. At the same time, the potential use of tactical nuclear weapons also carried significant risk of rapidly escalating a regional conflict beyond its expected limits, moving battles across borders into the realm of international warfare, and eventually leading to the use of even more devastating strategic nuclear weapons like ICBMs. Nevertheless, military strategists ultimately recognized the basic necessity of training American soldiers in nuclear weapons use as the likelihood of their use grew along with rising political tensions in Southeast Asia and Western Europe. Unfortunately, realistic training scenarios necessitated that troops witness a nuclear explosion at relatively close proximity in order to experience the physical and psychological effects of the detonation, so that they could cope with the bomb in combat. Seeking simultaneously to test tactical atomic weapons attack scenarios and drill American troops in the practices of nuclear warfare, the U.S. Army established Camp Desert Rock (CDR).

CDR was built on a 450-acre tract in a gently sloping desert valley roughly 60 miles northwest of Las Vegas, just inside the southern border of what was then known as the Nevada Proving Ground. The camp lay two miles southwest of the previously established AEC town of Mercury, the administrative center of the Proving Grounds, which at the time was called Camp Mercury. Established in September 1951, CDR was the primary cantonment for all U.S. Army forces attending and observing the atomic tests and, occasionally, for a visiting Marine Corps unit. Ten miles north of Mercury lay Frenchman Flat and Yucca Flat, two bone-dry, ancient lakebeds where 60,000 soldiers would ultimately train from 1951 to 1957 in a series of eight atomic military exercises. Soldiers were typically briefed at Camp Desert Rock prior to being deployed, often in the dead of night, to witness the next morning's atomic detonations. After observing the explosion, sometimes from as close as several thousand yards, soldiers then marched or were transported by bus to ground zero to witness firsthand the effects of the nuclear explosion on military equipment and structures (Edwards 1997:130; Fehner and Gosling 2006).

The first, and to date the only, archaeological study of CDR was conducted in the late 1990s. While little remained of the site when Susan Edwards (1997) made her initial archaeological survey in 1997, that survey nonetheless identified and documented concrete building foundations, rock-lined tent platforms, filled-in trench latrines, and paved and unpaved roadways and paths, as well as debris piles, trash scatters, and the remnants of the site's water, electrical, and communications infrastructure. These features and artifacts would ultimately contribute to a surprisingly intimate reading and interpretation of the site. Seeking to identify and describe the material remains of CDR while testing the utility of a historic ethnographic approach to the study of Cold War archaeological sites, Edwards successfully integrated archival records and oral histories with field research. Accessing a substantial collection of primary sources in the form of public and official documents archived by the U.S. Department of Energy (DOE) Coordination and Information Center in Las Vegas, Nevada, Edwards narrowed her review of the more than 1,000 documents relating to CDR operations in the Coordination and Information Center archive to a practical and functional subset of records. Focusing on types of documents most likely to contain information relevant to the construction, layout, and operation of the camp across the full period of its occupation, her final resource collection included reports, operational plans, maps, photographs, testing schedules, and newspaper and magazine articles from the period. To supplement this archival research, she interviewed individuals who either participated in the CDR exercises or had other intimate knowledge of CDR and its operations. The interviews proved invaluable in validating the content of archival documents and corroborating official accounts of CDR exercises.

Dubbed Desert Rock Exercises I through VIII, the military's atomic training exercises were in actuality extensions of planned weapons design and development tests in the AEC testing program. As a result, while the AEC scientists focused on nuclear weapon functionality and data collection, the military was concerned with understanding the psychologically disruptive and physically destructive effects of blast forces, radiation, and heat. The Desert Rock Exercises I, II, and III of 1951 were carried out as an element of the AEC's Operation Buster-Jangle atomic tests, or shots. Code-named Dog, Sugar, and Uncle, the shots were used to determine the damaging effects of nuclear detonations on military men and equipment and field fortifications. CDR exercise participants watched the detonations from trenches located seven miles from ground zero, then moved into the blast area after the explosion to inspect the damage to equipment. The following year, under Operation Tumbler-Snapper, the Army took its Desert Rock IV Exercises to a dangerous new level, by positioning the observer troops in foxholes just 7,000 yards from ground zero during four shots code-named Charlie, Dog, Fox, and George. In 1953, Desert Rock V added tactical troop maneuvers and operational helicopter tests to the normal observer and damage assessment training program during Operation Upshot-Knothole. Again, the Army upped the atomic ante by entrenched some battalions as close as 4,000 yards from ground zero and placing selected volunteers in foxholes as close as 2,000 yards to the Badger shot. Soldiers participating in Desert Rock V exercises conducted tactical maneuvers involving mock battles under the mushroom clouds in 6 of the 11 Upshot-Knothole shots. Under the auspices of Operation Teapot, the Desert Rock VI Exercises in 1955 involved observer programs for the Wasp, Moth, Tesla, Turk, Ess, and Apple 1 shots, as well as tactical attack maneuvers following the Bee and Apple 2 shots.

The Desert Rock VII and VIII exercises, under Operation Plumbbob in 1957, were not only the last tests to see troops encamped at CDR but also some of the largest nuclear shots ever associated with U.S. military training maneuvers. The troop maneuvers conducted during the Hood, Smoky, and Galileo shots involved the use of helicopters for tactical air support. Shot Hood, in particular, was notable as one of the largest atmospheric nuclear tests ever conducted at NTS, with a blast so powerful it collapsed several of the trenches in which marines were taking cover 5,000 yards from ground zero. During the 24 atomic tests of Operation Plumbbob, more than 20,000 troops participated in the CDR exercises, making it the largest tactical nuclear training event in American military history (Fehner and Gosling 2006).

Edwards's study revealed that life at CDR was particularly difficult in the early years, even beyond the encounters with nuclear explosions. Housing for both camp staff and exercise participants consisted of 12-man canvas tents with dirt floors. In the absence of a sewer system, troops in 1951 used open-trench latrines. Water was trucked to the camp from nearby Indian Springs after attempts to drill local wells proved futile. Drinking water was distributed in Lyster bags—36-gallon canvas bags with calcium hypochlorite added to chemically purify the water—that hung on wooden posts throughout the camp. Showers consisted of portable canvas shower bags hanging from poles (Edwards 1997:131).

Over the course of CDR's six-year life, however, conditions steadily improved. A medical dispensary capable of treating minor injuries and dental problems was added, as were a barbershop, open-air movie theater, chapel, and beer tent, albeit all in canvas tents. Electrical power, a phone system, and a water distribution system (still without local wells) were also added to the camp infrastructure. Eventually, concrete-floored Quonset huts and Butler prefabricated buildings were built to serve as administrative offices and mess halls, as well as a library and a main assembly hall. Personnel tents were winterized with wooden floors and kerosene-burning heaters. Butler buildings eventually replaced the canvas tent latrines. By 1955 CDR had more than 150 permanent buildings and provided a full range of services, including field hospital, postal, pharmacy, and dry cleaning and laundry services (see Figure 4.9; Edwards 1997).

Among Edwards's archaeological findings, two stand out. First, the building foundations she surveyed proved to be surprisingly revealing, despite their advanced age and deteriorated condition. Close examination of the foundations revealed obvious spatial divisions within the former structures that had not been described in the archival records or discussed in the oral histories. One structure in particular, identified in archival documents as a VIP latrine, showed indications in its foundation of multiple building additions having been made to the original central structure

Figure 4.9. Aerial view of Camp Desert Rock, Nevada Test Site, in 1955. By permission of the U.S. Department of the Army.

at different times. Not only did these additions increase the building's size and total number of toilets from 3 to 9, showers from 2 to 6, and sinks from 1 to 6, but the new layout added a changing room/locker area to the structure (Edwards 1997:190). These additions suggest an increasing number of VIP visitors to CDR over time, requiring additional facilities. The separation of the showers from the changing area provided a degree of privacy unavailable in either the enlisted men's or officers' latrines, suggesting that the conventions of military life may not have been suitable to all atomic test observers. This kind of archaeological discovery underlines the specific value of archaeology in accessing information that may have been deemed not worthy of remembering or recording in the past, or may have been everyday knowledge that was simply lost to history.

A second fieldwork discovery revealed discrepancies between archival documents, which attributed the construction of one of CDR's primary mess halls to the Army 95th Engineering Battalion in 1955, and inscriptions workers made in the foundation's wet concrete, which indicate the building was in fact built by the 412th Engineering Construction Battalion in 1953 (Edwards 1997). Though this is perhaps a negligible historical gaffe, it is nonetheless indicative of the benefits that archaeological fieldwork can bring to the study of the Cold War past by enriching the interpretive context and, as Edwards writes, "by expanding, clarifying, reaffirming, and even correcting the documentary record" (1997:206).

As an atomic-age training camp, the CDR site was unusual but not unparalleled. In the Soviet Union, troops were also being trained to fight on the atomic battlefield. At the site of an eighteenth-century military camp and field exercise area in southwestern Russia, along the border of the former Kazakh Soviet Socialist Republic, the USSR conducted Exercise Snezhok (Snowball) in September 1954. Chosen because its topography was similar to that of West Germany, Snezhok exposed Soviet troops to blast forces and radiation from a 40-kiloton atomic bomb dropped on a site roughly eight miles from the Russian town of Totskoye. Informed that Snezhok was simply a regular military exercise with a mock nuclear explosion, the 45,000 Soviet soldiers and officers in attendance were not issued protective gear. In addition to the troops, a massive contingent of some 320 planes, 600 tanks, and 600 armored personnel carriers were involved (Feskov et al. 2004). The objective of the exercise was to break through heavily fortified enemy defensive lines using nuclear weapons, a situation not unlike the tactical training and mock battle scenarios of CDR exercises. Soviet planes bombed ground zero with conventional bombs minutes after the explosion, and armored personnel carriers moved troops to the site mere hours later to fight a mock battle. As a consequence, tens of thousands of Soviet soldiers were exposed to high levels of ionizing radiation.

The similarities between CDR and the atomic training grounds at Totskoye provide an uncanny example of an intrinsic pattern of parallelism during the Cold War. Whether they resulted from acts of espionage or simply the logical course of scientific and technical development, numerous architecturally similar scientific facilities, analogous military activities, and often functionally identical military sites were built to support the atomic bomb on both sides of the Cold War conflict landscape.

By 1958, CDR was all but abandoned. By 1964, all the permanent buildings had been moved or dismantled, leaving only traces on the landscape and memories for those who were once stationed there (Edwards 1997).

Frenchman Flat, Nevada Test Site

Few sites in the archaeology of the Cold War embody the violent and fearsome character of that conflict like Frenchman Flat. Situated in the southeastern corner of the NTS, Frenchman Flat is a dry lakebed, or playa, encompassing 110 square miles of high desert terrain. Occupied from 1951 until 1958 for 14 atmospheric nuclear weapons tests, and in later years for five underground nuclear tests, the playa is strewn with the evidence of early Cold War nuclear weapons research and civil defense studies. From the rusting remains of a freestanding bank vault, its protective steel and concrete skin ripped away, to the rootless stumps of trees planted in concrete to study blast-wave effects, the nuclear testing features and artifacts of Frenchman Flat are positively surreal in their unexpected juxtapositions and seeming non sequiturs of context.

The first experimental nuclear shots at NTS were conducted at Frenchman Flat. Five tests comprised the Operation Ranger test series in 1951, all involving airdrops of atomic bombs from Boeing B-50 Superfortress bombers. These tests were used to help design what would become the second generation of atomic fission weapons. Unlike later nuclear tests—which would be monitored, measured, and analyzed with scientific precision—the Ranger tests were designed simply to determine the new weapons functioned as designed, and a rudimentary instrumentation infrastructure reflected that goal (Fehner and Gosling 2000).

Following the Ranger test series came Operation Tumbler shot Able in 1952, an airdrop test designed to study the optimum detonation height for bombs. Then came shot Encore of Operation Knothole in 1953, an airdrop designed to test weapons effects (blast, radiation, and thermal phenomena) on aspects of the natural and built landscape, including various industrial structures; sections of an open-deck, single-track truss railroad bridge; 27 vehicles; and perhaps most surprisingly, an artificial forest of pine trees transplanted on Frenchman Flat by the U.S. Forest Service. Military personnel observed Encore from trenches located 10,000 feet from ground zero as part of Exercise Desert Rock. Sheep were likewise placed in bunkers, foxholes, and trenches, and out in the open, around ground zero. Operation Knothole Shot Grable, also in 1953, took the form of a 280 mm nuclear artillery shell fired over Frenchman Flat from a cannon. Grable was designed to test not only the performance of the M65 Atomic Cannon, but the blast, radiation, and thermal effects of the

Figure 4.10. Officers in the Desert Rock Exercises watch the Teapot MET shot from Frenchman Flat in April 1955. By permission of the National Nuclear Security Administration, Nevada Field Office.

atomic artillery shell on military equipment and roughly 4,000 Exercise Desert Rock observers (Massie et al. 1982). In 1955 the Military Effects Test (MET) of Operation Teapot became the Flat's tenth nuclear test (Figure 4.10). MET was the first tower detonation at Frenchman Flat. Fired from a 400-foot steel tower, the MET shot involved 38 different scientific experiments, the largest number of any shot in the 15-shot Teapot series, all of which involved considerable preparation. Preparations for MET included the construction of a testing area with three different ground surfaces surrounding the tower: water, asphalt, and desert. A shallow pool of water 800 feet wide and 3,000 feet long was constructed north of the tower, while a similarly sized area to the south of the tower was paved with asphalt, with desert in between. Placement of instrumentation, vehicles, military field fortifications, and structures of various types was replicated all three areas to obtain equivalent data. Vehicles, fortifications, and structures on the desert surface were most severely damaged, leaving that area strewn with wreckage (Ponton et al. 1981).

Teapot MET was followed in 1957 by the Priscilla shot of Operation Plumbbob, a balloon-launched shot with 34 associated military effects projects and various civil defense experiments. During Priscilla, the Federal Civil Defense Administration conducted projects intended to evaluate Civil Defense emergency preparedness and to assess the effects of nuclear detonations on aspects of the civilian infrastructure. Ultimately, the Priscilla test produced some of the most unusual features and artifacts left on the Flat, including the remains of a bank vault, metal and concrete domes, and architectural structures of various kinds and sizes (Viscuso et al. 1981). The next nuclear weapons tests at Frenchman Flat were the Hamilton, Wrangell, and Sanford shots of Operation Hardtack II in 1958, and the final atmospheric nuclear test ever conducted at Frenchman Flat was a low-nuclear-yield shot as part of Operation Sunbeam in 1962, dubbed Small Boy (Ponton et al. 1983).

Archaeologists from DRI conducted investigations of Cold War activities at Frenchman Flat over the course of several years. Principally employing processual theoretical frameworks, they identified and documented Cold War work sites in field surveys conducted from 1993 to 1996. Following this, field photography, analysis, and report-writing activities stretched into 2000. They began their work with comprehensive studies of archival records, including extensive examination of thousands of engineering records detailing site layouts, experimental designs, and construction of structures and buildings. Oral histories were taken from informants who participated directly in the nuclear testing activities at Frenchman Flat (Johnson et al. 2000). From this work, structures and features were identified for fieldwork research. Although DRI investigators commonly grouped field sites at Frenchman Flat into sets based on known association with specific projects or nuclear test series (e.g., the Operation Ranger series), the widely dispersed nature of the more than 157 identified features led them to consider the entire 95-square-mile site a historical unit called the Frenchman Flat Historic District. Whereas nuclear testing at the Pacific Proving Grounds had focused on the development of powerful multi-megaton weapons, testing at Frenchman Flat generally focused on the effects of nuclear weapons in the smaller kiloton-range detonations. Many of the nuclear tests conducted at Frenchman Flat were historically and scientifically unique, with neither precedents nor antecedents.

Though the features and sites of the Frenchman Flat Historic District constitute a broad collection of historic finds, three artifact assemblages offer unique perspectives into the material nature of historic nuclear weapons testing activities there. The first of these assemblages contains the artifacts and features generally associated with the creation of a nuclear testing infrastructure at NTS. Broadly defined as everything needed to make nuclear testing possible, this infrastructure ranged from the basics—roads, water supplies, electrical and communications systems, housing, and dining facilities—to the relatively arcane—shot towers, subterranean bunkers, instrumentation, camera stations, and even bleachers providing a (relatively) safe and comfortable place to view atomic tests.

One of the first test structures built on Frenchman Flat was the Kay Blockhouse, a concrete-encased 300-square-foot steel vault buried near the center of the flat flush to ground level and covered over with a 10-foot-thick soil berm. With 25-inch-thick walls and 55-inch-thick roof and floor, the Blockhouse was, quite literally, blast proof and provided protection for delicate data-recording instrumentation during the Ranger tests. The Blockhouse's immutability was critical to testing the air-dropped Ranger atomic devices, as it provided protection in case the bombs missed their intended targets (as at least one did). Destruction of a bunker in the blast would have meant both a bomb wasted (remember, atomic devices were in short supply in the early years of the Cold War) and the loss of valuable scientific data.

In addition to the Kay Blockhouse, DRI archaeologists identified a number of other features associated with the testing infrastructure assemblage, including several two-room, subterranean bunkers used for holding experiments, which may have included animal test subjects, and numerous camera and instrumentation stations. While the instrumentation stations contained numerous types of data-collection devices, some of the most common were the so-called Q gauges, which were used for measuring dynamic air-blast pressures over various ground surfaces. Consisting of steel plates ranging from 2 to 30 inches in diameter, the plates, and their accompanying pressure gauges, were placed in various orientations and at various distances from ground zero. Some were placed on stands with the plate perpendicular to the ground surface facing the blast, while others were set into holes in concrete pads, parallel to and flush with the ground surface. Camera stations were constructed at various locations on the flat to protect the cameras used to photograph atomic explosions. Consisting of a 30-inch-square steel box encased in a 10-foot-wide by 4-foot-high block of reinforced concrete, each station had a small leaded-glass window in the front of the block, allowing a high-speed camera to be placed in the steel box from the rear. In addition to several camera stations, more than 100 steel towers, ranging in height from 6 to 25 feet and positioned at various locations across Frenchman Flat, were built with remote-controlled cameras mounted on them to photograph the blasts.

Two sets of wooden bleachers were constructed roughly 200 yards apart on a north-facing hillside overlooking Frenchman Flat (Figure 4.11). Consisting of 11 and 12 rows, respectively, of 32-foot-long benches, the bleachers pictured in figure 4.11 were built to provide a viewing area out of harm's way for members of the U.S. Congress, military officials, and other VIPs during atomic tests for the Operation Ranger series.

In a second notable assemblage, features belonging to the AEC's Civil Effects Test Operations (CETO) program provide substantive evidence of a scientifically unique research agenda aimed at exploring some of the nonmilitary effects of atomic weapons. These tests were often designed to push structural limits, and thus most structures were damaged or destroyed, but nearly all remain in some form. Such is the case with the concrete and aluminum domes built for the CETO blast-effects experiments for Shot Priscilla of Operation Plumbbob. Priscilla's explosive force collapsed two of three reinforced concrete domes with six-inch-thick walls, and flattened two 16-foot-diameter aluminum domes designed and built

Figure 4.11. British and Canadian VIPs are photographed by the flash of an atomic test at Frenchman Flat in 1955. By permission of the National Nuclear Security Administration/Nevada Field Office.

by American Machine and Foundry Company—with one-half-inch and one-inch-thick walls, respectively—that were being tested as possible bomb shelters for the national shelter program. Two larger domes, 73 feet in diameter with 24-inch-thick reinforced concrete walls, survived Priscilla's destructive attack (Viscuso et al. 1981).

Not far from the CETO domes are the remains of another of Priscilla's more unusual effects experiments. The First National Bank of Frenchman Flat is a free-standing bank vault built by the Mosler Safe Company of San Francisco to study the thermal effects of a nuclear blast on vital records and valuables, including stacks of simulated paper currency. The 12-foot by 8-foot reinforced concrete vault was built with a 10-inch-thick door mounted on a steel frame weighing 14 tons. With the door missing (removed sometime after the test) and the vault's exterior concrete violently peeled away to expose the rusting rebar, the wreckage is misleading. Despite the blast damage, the vault door opened after test, the contents were intact, and the experiment was considered a success (Fehner and Gosling 2006).

On the eastern side of Frenchman Flat are the remains of yet another curious air-blast-effects experiment. The Forest is an array of 135 tree stumps, the decaying remains of an experiment conducted during the Encore shot by the U.S. Department of Agriculture and the U.S. Forest Service in which 145 mature ponderosa pines were harvested from Kyle Canyon on nearby Mount Charleston and placed on Frenchman Flat in concrete-filled holes to create an artificial forest. The purpose of the test was study the effects of an atomic attack on a forest in which military forces might seek cover. The initial release of thermal radiation from the Encore blast charred some of the trees but did not ignite any, and the subsequent shockwaves broke only a small percentage of trees.

Certainly the most chilling archaeological assemblage of Cold War nuclear testing activities at Frenchman Flat are those features associated with the biological effects experiments conducted as part of Upshot-Knothole Encore, Plumbbob Priscilla, and Hardtack II Hamilton tests. Surveys by DRI archaeologists located remains of six elevated drumlike aluminum cylinders used for studying biological effects of nuclear weapons. Spaced at roughly 200-foot intervals along a line running from 1,900 to 4,000 yards from ground zero, the cages were only a few of the enclosures in which rats, dogs, and pigs were placed to evaluate the thermal effects of a nuclear explosion. Outfitted with specially made Army uniforms made of various cloth materials, pigs were placed in the cages in order to ascertain which fabric provided the best protection from thermal radiation produced by the nuclear detonation. Archaeologists also identified 16 barbed-wire animal pens, both rectangular and circular in shape, associated with the use of pigs and sheep during blast-effects studies in nuclear testing, most notably in the Priscilla and Hamilton nuclear tests (Johnson et al. 2000; Viscuso et al. 1981). Measuring from 200 to nearly 4,000 square feet in area, the largest of these pens held as many as 145 animals during the Priscilla tests.

As extensive as the archaeological investigations at Frenchman Flat have been, DRI staff still consider their work to be preliminary in nature, with a number of Frenchman Flat sites meriting study in greater depth and several more recent Cold War nuclear testing features yet to document. Countless questions concerning the nature of scientific activities at Frenchman Flat await answers as historical archaeologists attempt to more fully understand the material aspects of American nuclear weapons testing.

Peace Camp, Nevada Test Site

Among the North American peace camps introduced in the previous chapter, the Peace Camp at NTS stands as the only American site known to have been studied by archeologists of the Cold War. The camp is still in occasional use for protests against ongoing nuclear weapons research at NTS by various faith-based protest alliances and environmental groups and the people of the Newe (Western Shoshone) Native American nation, on whose ancestral land both the Peace Camp and NTS lie. Established by virtue of historic and routine communal use, the Peace Camp extends along approximately 1¼ miles of U.S. Route 95, roughly 65 miles northwest of Las Vegas, Nevada. Lying on the south side of the highway, directly opposite the main entrance road to the NTS, the Peace Camp site grew from a small initial roadside occupation to ultimately encompass roughly 600 acres of undeveloped state public land. The NTS is accessed from the camp by way of a vehicle underpass and a large concrete drainage tunnel that passes beneath both eastbound and westbound lanes of the highway. Other than two dirt access roads, which run parallel to the highway, there are no roads or utilities at the camp. Low stony ridges cross the Peace Camp's desert terrain, with the sparse vegetation of native sagebrush, yucca, and cactus confined almost exclusively to the ridge crests. At the far southwestern corner of the Peace Camp site is an elevated area dubbed Pagoda Hill by protestors (Beck et al. 2007).

Among Cold War protest sites in the United States, the NTS camp is unique as the only site repeatedly occupied by a number of different antinuclear protest groups over the course of its 30-year history (Beck et al. 2011:95). Beginning in the 1950s, small groups of protestors voicing their opposition to nuclear weapons walked from Las Vegas in peace marches to the NTS entrance. The Peace Camp often provided temporary (usually overnight) accommodations for the protestors. With a global rebirth of antinuclear activism in the early 1980s, NTS became a focal point for larger, longer protests. As early as 1982, the Peace Camp site served as an encampment for protestors affiliated with groups including the Nevada Desert Experience, American Peace Test (APT), Greenpeace, Physicians for Social Responsibility, Nuclear Freeze/SANE, Peace Committee of the American Public Health Association, and others conducting protests at NTS. Throughout the 1980s, hundreds of individual protests organized by these and other groups would attract thousands of participants in civil disobedience actions often lasting a week or more and regularly resulting in hundreds of protestors being arrested for trespassing or resisting arrest. These protest actions reached a zenith in 1988, when a protest organized by APT dubbed "Reclaim the Test Site" attracted in excess of 8,000 participants, including a number of celebrities and political figures. The protest resulted in more than 2,000 arrests and was the largest civil disobedience action in American history to that time (Coates 1988; Gusterson 1996). During these protests, the NTS Peace Camp took shape.

Archaeological surveys of the Peace Camp were conducted in 2002 by DRI archaeologists Colleen Beck, Harold Drollinger, and John Schofield, former head of Military and Naval Evaluation Programs at English Heritage, the charitable trust charged with overseeing the United Kingdom's national heritage sites. With extensive experience in both the archaeology of the Cold War at the NTS itself and the archaeology of Cold War social dissidence at Greenham Common (Schofield and Anderton 2000), the team set out to better understand not only what made the Peace Camp distinctive as a settlement type, but how the archaeological traces might represent changes in the philosophy or actions of the protestors over the years and how the opposition to nuclear weapons testing was represented in the material record (Beck et al. 2011).

Their surveys revealed a well-preserved site with nearly 800 distinct surface features, ranging in type from graffiti and rock art to campsites and detention structures, distributed across five temporally and spatially defined areas of occupation. Dating from the mid-1950s, the first Peace Camp site was little more than a rallying point and transit camp for the small groups of protestors who undertook regular peace marches from Las Vegas to the site. Relatively small and intermittently occupied, the original campsite was located close to the access roads and only several hundred feet west of the entrance to the NTS, near the US 95 underpass tunnel. The camp is characterized by a relatively sparse and random layout of fire rings constructed of local stone and of tent pads, which are flat ground areas cleared of rocks, vegetation, and tree roots and slightly sloped in order that rainwater runs off.

A second, somewhat larger Peace Camp site was later established just to the east of the original site; this area was permanently occupied during the protests of the late 1980s. Encompassing roughly 200 acres, new campsite was more intentional and better planned in physical layout, with field surveys showing certain areas clearly being used for habitation (with stone

Figure 4.12. Located across the highway from what was once the Mercury gate of the NTS in Mercury, Nevada, the Shadow Children sculpture lies mostly in pieces at the NTS Peace Camp. Photo by the author.

fire rings, improvised cooking hearths, and multiple tent pads), while other areas had expansive open spaces and larger fire rings, possibly for use in communal and ceremonial activities. The area shows evidence of substantial landscaping along the low ridges that cross the site, principally with geomorphs representing human figures, doves, hearts, peace signs, and other symbols, as well as the words "Peace Camp" spelled out with stones. On one ridge, rocks are arranged to spell out the word "Peace" in English, Chinese, French, and Russian, the languages of the five so-called nuclear-weapon states in the 1980s. Not far away, a set of three life-sized plaster casts of children, known as the Shadow Children, lie enshrined in a stone circle (Figure 4.12). Believed to be associated with a visit to the site by protestors from Hiroshima, Japan, the Shadow Children casts are substantially weathered and deteriorating, yet retain a dramatic power of presence as an antinuclear protest symbol. Beyond the major features, the artifacts recorded at the Peace Camp site are extensive but not particularly abundant, and range from the sacred to the mundane. In general, the camp occupants' regard for the natural environment manifests itself in the overall lack of customary refuse and litter at the site. Aside from the various artistic works and sacred and pseudo-sacred objects intentionally left behind as sustaining evidence of the peace movement, discarded items are rare, offering relatively little artifactual evidence of the site's sizeable, multi-decadal occupation.

DRI archaeologists identified a third area of the Peace Camp associated with antinuclear protests; namely, a pair of tunnels running beneath the two lanes of US 95 near the main Peace Camp site. Lining the walls of the soi-disant "Tunnel of Love" is graphic evidence from 20 years of the Peace Camp's occupation (Figure 4.13), constituting numerous painted peace signs, literary quotations, notes, poems, and drawings, as well as various prosaic informational messages related to Peace Camp actions (Schofield, Beck, and Drollinger 2006).

Features associated with the entrance road and gate to the NTS property itself constitute a fourth major Peace Camp area. Principally these are features of engagement, arrest, and confinement. Like many rural roads in the American West, where steel cattle guards are installed in lieu of gates when the road crosses through a fence line to prevent the transit of

Figure 4.13. A central access point to the NTS, the underpass tunnel now serves as a popular venue for antinuclear activist graffiti and messages. By permission of Harold Drollinger, Desert Research Institute.

Figure 4.14. The Red Lady sculpture on Pagoda Hill at the NTS Peace Camp. By permission of Harold Drollinger, Desert Research Institute.

grazing livestock, Mercury Road, the two-lane access road to the NTS, once had a cattle guard. This represents the point along Mercury Road beyond which protesters were forbidden to pass. Throughout the 1980s and 1990s the cattle guard served as a rallying spot for protesters and was a site of symbolic engagement with NTS security and Nye County law enforcement. During protests, security guards from NTS stationed themselves on one side of the cattle guard and arrested for trespassing anyone who crossed it. In 1996 the cattle guard was replaced with a simple painted white line on the roadway to keep protesters from chaining themselves to the bars of the guard. Immediately to the northwest of the former cattle guard site are two large fenced areas designated as protestor holding pens. Ostensibly, these detention structures are features shared between the Peace Camp and the NTS, since the DOE built them inside the official NTS boundary, but because of their historical use for the confinement of protestors during protest actions, they are often considered part of the Peace Camp. The DOE built the first of two 100-foot by 220-foot enclosures in 1988 using chain-link fencing topped with barbed wire (Coates 1988). The second fenced area was built later to allow for the segregation of detainees by sex. Neither enclosure contains any furniture or structures, except for a single portable toilet located in the center of the space.

In the far southwest corner of the Peace Camp is a fifth feature area that is ostensibly a more secluded, possibly even ceremonial, place for camp occupants. Known to protestors as Pagoda Hill, the site is the highest point in the camp. Conical in shape, Pagoda Hill provides a commanding view of the Peace Camp itself and of much of the NTS that lies to the north. At its crest are three rock cairns, two more than 2 meters in height, which were constructed over several years by protestors carrying stones up to the hilltop. Votive offerings, including a variety of quartz crystals, seashells, colored stones, amulets, yarn, and handwritten notes, have been placed within the interstices of the cairns' rocks. Symbolizing the very personalized aspects of the opposition to nuclear weapons development and testing, the cairns' artifacts are, quite literally, peace offerings. Another notable feature on the western side of Pagoda Hill is a large red clay sculpture of a reclining pregnant female figure set into the ground (Figure 4.14). Encircled with stones, the figure is inscribed with radioactive symbols and wears an amulet around her neck bearing the words "DOE Nuke Waste Dump" (Schofield 2009).

DRI archaeologists determined in 2007 that the Peace Camp met the criteria for NRHP eligibility both for its association with events that have made a significant contribution to the broad patterns of American history and for its embodiment of distinctive characteristics that possess high artistic value. While the continuing use of the Peace Camp site, coupled with the adversarial and polarizing nature of nuclear protest, makes the likelihood of formal legislative protection of the Peace Camp site complicated, it exists as a unique and relevant symbol of twentieth-century American civil disobedience and creative resistance against hegemonic power.

Nuclear Rocket Development Site, Nevada Test Site

While the NTS has long been widely associated with nuclear weapons testing and the arms race, the site also played a role in America's Space Race. Not only did Apollo astronauts test some of their equipment in the desolate expanse of the NTS before going to the moon, it housed activities aimed at the development of a nuclear-powered rocket engine for space propulsion. Carried out under the designation Project Rover, rocket development and testing activities such as those shown in Figure 4.15 were conducted from 1959 to 1973 at the Nuclear Rocket Development Station (NRDS), a roughly 30-square-mile expanse of Jackass Flats in the southwest corner of the NTS.

Funded to the tune of nearly $1.5 billion (Dewar 2004), Project Rover's mission was to produce a nuclear thermal engine capable of greater propulsion performance than the liquid or solid fuel chemical rocket engines of the era. The operating principles behind the nuclear thermal engine were fairly simple. Because a nuclear reactor's core generates tremendous heat, it can raise the temperature of any gas flowing through it to temperatures in excess of 2,000 degrees Celsius. When a gas with a low molecular weight, such as hydrogen, is pumped through the nuclear reactor's hot fuel elements, it vaporizes and expands. Funneling the escaping gas through a nozzle produces a massive amount of thrust.

Calculations done at the time by LASL scientists predicted that a nuclear thermal engine could achieve a far greater power density than one fueled by chemical reactions. Thus, for a given amount of engine and fuel weight, the nuclear engine could produce more thrust, resulting in not only farther travel distances through interstellar space, but also heavier payload carrying capacities. An ancillary but impressive advantage of the nuclear rocket engine was that it could be reliably stopped and restarted in flight, unlike the conventional rocket engines of that era. A substantial downside, however, was that because the gas coming from the rocket was radioactive it would likely prove impractical as a booster-stage engine for any terrestrial launched rockets.

Project Rover passed through a number of engine development stages, which were roughly defined at the time by the engine code names. The initial development consisted of eight reactors built between 1959 and 1964 and code-named Kiwi-A and Kiwi-B, referencing New Zealand's flightless bird because the rockets were considered to be earthbound and

Figure 4.15. LASL scientists and technicians at work in the Project Rover control room at the NTS during a 1959 test of a Kiwi reactor. By permission of Los Alamos National Laboratory.

used only for research and theory validation. By 1963, faith in the economic and technological potential of Project Rover was sufficient to lead Congress to hold hearings to consider the construction of an entire residential community at the NTS to accommodate what was then believed to be the future of American space propulsion (U.S. Congress 1963). The NRDS community was ultimately never built, but in 1965 a second phase of research began under the project name Phoebus. Lasting until 1968, the Phoebus research produced a new generation of more powerful and sophisticated thermal nuclear engines that, although never actually tested, were likely capable of spaceflight. The final engine in the Project Rover development project was PeeWee, built in 1968 as an attempt to make a more compact engine using various different nuclear fuel compositions. While all of the Rover rockets were designed and constructed at LASL, all of the testing took place at the NTS.

Consisting of five large building complexes, the NRDS was constructed in phases to accommodate the evolution of nuclear engine research work during Project Rover. DRI archaeologists, assisted by architectural historians, assessed and documented the NRDS in the mid-1990s in anticipation

Figure 4.16. View of the NRDS R-MAD facility in 1996. While R-MAD was considered eligible for nomination to the NRHP and was recommended for such designation, it was demolished in April 2010. By permission of the U.S. Department of Energy.

of the future demolition of the complexes. One of these sites was R-MAD, the Reactor Maintenance and Disassembly facility (Figure 4.16). Constructed in 1958, the R-MAD complex provided research space for the Kiwi series of engines, which focused on refining and testing reactor designs and validating theories that a nuclear thermal reactor could develop sufficient thrust to propel a rocket. The facility encompassed roughly 53 acres of floor space for administrative, reactor assembly, and disassembly areas. A massive, self-propelled and remote-controlled robot called Beetle was maintained at R-MAD for use in handling radioactively contaminated Kiwi reactors.

A second NRDS facility documented by archaeologists was E-MAD, the Engine Maintenance and Disassembly facility. A windowless reinforced concrete facility similar in design to R-MAD but larger, E-MAD was built in 1965 to facilitate the development of Phoebus, a series of more powerful engines capable of operating for longer periods. E-MAD contained offices, workshops, assembly and disassembly bays, hot cells, a machine shop, and what was once the world's largest hot cell for use in disassembling the Phoebus engines (Beck et al. 1996). E-MAD was unique in that it had bays designed to accommodate the specially modified railroad system shown in Figure 4.17, dubbed the Jackass & Western Rail Line, and used for transporting the multi-ton nuclear engines to and from the test cell, two miles away. DRI archaeologists examined and documented not only the facilities at E-MAD, but the locomotive, railcar, and rail tracks of the railroad transport system as well.

The archaeological investigation and documentation of the rail transport system at NRDS are tied to the survey and documentation of two

Figure 4.17. The Phoebus engine being prepared for testing in 1967 at Test Cell C. Project Rover's rockets were test-fired with the nozzles pointing upward to better calculate thrust and to keep the engines on the ground. The two-mile rail system enabled transport of the rocket engines around the E-MAD complex. By permission of Los Alamos National Laboratory.

engine test cells prior to decommissioning and demolition. Test Cell A was built to test whether the thermal nuclear engine could start on its own and then run at full power for an extended period. The test cell consisted of a main building, covering roughly 5,000 square feet, along with a number of ancillary structures, including a large spherical dewar for holding liquid hydrogen (Beck et al. 2000). Built in 1961, Test Cell C (see Figure 4.17) was virtually twice the size of Test Cell A in order to incorporate a number of additional features necessary to handle newer, more advanced nuclear reactor and engine designs. Tests were conducted at Test Cell C from 1962 to 1972 (Drollinger et al. 2000). Project Rover was ultimately terminated in 1973 for lack of funding.

The archaeological studies of Project Rover and the NRDS emerge as archaeologies of Cold War science by virtue of their explication of sites of historic scientific advancements in the fields of high-temperature chemistry, nuclear physics, and metallurgy. Although archaeological research at NRDS was conducted expressly to document the facilities as elements of the HAER prior to decommissioning and demolition, the data gathered provides broader insights into the site's setting, construction, and use, especially in terms of illustrating the deviations or adaptations of facilities from the construction blueprints or as-built drawings. Dewar (2004) posits that the scientific advancements achieved during Project Rover, which have been transferred to the American military and civilian space programs, will ultimately lead to a nuclear rocket for space travel. Notable among Rover's technological advancements was the production, transport, and storage of hydrogen and its isotopes in large quantities, capabilities that may someday be useful if hydrogen becomes America's primary automotive fuel.

McGregor Range, New Mexico

Early in the Cold War it became apparent that the new weapons technologies being developed would require ongoing testing and maintenance to ensure their battle readiness after extended periods of inactivity. Likewise, the crews operating them would need to be periodically retrained in live-fire exercises. While Vandenberg AFB would provide opportunities for ICBM crews to test-launch missiles in so-called glory trips, for the Nike and later variations of SAM systems, both the missiles and missile crews would be tested at McGregor Range in New Mexico. Operated by the

U.S. Army's Fort Bliss, McGregor Range began operations in 1949 as the Army's air defense training range. Encompassing 670,000 acres in south-central New Mexico, McGregor Range lies along the New Mexico–Texas state line with its northern border abutting the southern border of White Sands Missile Range. These two ranges combined provide nearly 4,000 square miles of contiguous land for military training and testing exercises.

The first air defense training exercises conducted at McGregor were for crews manning conventional antiaircraft artillery, principally the 90 mm radar-directed and 120 mm Stratosphere artillery cannons (Nowlan 1999:16). Later, training was added for crews operating the 75 mm Skysweeper gun. As conventional antiaircraft artillery batteries were replaced by Nike SAMs, training at Fort Bliss shifted again to accommodate the new missile technologies. In the decades that followed, McGregor Range provided air defense forces training for the Lark, Chaparral, Nike, Hawk, Patriot, Sprint, Redeye, and Stinger missiles (Hawthorne-Tagg 2001). For these tests, McGregor Range was divided into three distinct firing range areas: South McGregor, Desert Range, and North McGregor.

North McGregor began air defense training operations in 1949 with 32 separate 90 mm antiaircraft artillery firing points located along the east side of U.S. Highway 54, all firing their guns in an eastward direction across the desert. Archaeologists found sparse facilities at North McGregor: two 16 × 16 foot storage hutments, a steel observation tower, and a pit latrine. Located 10 miles south of North McGregor, again with all its firing points positioned along the east side of US 54, Desert Range had 16 firing points for 90 mm and 120 mm guns and 24 points for 75 mm Skysweeper guns, all firing eastward. Desert Range was the primary antiaircraft artillery training area at McGregor; surveying archaeologists found 23 wood-frame structures built at the site by 1954, including six kitchens, five 10-seat pit latrines, multiple storage sheds, an observation tower, and a radio-controlled aerial target (RCAT) rotary launch facility. By 1955, South McGregor had 16 firing points each for 90 mm and 75 mm Skysweeper guns, but initially it had no support facilities. Eventually, South McGregor would become the site of the McGregor Range Camp and would host most of the missile training launch sites.

Archaeological research indicates that construction of McGregor Range Camp facilities began in earnest at South McGregor in 1956 in parallel with the increasingly important Nike missile training range headquarters, range control, and missile assembly buildings. Features that were revealed through fieldwork include several compacted earth revetments used for the storage of missile fuel and warheads, and for readying missiles (Nowlan 1999). By 1960, the camp had 26 large concrete and brick barracks, each with an attached mess hall. Over the next five years, other structures were constructed, including headquarters buildings, a sentry station, and a permanent radar facility, as well as a softball field, a bathhouse, and an outdoor swimming pool. These buildings were built almost exclusively of concrete or brick, which as Lowry and Henry (1997:147–148) noted, reflected the increasingly permanent nature of the camp. Antiaircraft artillery crew officers, operations assistants, fire control crews, and radar operators from across the nation came to all three areas to receive technical instruction relevant to their rank and station in target acquisition, directing fire, radio communications, field techniques, and artillery gun maintenance and repair.

Archaeological investigations of the Cold War at McGregor Range began in the late 1990s, when Lowry and Henry (1997) examined evidence associated with missile systems training at McGregor Range Camp and with the Firebee-Towbee and Redhead/Roadrunner missile launch sites. Nowlan (1999) would later identify 55 archaeological features at McGregor Range that were directly related to historic Army Cold War activities, including a former Nike AN/FPS-36 radar and control building and 26 former Nike launch sites with their corresponding Integrated Fire Control sites.

Located approximately a half mile north of the McGregor Range Base Camp, the AN/FPS-36 radar site consisted of a rotating scan radar antenna mounted on a steel crossbeam tower alongside an 850-square-foot reinforced concrete radar control building. Built in 1961 specifically to support the Nike missile system training program, the AN/FPS-36 radar had a range of 200 miles, making it optimal for acquisition of training targets over McGregor.

In 1957, only six Nike launch sites, each with radar facilities and two launchers, were in operation at McGregor. By the end of 1959, 26 Nike sites had been built, each with two Nike launchers and a small subterranean concrete blockhouse, all along a roughly north-south line approximately three miles east of the Base Camp. Unique to the Nike training sites at McGregor Range, the blockhouses served as control centers during launches. A mile west of the line of missile launch sites was a corresponding parallel line of Integrated Fire Control sites, with hardstand areas for the portable radar control, generator, and maintenance trailers for each Nike missile launcher (Nowlan 1999).

In 2000 archaeologists working for Lone Mountain Archaeological Services identified, surveyed, and recorded three previously unknown and particularly notable McGregor Range sites. Designated LA 132327, LA 132328, and LA 110871 under the New Mexico Cultural Resource Information System Archaeological Records Management Section, the sites were functionally linked with training uses in their Cold War air defense context. Site LA 132327 is a former antiaircraft artillery range firing point and command center for artillery field maneuvers at Desert Range, where soldiers tested their antiaircraft artillery skills in a simulated combat environment. Consisting of bunkers, firing points, and the remains of encampment structures, site LA 132328 is a former Continental Air Defense antiaircraft artillery target practice site from 1954. Established at Desert Range in 1953 for the training of ARAACOM units, site LA 110871 is a former structured target practice area, consisting of a target launch area, artillery firing points, and the remains of a small base camp (Hawthorne-Tagg 2001).

Archaeological surveys of LA 132327 documented 24 Cold War features, including 27 earthen berms or mounds, some as large as 60 feet in diameter; 15 foxholes; and 5 artillery firing points situated in large horseshoe-shaped excavations. Also discovered were two 12-seat latrines and an underground bunker. Artifacts and features at LA 132327 suggest that it was the site of a former command center for Desert Range field maneuvers. The site contained a 100-foot by 70-foot oval depression, or pit excavation, sufficient to shelter military communications equipment trucks from errant artillery or small-arms fire. Large wooden spools that once contained electric cable typically used with radar and communication equipment, and defensive gun emplacements, sit amid six-man foxholes and several crew-served machine gun emplacement mounds. A unique berm and trench feature indicative of an emplacement for bazookas seems to have been built for the protection of the Desert Range command center, hinting at the site's role in simulated combat situations that were performed simultaneous with target practice by antiaircraft artillery crews. Although the shallow, horseshoe-shaped excavation indicates the location of the antiaircraft artillery firing point, no artillery shells were found, which is perhaps not unusual as such shells were no doubt recycled. Nearby, however, machine gun emplacements and foxholes showed evidence of both automatic and semiautomatic small arms fire, with hundreds of machine gun shell casings and belt links scattered across one site, and M1 Garand rifle magazines and cartridge casings scattered at another.

Although LA 132327 remains in fair condition overall, despite some features being partially buried and others disintegrating due to natural weathering, the site was too young at the time the research was done to be eligible for nomination to the NRHP as the site of the earliest antiaircraft artillery training at Fort Bliss. Possessing both archaeological and historical research potential and local significance, the site was recommended as potentially eligible, pending additional archaeological research (Hawthorne-Tagg 2001).

LA 132328 is located roughly 1,000 yards southwest of LA 132327 and is characterized by 48 documented Cold War features, including numerous shallow excavations; four underground wooden bunkers roofed with tarpaper, dirt, and limestone cobbles; and 24 separate foxholes encircling the bunkers. The site also has two 12-seat pit latrines situated on the far western and eastern boundaries of the site; these show structural features similar to those found at LA 132327: wood-frame benches built over trenches, and urinals consisting of two funnels nailed to poles sunk into the ground near the latrines. A significant archaeological discovery at the site were excavations lined with 55-gallon steel drums, which were presumed to have been filled with water to help cool the spaces where electronic equipment was used. The archaeology of LA 132328 also indicates a site where conventional antiaircraft weapons systems might have been used in association with a simulated combat environment based on a surface assemblage containing hundreds of 30- and 50-caliber shell casings found at several mounds and foxhole locations (Hawthorne-Tagg 2001:109).

Desert Range site LA 110871 was likely built in 1953 to provide structured target practice. In structured target practice, aerial targets would have been launched from the site and shot down by antiaircraft artillery. Archaeological evidence at the site includes a graded strip of land capable of providing temporary firing points for as many as 24 Skysweeper 75 mm artillery guns, along with 26 underground bunkers and the structural remains of 13 buildings. The remains of a wooden observation tower and RCAT launch site supported the hypothesis of a structured target practice function.

Perhaps the most notable feature discovered was the RCAT launch area, which consists of a 200-foot-diameter graded circle encircled by an asphalt-paved perimeter road. Located approximately 360 meters north of the Skysweeper firing line, the RCAT was used to launch drone aircraft for artillery target use. The LA 110871 RCAT is a fairly well-preserved Model A-2 rotary launcher. To launch a drone—which was essentially a small single-engine airplane with a 12-foot wingspan and no landing gear—the drone was placed on a three-wheeled dolly or car that circled the site's asphalt track while tethered to a central pole by a cable. The drone and dolly would travel around the circular track until the drone became airborne. The drone was then remotely released from the dolly and would continue to accelerate in flight, held in a circular course by the pole until it reached a critical launch speed. When the tether was released, the drone launched and was flown remotely into artillery crew training exercises at McGregor Range. The OQ-19 drones had a range of 65 miles and could reach a maximum altitude of 23,000 feet while flying at 200 miles per hour (Hawthorne-Tagg 2001).

The vast landscape that comprises McGregor Range has witnessed significant Cold War archaeology study, but much is yet to be revealed about its role in air defense. McGregor was a central site for missile force training throughout the Cold War, including practice with Patriot and Stinger missiles in the 1980s, and further archaeological investigations are needed.

Cape Canaveral, Florida

Insomuch as the Space Race was an elemental part of the Cold War, archaeological studies of sites related to the research, development, testing, launch, operations, and recovery of manned and unmanned rockets and space vehicles have become essential components of the archaeology of the Cold War. Internationally, a broad range of studies has recently explored the diverse material aspects of the Cold War Space Race on the ground (e.g., Donaldson 2015), in Earth orbit (e.g., Gorman 2009, 2015), and beyond (e.g., Capelotti 2010; Gold 2009; Gorman 2005; Gorman and O'Leary 2007). Nowhere is the archaeology of the Space Race in North America better represented, however, than at Cape Canaveral.

Arguably, no site in North America captures the quintessence of the

Cold War Space Race like Cape Canaveral. Established in 1949 on the barrier islands along Florida's Atlantic coast as the Joint Long Range Proving Grounds at Cape Canaveral, the site was renamed the Cape Canaveral Auxiliary AFB in 1951. The base later became Cape Canaveral AFS and Station One of the Florida Missile Test Range, but from 1963 to 1973 it went by the name of Cape Kennedy, in honor of President John F. Kennedy. During the Cold War, Atlas, Titan, Thor, Jupiter, Matador, Bomarc, Snark, Navaho, and Navy Polaris missiles were all tested at Cape Canaveral (Cleary 1991). With the birth of the National Aeronautics and Space Administration (NASA) and the creation of America's civilian (nonmilitary) space program in 1958 came the construction of Launch Complex 39 on Merritt Island at Cape Canaveral, from which the Project Apollo missions would put 12 Americans on the Moon.

As Map 4.3 illustrates, Cape Canaveral AFS served as the point of origin for the EMTR, which extended southeastward across the Atlantic Ocean for 5,000 miles and consisted of the launch complexes at Cape Canaveral and missile tracking stations on the islands of Grand Bahama, Eleuthera, San Salvador, Mayaguana, Grand Turk, the Dominican Republic, and Puerto Rico. The purpose of the radar tracking stations was to receive flight telemetry on the missile's speed, direction, altitude, location, and operating conditions. Missiles were tested on the EMTR from 1956 through the end of the Cold War (Cleary 1991).

Archaeological investigations of Cape Canaveral's Cold War activities have been conducted for nearly a decade by cultural resource professionals working under the U.S. Air Force 45th Space Wing Civil Engineering Squadron at Cape Canaveral AFS. Employing a range of theoretical frameworks, these archaeological studies of Cape Canaveral AFS represent some of the most innovative work being accomplished in modern conflict archaeology. Reflecting both the efficacy of well-conceived research designs and the emerging historic preservation applications of laser scanning technologies, the current archaeological work at Cape Canaveral is both solving mysteries and helping protect some of Cold War America's historic aerospace landmarks.

Occupying approximately 15,800 acres on Florida's barrier islands, Cape Canaveral AFS is notable for its role in America's early Cold War ballistic missile testing program. Home to more than 20 active and abandoned launch complexes, the Cape Canaveral site is also significant for the 138 missile launch failures that occurred during the testing and left the

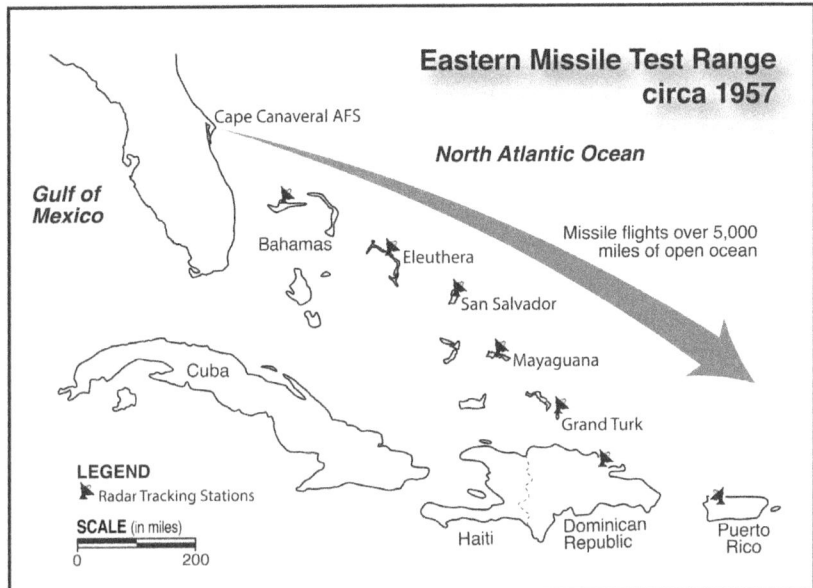

Map 4.3. Eastern Missile Test Range and environs during the Cold War. Map by the author.

adjacent coastal landscape and ocean floor littered with the wreckage of failed missions. In 2007, Cape Canaveral archaeologists initiated a study of one of these failed mission crash sites.

Located and documented but never investigated by previous cultural resource inventories of Cape Canaveral AFS, the Jupiter Missile Crash Site (designated 8BR2087) lies in the overwash plain between the dune and swale areas of the Atlantic Ocean, approximately 300 meters from the shoreline. Marked by an impact crater approximately 15 meters in diameter and 3 meters deep, the area is surrounded by a 1-meter-high raised rim of ejected material (sand) within a field of missile crash debris extending to the south and southwest. Researchers speculated that the crater was created by the crash of a Jupiter intermediate range ballistic missile, but the theory had never been substantiated because a number of Cape Canaveral AFS missile crashes were potential candidates (Penders 2012).

Measuring 60 feet long and 8½ feet in diameter, Jupiter missiles used a gimbaled rocket engine powered by a liquid oxygen and liquid kerosene fuel mixture known as RP-1. Jupiter intermediate range ballistic missiles were predominantly launched at Cape Canaveral AFS from launch complexes built specifically for the Jupiter program in 1955 and 1956 and designated as Launch Complexes 5 and 6 (LC-5/6) and, just to their north, Launch Complex (LC-26). These ballistic missile launch complexes consisted of a single blockhouse flanked by twin flat concrete pads. Jupiter played an important role in the Cold War as America's first widely deployed intermediate range ballistic missile. In 1961, the NATO deployment of Jupiter missiles in Turkey was one of the precipitating causes of the Cuban Missile Crisis, and their removal from Turkey was a stipulation of the agreement that resolved the crisis.

Because of the number of missile launch complexes (eight complexes, each with two launch pads) located within a one-mile radius of the crash site, researchers were initially unable to verify that site 8BR2087 was the location of a Jupiter missile failure. The crater and debris field could have been created by any number of failed Cold War missile launches. To reduce the number of potential crash candidates, Thomas Penders (2012) conducted a data search that cross-referenced all launch accidents with their associated launch complexes. By combining documented descriptions of the individual mishaps from each launch complex with evidence gathered during field surveys Penders narrowed the crater's possible origin to five potential missile failures.

A pedestrian reconnaissance survey of site 8BR2087 conducted in 2008 recovered 412 artifacts from a 280-meter by 150-meter debris field. After excluding the modern debris (e.g., aluminum cans, plastic and glass bottles, and pieces of wood) that were clearly unrelated to the crash, 358 items could be attributed to a Jupiter missile crash, including 325 aluminum or steel alloy items identified as exterior skin or tank fragments, 26 baffles from inside the liquid oxygen and fuel tanks, and one exhaust port from the base portion of the missile. Researchers performing the surface survey photographed all artifacts discovered in the field with a digital camera, marked the artifacts with pin flags, then georeferenced the pin flag locations with a GPS unit. Because accordion tank baffles were installed on the Jupiter missiles in 1957 to prevent fuel from sloshing around in the missile's tank during flight, the presence of tank baffle fragments at the site pointed to a post-1957 Jupiter missile crash. Ultimately, two Jupiter launches from LC-26 were considered potential crash candidates. Archival video footage of one of these crashes on LC-26 reduced the candidates to a missile designated Jupiter AM-23 launched from LC-26B on September 15, 1959.

While the 2008 survey concentrated on identifying and documenting the distribution of artifacts across the crash site, a subsequent investigation in May 2012 focused on identifying and analyzing the locations of specific missile debris in proximity relationship to the impact crater, in order to ascertain certain details about the crash. The research design employed combined traditional archaeological methods with practices established by various aviation agencies for use in aircraft and spacecraft accident investigations. In this design, the first step was to assess the morphology of the crater. The morphology of the crash site combined with land surveys and examination of a 1960 aerial photograph indicated that the Jupiter missile impacted at a high angle at or near the surface, thereby creating the circular crater shown in Figure 4.18. Based on the fact that missile crashes typically cause debris to be dispersed over a limited spatial

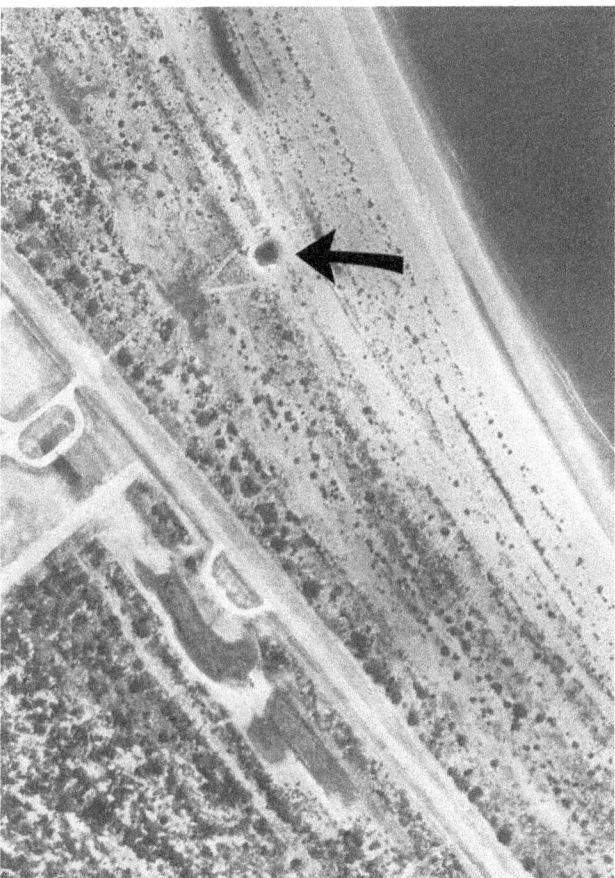

Figure 4.18. Aerial photograph from 1960 of the crater left by a Jupiter AM-23 missile that crashed after being launched from Cape Canaveral Launch Complex 26-B on September 15, 1959. By permission of the U.S. Air Force.

area in a non-uniform fan-shaped pattern pointing in the direction of impact, examination of the debris field around the crater subsequently allowed Cape Canaveral AFS researchers to determine the flight direction of the missile at impact.

To determine the missile's original flight orientation, Cape Canaveral AFS investigators strung a line between two stakes installed along the main axis of the impact crater, effectively dividing the crater and its accompanying debris field into symmetrical halves. This axis was oriented toward the southwest, which was consistent with the crash record for the Jupiter AM-23 launch. That missile lifted off and quickly veered from its easterly flight path toward the southwest before crashing. The crash created a high-angle circular impact crater with a debris field scattered in a southwesterly direction.

Pender's archaeological study attributing this Jupiter missile crash site to the launch of Jupiter AM-23 solves one of the Cold War's minor mysteries. More importantly, it serves as an exemplary study of a missile crash site, highlighting the ongoing need to study, document, and protect such sites. Cold War missile crash sites provide an invaluable means for reconstructing, and in some cases reassessing, our understanding of the course of America's missile and rocket development programs under conditions where historic details may be lacking. As Penders notes, "The physical remains at crash sites can offer information on manufacturing processes, materials, internal fittings, modifications, and even paint finishes, information not available from other sources" (2012:232).

Paralleling conventional archaeological and historic preservation activities at Cape Canaveral is a project aimed at documenting, conserving, and preserving several important Cold War landmarks through high-definition digital documentation (H3D), a systematic, technology-based approach to the acquisition, processing, and visualization of high-resolution, 3-D spatial data for archaeological research, cultural heritage management, and educational uses.

The H3D approach allows spatial and structural aspects of the archaeological record to be documented and archived at artifact, feature, site, and landscape scales, creating a comprehensive, multifunctional digital record for a number of uses, such as making CAD drawings and 3-D models. Digital models of features and landscapes based on terrestrial laser scanning surveys can be integrated with aerial lidar (remote sensing) data, GPS photographs taken of survey target points, topographic mapping data, and aerial and satellite imagery. Spatially referenced data gathered from ground-penetrating radar and magnetometer, electroconductivity, and spectroscopic surveys can also be incorporated into H3D datasets (Collins and Doering 2013).

The H3D process is particularly useful for making recurrent assessments of complex sites or for recording sites that may be difficult to fully document by other means due to issues of safety and accessibility. Working in collaboration with the University of South Florida Alliance for Integrated Spatial Technologies, in 2014 Penders and colleagues created baseline surveys of six historic Cape Canaveral AFS launch complexes as part of a five-year study of the sites. Using FARO Technologies LS880 Phase-shift Mid-Range laser scanners capable of collecting one million data cloud points per second, researchers captured millimeter-scale (± 2 mm), gigapixel, 3-D data on each of the launch complexes for potential use in creating CAD drawings and 3-D models for historic preservation site documentation, structural and environmental monitoring, and historic restoration needs. The research strategy is to make annual scans and condition assessments of the launch complexes, which have been affected by erosion, corrosion, and the destructive effects of invasive plant species. The nondestructive scans for degradation, erosion, or deterioration of features and sites due to age, weather, or vegetation growth—which could ultimately undermine the site's structural integrity, appearance, and historical value—will help Cape Canaveral AFS archaeologists monitor the condition of sites and set priorities for preservation efforts (Penders et al. 2009).

An exemplar of the H3D collaboration at Cape Canaveral is the digital documentation of the LC-31/32 "beehive" blockhouses. Dubbed "beehives" based on their appearance, the two 30-foot-high reinforced concrete domes were constructed in 1960 to provide launch control facilities for Minuteman missile tests (Figure 4.19). The unique exteriors result from a construction method in which layers of wet, concrete-filled sandbags were stacked against the exterior of rebar-reinforced concrete domes to provide added protection. Exterior steel staircases provide access to the upper levels of each blockhouse. Although the three-foot-thick shell of concrete bags added increased blast protection, the design also left the blockhouses prone to the erosion and slumping of the sandbags, rusting and corrosion of the stairway, and the detrimental effects of invasive vegetation growth. The annual laser scans of the blockhouses will help

Figure 4.19. One of two 30-foot-high reinforced concrete "beehive" blockhouses at LC-31/32, Cape Canaveral AFS. The domes were built in 1960 to provide launch control facilities for Minuteman ICBM tests. By permission of the U.S. Air Force.

researchers monitor for deterioration or degradation of their condition, especially changes in structural integrity associated with weathering or vegetation growth, by revealing even the smallest (sub-centimeter scale) variations in site configuration. These are changes at scales that even the most perceptive archeologists might find difficult to observe and quantify (Penders et al. 2009).

The data captured as part of this H3D effort provides exceptionally accurate and robust spatial information with which to construct digital models, 3-D fly-through videos, and visualizations of some of Cape Canaveral's most important heritage sites for use in a wide variety of applications, from structural health assessments to virtual walkthroughs for interpretive opportunities, education, and tourism (Figure 4.20).

Summary

Employing a diverse range of theoretical constructs from the fields of conflict archaeology, contemporary archaeology, and the archaeology of science, the research described in this chapter provides compelling models for future studies of Cold War materiality. Applying conflict archaeology constructs to the study of the McGregor Range in New Mexico, Nowlan and Hawthorne-Tagg not only documented a shift from antiaircraft artillery to Nike SAM missile training sites, but also offered insights into the complex functional aspects of that training. Using frameworks from contemporary archaeology, Diez Acosta, Burström, and their colleagues not only produced new knowledge relative to the Soviet missile sites in Cuba, but also yielded information about the reuse of various Cold War material remains and provided a venue for conversations with Cuban residents about how the Crisis de Octubre was experienced and lived locally. Theoretically grounded in the archaeology of science, Delgado's and Brown's investigations of atomic tests at Bikini Atoll, and specifically their studies of the bunkers, measurement devices, and instruments that remain in situ, offer intriguing evidence of the technological adaptations American nuclear weapons scientists used to quantify some of the most

Figure 4.20. A terrestrial laser scanning survey in progress in 2014 at Cape Canaveral's LC-14. LC-14 is best known for the 1962 launch of Friendship 7, the flight that put the first American in Earth orbit. By permission of the U.S. Air Force.

basic physical characteristics of nuclear weapons explosions and, ultimately, how to measure those blasts.

In the next chapter, I look beyond specific sites to explore some of the issues related to the archaeological study and stewardship of America's Cold War landscape.

5

COLD WAR ARCHAEOLOGY

Study and Stewardship Issues

In previous chapters, I traced how an extensive and expensive American Cold War built landscape evolved from the remains of a hastily aggregated World War Two defense industry into a vast military-industrial complex, as well as how archaeologists have approached the study of properties within that landscape from different methodological and theoretical perspectives. In this chapter, I examine some of the fundamental issues related to the archaeological study of that landscape, broadly defined as North America's Cold War cultural heritage. In particular, I look at some of the challenges facing those interested in researching, exploring, and preserving that heritage. I look as well at the rise of the atomic tourism phenomenon, its implications for Cold War material culture studies, and the potential role of Cold War veterans in heritage study and stewardship.

Challenges to the Study of Cold War Remains

In many ways archaeological studies are the wheel upon which heritage stewardship turns. It is through the interpretation of tangible and intangible cultural history that we are best able to meaningfully understand, represent, and manage the artifacts and monuments of our past. As a war that was fought globally yet produced tangible and profound local effects in many places, the Cold War offers a bafflingly complex legacy for archaeological studies. Driven as much by political and ideological divisions as by a range of psychological, technological, economic, cultural, and social issues, it produced landscapes of immense range and complexity. Within these vast and complex landscapes, even the smallest Cold War sites often have something valuable to tell us about such things as the subversive material character of political protest, the lifestyles of U.S. armed forces in challenging environments, and the material nature of technical ingenuity. Because the challenges facing the archaeological study of Cold War cultural history turn so predominantly upon aspects of access, safety, and secrecy, I examine each issue in turn.

Challenges of Access

A range of challenges can limit or even prevent an archaeologist's access to Cold War sites, including the remoteness of sites, physical hazards, and location issues. While the scope of Cold War sites available for study is broad and international in extent, one of the most advantageous aspects of archaeologies of the Cold War is the fact that no region of the United States is without its own, often archaeologically unstudied, Cold War sites. As a result, investigations of North American Cold War material culture can often occur, quite literally, in one's own backyard. Many important sites are, however, quite remote as a direct result of the ways in which Canada and the United States prepared for and fought the Cold War at a distance. Preparing a Cold War continental defense required positioning strategic resources (radar installations, air bases, and defensive missile launch sites) along the continental perimeter, and most of these defense facilities also required large tracts of land. Massive airfield runways, capable of supporting the largest, heaviest bombers ever built; missile launch complexes with silos distributed across hundreds of square miles; and weapons production facilities, all needing to be surrounded by extensive safety envelopes and security perimeters, consumed vast amounts of the Cold War landscape. In some cases, even more extreme isolation was necessary. Weapons of mass destruction required testing in areas where the fewest possible number of people would be impacted, and the geographic locations ultimately chosen for test sites were carefully vetted. While conventional wisdom holds that relatively few people were affected by such Cold War activities as nuclear weapons testing, the numbers affected were not trivial, and the resulting negative consequences for those individuals, their communities, and their former ways of life were both profound and enduring, leaving the morality of these territorial appropriations in considerable debate. As a result, archaeological investigations of these appropriated locations where weapons were tested, missiles were deployed, and remote surveillance outposts were built and staffed not only constitute some of the field's most engaging challenges, but are constituent to a consequential scholarly dialogue in which archaeologies of the Cold War can add much-needed materiality.

While certainly not all archaeologies of the Cold War need be studies of far-flung spaces, investigations of former nuclear testing sites in the Republic of the Marshall Islands or the DEW line radar stations in the Canadian Arctic seem to hold great promise for understanding the rare and distinctive nature of Cold War work and life. As James Delgado (personal communication 2015) notes, some of the most remote of these North American Cold War sites are those found in the deep ocean, including the SOSUS arrays (or the remains thereof) and several submarine wrecks. Cold War American wrecks such as the USS *Thresher* and USS *Scorpion* are joined by the wrecks of Soviet submarines such as *K-129*, which Delgado calls the "penultimate Cold War shipwreck site" inasmuch as it was a catastrophic operational loss and the object of Project Azorian, a secret American salvage operation in 1974. Although the intellectual consequence of the research can exceed the effort required to access even these remote sites, the challenges of remoteness should, whenever possible, neither limit nor impede the archaeologist's access. This is particularly important since issues of remoteness can often pale in comparison to some of the physical hazards of access.

Safety and the Physical Hazards of Cold War Sites

The physical hazards encountered while conducting archaeological investigations of Cold War sites are both real and serious. These hazards include not only the typical field research perils of bug bites, cuts, and falls, but a range of hazards that are both unique and inherent to the Cold War legacy. The Cold War left us with not only dangers tied to the sites of production, deployment, maintenance, storage, and testing of nuclear, biological, chemical, and conventional weapons, but hazards associated with the abandonment and ruination of these sites as well.

The potential for exposure to latent ionizing radiation is one of the primary, albeit often overestimated, Cold War site hazards. While the radioactive materials used at nuclear weapons laboratories and military sites were tightly controlled throughout the Cold War, radioactive contamination remains a potential health threat, although almost exclusively at former nuclear weapons–related production or testing sites. Here the dangers lie in the potential inhalation of trace amounts of residual radioactive material left in the soil. In fact, the greatest potential radiological danger for archaeologists at the NTS or former test sites in the Marshall Islands comes from the possibility of stirring up old radioactive fallout during excavation. At these sites, nuclear explosions sucked up tons of sand or coral in their debris clouds and contaminated and intermixed that material with nuclear isotopes before depositing it as radioactive fallout anywhere from several hundred feet to several thousand miles from the detonation point. Although the highest concentrations of radioactive fallout were closest to ground zero, digging in soil deposited 50 years ago almost anywhere in the world might expose you to some latent trace amount of radioactive fallout from nuclear testing. Of course, digging in this layer of soil at the NTS or on Bikini Atoll is almost certain to expose you to far more radiation. And because archaeological field research practices frequently involve digging, it would seem that fallout poses a real, albeit manageable, peril for Cold War archaeologists.

Most Cold War sites have been or are the process of being cleaned up and remediated of radiation. The sites of the earliest Cold War radiological contaminations, however, are likely to be less thoroughly cleaned up than later-era sites, since the standard definition of a "clean" site has changed over time while continuing to evolve toward increasingly rigorous remediation. At nuclear weapons storage or deployment sites, such as former ICBM launch sites or strategic bomber bases, the dangers of radioactive contamination from Cold War sources is almost nonexistent because barring an accident, nuclear warhead casings were never opened in hangars or missile silos. Fortunately, one of the most advantageous characteristics of radiological materials is that their presence can be easily detected, and contamination avoided, using radiological detection devices such as Geiger counters. In rare cases, however, extreme protective measures might be required. For the study of the NRDS, the DRI researchers were trained in radiological protection methods in order to undertake their field research wearing anti-contamination suits (or anti-Cs; see Figure 5.1) that kept their potential radiation exposure low. The data they collected and knowledge they gained about the NRDS, while perhaps risky to obtain, was critical to recording the site for HAER before it was demolished.

Figure 5.1. Members of the DRI Cold War archaeology team in protective clothing at the Radioactive Material Storage Facility at the NRDS. By permission of Harold Drollinger, Desert Research Institute.

Developing a research plan that identifies any potential radiological exposure hazards, requires the wearing of proper protective equipment, and includes a qualified radiological control technician on the research team goes a long way toward creating a reasonably safe archaeological field research experience at radiologically hazardous sites.

In reality, the greatest dangers to fieldworkers at most Cold War sites are the mundane yet potentially deadly, industrial-type hazards that can lead to lacerations, falls, and exposure to residual solvents and fuels. There are incalculable perils posed by time-weakened and rusting railings and walkways, collapse-prone underground tunnels and passageways, and open but hidden holes, trenches, and pits filled with polluted water and even chemical wastes. Chlorinated organic solvents such as trichloroethylene and carbon tetrachloride were used for cleaning in missile silos. Dangerous chemical compounds, including perchlorates, nitrogen tetroxide, aniline, and hydrazine, were frequently used in Cold War jet fuels and liquid rocket fuel for missiles (Sutton 2003). Polychlorinated biphenyls and lead-based compounds were also widely used in industrial products, from motor lubricants and coolants for electrical transformers to caulking compounds and paint. Despite decades of ongoing efforts to remediate these legacy wastes, residues of these and other chemical compounds remain in the sites and soils surrounding numerous Cold War sites. Another rare but potential hazard in conducting Cold War archaeological field research is the unearthing of unexploded small arms cartridges, blasting caps and high explosives, and unexploded ordnance. Other common physical and environmental threats include insect, rodent, or reptile infestations of abandoned buildings and underground facilities, as well as the presence of asbestos, a construction material that was widely used in Cold War–era buildings for ceiling and floor tiles, roofing, pipe insulation, and in aircraft, tanks, and ships.

While all these hazards obviously vary by location, the point here is that almost all Cold War sites pose threats that are not normally found in other historic or prehistoric archaeology research. And although certain individuals—such as graffiti taggers, scrap metal scavengers, and urban explorers—who have gained unauthorized access might be willing to assume these risks, professional and avocational archaeologists conducting fieldwork must recognize and thoughtfully evaluate the potential physical and environmental risks created by a decaying Cold War infrastructure. Ultimately, proper personal protective equipment including masks, safety glasses, hardhats, gloves, steel-toed boots, and other protective clothing, coupled with strong project planning, can help keep Cold War archaeologists safe in the field.

Secrets and Secret-Keeping

Perhaps more than any other conflict before it, the Cold War was a war of secrets and secret-keeping. Even the traditionally covert nature of warfare was redefined by the paranoia-soaked Cold War ideologies of secrecy once considered essential to protecting national security. Under a veil of secrecy, billions of tax dollars were spent on military technologies about which even those in high-level government positions often knew little. Massive Cold War construction projects were carried out with little public awareness or access. American soldiers and sailors were sworn under penalty of death to keep secret the workings of nuclear weapons, spy planes, submarines, and all kinds of other advanced military technologies. Meanwhile all across America tens of thousands of civilian workers secretly toiled in nondescript buildings in unremarkable towns designing new weapons, building military technologies, and generally drawing up plans for Doomsday. Secrecy became a standard practice in many areas of business, politics, and government.

Because of secrecy's central role in the conflict, issues of secrets and secret-keeping confront archaeologists of the Cold War every day and seem likely to confound the archaeological study of the conflict for decades to come, even as the secrets are revealed over time. Cameron (1994) notes that immediately after the end of the Cold War the federal system that declassifies national security records was "hopelessly clogged" (29) and cited as an example the estimated 325 million pages, or 100,000 cubic feet, of records containing classified information held by the National Archives and Records Administration (NARA) alone. NARA estimated in 1992 that even if no further classified records were acquired by the agency, the declassification process could take another decade. That estimate not only did not predict changes to national security policies and procedures resulting from the 9/11 terrorist attacks, which slowed the pace of declassification, but also did not include classified records held by the DoD, DOE, CIA, and other national security agencies at the time (Cameron 1994).

Because of this initial backlog, continuing funding challenges, and a post-9/11 increase in classified information, federal agencies often cannot allocate the intellectual resources necessary to randomly declassify documents. As a result, gaining access to classified information has become a continuing challenge for archaeologists. Archaeologists of the Cold War will need to use the Freedom of Information Act to compel government agencies to declassify and release needed historical material, or to rely on existing, often redacted, versions of documents along with alternative resources, such as oral histories, to conduct archaeological investigations.

Unfortunately, oral history tends to be a dwindling resource, as the generation of Americans who served in the Cold War ages and passes away. With increasing numbers of potential informants going to their graves never having revealed the secrets with which they were once entrusted, oral history becomes a lost legacy of the Cold War. Among the still-living Cold War veterans, the challenge is to persuade them to share their stories. This can be difficult, as it is not uncommon for participants in the various Cold War programs, projects, groups, and missions to believe that the operations in which they were once involved might still be considered classified. While classified status once meant that all the details of the operation were to be kept secret, or even top secret, the fact is that not all aspects of every operation were secret, nor need they continue to be so. In practice, it was typical that only the details of an operation having immediate strategic benefit to an enemy need be considered secret. That fact notwithstanding, the participants in Cold War operations were routinely told to keep secret all information regarding the operation, and by implication their very participation in it, until told otherwise. Time has had a hand in changing that reality, however, especially as former Cold War enemies have long since become trading partners, allies, and even friends. And while the strategic value of these secrets might once have been considerable, in most cases they are now much less significant. For example, many of the relatively mundane details about the nuclear testing operations at Bikini Atoll—such as device yields, code names, dates, times, and participating agencies—are no longer considered secret. Likewise, information on the types and names of ships involved, the kinds of clothing test participants wore, the kinds of food they ate, and what living conditions were like on the ships or atolls were never actually secret. Now such details should be shared, because it is in these seemingly mundane moments of life that greater understanding of twentieth-century nuclear testing work can be found. Without accessing the knowledge held by American veterans, it seems likely that we may someday know less about everyday work at a Cold War Nike missile or nuclear weapons testing site than we do about daily life in ancient Rome.

Atomic Tourism

Both complicating and complementing the study and stewardship of the global Cold War landscape is a burgeoning popular interest in visiting, exploring, photographing, and understanding better the material history of twentieth-century nuclear heritage sites. Colloquially referred to as "atomic tourism," the pastime involves leisure travel to significant sites in the history of both civilian nuclear energy and nuclear weapons design, development, manufacture, testing, deployment, delivery, and use. In a tourism context, these transient experiences are broadly framed as personal, experiential studies of the so-called atomic age.[7]

In every important respect, atomic tourism in the United States began shortly after the detonation of the atomic bomb, when reporters and photographers, eager to feed a nation hungry for news about how and where the atom bomb had been developed, toured the still highly radioactive Trinity Site on September 11, 1945, with General Groves, the military leader of the Manhattan Project. In the weeks and months following the Groves tour, news stories about the Trinity Site and the people and places of the Manhattan Project populated newspapers and magazines, and names like Trinity, Los Alamos, Hanford, and Oak Ridge were forever etched into the American memory. With several Manhattan Project secret cities still under military control or closed to the public—the town of Los Alamos remained closed to outsiders until 1957—and with few Americans able to afford leisure travel in the years immediately following the war, travel to these atomic sites was mostly vicarious. Nonetheless, an interest had been kindled, and Americans would remain fascinated with places and things atomic for decades to come.

For its part, the mainstream news media would reinforce the fascination starting on April 22, 1952, when some 200 reporters and photographers from the nation's leading news media witnessed an atomic bomb test at the NTS (see Figure 5.2). Perched on a craggy knoll of rock known as News Knob that offered a panoramic view of Yucca Flat, the media provided the first televised coverage of an atomic explosion during "Operation Big Shot," officially known as the Charlie test of Operation Tumbler-Snapper. An estimated five million Americans watched the explosion, and many more read about it in newspapers and magazines in the days and weeks that followed. Operation Big Shot was part of a public relations campaign organized by the AEC to calm growing public fears over atomic testing and placate Las Vegas businesses, which had been upset since the start of testing in 1951 over store windows being broken by the blasts and were appropriately concerned about the threat of mushroom clouds drifting over the city.

Las Vegas businesses quickly learned to capitalize on the popularity of atomic shots among visiting tourists, and began to promote the atomic tests as tourism through an embarrassment of atomic-themed cocktails, women's hairdos, beauty pageants, store sales, vacation packages, bomb-viewing parties, and other atom bomb–themed events (Titus 1986). As the Cold War progressed, nuclear weapons testing at the NTS moved underground and mushroom cloud rubbernecking in Las Vegas became a thing of the past. In fact, due to a growing peace movement in the United States fueled by resistance to the Vietnam conflict, atomic tourist travel to all Cold War sites dwindled in the 1970s.

Figure 5.2. Tumbler-Snapper shot Charlie. On April 22, 1952, some 200 reporters and photographers from the nation's leading media were invited to witness an atomic bomb test in Nevada. By permission of the U.S. Department of Energy.

With the deterioration of U.S.-Soviet relations and a resurgence in the arms race, atomic tourism reemerged in the early 1980s as a form of antinuclear activism. The first publication to provide substantial guidance for this atomic tourism was *Nuclear Heartland: A Guide to the 1,000 Missile Silos of the United States*, a 1988 work edited by reporter, editor, and political activist Samuel H. Day. From 1985 to 1987, activists working with Day, who was then the director of Nukewatch, a Wisconsin-based public interest group, compiled a list of the Minuteman ICBM launch sites spread across the U.S. Great Plains. Based on visits to the sites, and complete with maps and specific directions to their locations, the book was aimed at general readers but raised considerable interest among antinuclear activists interested in traveling to the sites for acts of civil disobedience. Meant to create greater public awareness of America's missile fields, Day's book was in itself something of an act of civil disobedience, as the exact locations of American missile sites were not widely known and visitors to the sites were, to say the least, discouraged. While publication of the book was not illegal, it was a part of Day's broader nuclear-consciousness-raising work. After Day's book, it would be more than a decade before another seminal work in atomic tourism emerged.

In 2002, James Maroncelli and Timothy Karpin, both experts in the environmental remediation of nuclear contamination, published *The Traveler's Guide to Nuclear Weapons: A Journey through America's Cold War Battlefields*. Meticulously researched, *The Traveler's Guide* was an ambitious compilation of detailed information on more than 150 factories, mills, research laboratories, and nuclear test detonation sites in the United States. Provided on a compact disc, the publication included scaled maps, site photographs, tour schedules, and site telephone numbers, which the authors thought would "provide atomic tourists with all they need to visit these historic locations" (Maroncelli and Karpin 2002). In the decade following the publication of Maroncelli and Karpin's guide, other books emerged to inspire both active and armchair atomic tourists. Most notable were works by Tom Vanderbilt (*Survival City: Adventures among the Ruins of Atomic America*) in 2002 and by Weinberger and Hodge (*A Nuclear Family Vacation: Travels in the World of Atomic Weaponry*) in 2008. While less specific in providing directions than Maroncelli and Karpin's publication, these and other works would further galvanize the public's interest in exploring America's nuclear landscape, while echoing Samuel Day's antinuclear call for greater awareness and knowledge of all Cold War sites.

Despite its American origins, atomic tourism is truly an international phenomenon. Adventurers, scholars, Cold War veterans, and students from countries around the world are even now exploring former Soviet missile sites in what was once East Germany, touring underground bunkers in Canada and the United Kingdom, and visiting a plethora of other obscure and remote Cold War sites. On these journeys, several sites have become quintessentially requisite destinations for the well-traveled atomic tourist. The foremost of these is Trinity Site, home of the first atomic bomb test. Located on the White Sands Missile Range in New Mexico, the site was listed as a National Historical Landmark in 1975 and features biannual tours in April and October, when normal range access restrictions are lifted for travel to Trinity ground zero. Also popular are the Japanese cities of Hiroshima and Nagasaki, where evidence of the atomic bombs' horrific effects has been preserved in the Nagasaki Atomic Bomb and Hiroshima Peace Memorial Museums. Other popular destinations are the Manhattan Project cities of Hanford, Los Alamos, and Oak Ridge. At Bikini Atoll, atomic tourists can witness the devastation of atomic explosions while scuba diving the wrecks of ships sunk during the Able and Baker atomic tests. Intrepid atomic tourists can even enlist one of the nearly dozen companies (as of 2014) offering day tours into the exclusion zone of the former Chernobyl nuclear power plant in Ukraine to see the consequences of the 1986 nuclear reactor rupture and fire.[8]

While the more popular sites on the atomic landscape bring visitors face-to-face with technologies of war, not all visitors are interested purely in technology. Hugh Gusterson, an anthropologist at George Washington University with expertise in the American nuclear weapons complex, describes the phenomenon of atomic tourism or, as he calls it, nuclear tourism, as offering "the promise of a glimpse into the sublime and forbidden" (2004:24). Gusterson draws upon the philosophies of eighteenth-century Irish statesman and philosopher Edmund Burke, who used the term "sublime" to describe the quality of artistic, aesthetic, or spiritual enormity in an object or process that goes beyond any prospect of measure or imitation. Burke's idea of the sublime as wonder and awe slightly tinged with terror informs Gusterson's notion of nuclear tourism as the pursuit of visceral knowledge and a way of imagining the real. For humans increasingly distanced from the Cold War's secrets and the nuclear sites and implements those secrets created, imagining the real is an atomic tourist's sublime experience. This enthusiasm for vicariously experiencing the dangers and fearsome purposes of the nuclear landscape shares a following with the practice known as "dark tourism."

Dark tourism is recreational travel to sites that have been directly or indirectly associated with significant events of human tragedy, suffering, disaster, violence, and death. Broadly these sites include cemeteries, places of imprisonment and internment (World War II concentration camps), sites of natural and human-caused accidents or disasters (the former Chernobyl nuclear reactor), and particularly bloody battlefields (Gettysburg). Also included are places of accidents, massacres, murders, and executions (Lennon and Foley 2000; Sharpley and Stone 2009). Although a hallmark of any dark tourism experience is authenticity, some of the actual dark sites are inaccessible. In those cases, the dark tourist's destination becomes a museum, which may or may not have been sanitized of the most controversial or macabre aspects of the site's history, but nonetheless remains representative of the event's or site's history. Scholars of dark tourism (Stone 2012; Stone and Sharpley 2008) suggest that one possible motivation for dark tourism's popularity is the fact that in most western societies today the fearsome realities of death and dying are mostly out of sight in everyday public life. Dark tourism allows individuals to explore the multiple meanings of suffering, tragedy, death, and human mortality in a socially acceptable and safe public context, and in ways they could not in private, where prolonged exposure and contemplation of such matters might be psychologically dangerous.

It is perhaps not surprising that sites associated with nuclear weapons testing and use are among the most highly regarded dark tourism destinations. Epitomized by sites such as Nagasaki and Hiroshima, whose sites offer compelling if macabre evidence of atomic history's darkest days, atomic tourism finds ominous new dark tourism meanings for visitors to sites of Cold War disaster, tragedy, and death. Such sites include landscapes destroyed by nuclear tests, missile launch complexes charred and scarred by accidental explosions, defunct nuclear power plants, military plane crashes, and landscapes poisoned by radioactive contamination, to name only a few. Ultimately, the dark tourist's attraction to such sites is not substantially different than the atomic tourist's interest in other Cold War sites, as both seek a deeper understanding of the Cold War through the pursuit of visceral knowledge of its secretive places and spaces.

Cold War Veterans

Augmenting the atomic tourist's recreational interest in America's Cold War built landscape are the heritage preservation concerns of those who served during the creation and occupation of that landscape. For the estimated 25 million Cold War veterans of the Air Force, Army, Coast Guard, Marine Corps, and Navy, the commemoration, and in some cases memorialization, of that military service is legitimately anticipated. The sum total of veterans' work spent defending the nation amounts to, even by conservative estimates, many billions of duty hours. That is by any measure a significant portion of twentieth-century American working life.

The existence of this large living cohort strongly benefits the archaeology of the Cold War. The knowledge held by Cold War veterans is elemental to understanding material aspects of twentieth-century military life but must also be recognized as a dwindling resource. Personal knowledge of aspects of the Cold War's arcane material culture makes veterans invaluable contributors to most archaeological research, as without the information they hold we may never know the exact technical functions of some devices or spaces.

Beyond being vital resources in the archaeological study of Cold War sites, veterans likewise constitute a strong natural part of historic preservation efforts. Veterans have the potential to contribute financially, intellectually, and physically to Cold War historic preservation projects. As holders of the lion's share of American wealth, Cold War veterans have a funding potential that is matched only by their potential intellectual contributions. Intimate knowledge of a Cold War site is crucial both to understanding the site occupants' worldviews and to making accurate NRHP assessments, especially in the highly subjective area of feeling criteria: the degree to which a feature or property accurately or faithfully expresses the Cold War aesthetic. As a community likely to benefit emotionally from historic preservation, Cold War veterans are often willing to contribute to preservation efforts. Working alone and in small groups, they have already become a driving force in the collection of oral histories and artifacts, and in the restoration and preservation of several Cold War–era sites. A notable example is Alaska's Nike Site Summit.

Site Summit is the last of three Nike Hercules missile sites built in 1959 to defend the U.S. Army's Fort Richardson, Elmendorf AFB, and the city of Anchorage from a Soviet air attack. Fifteen miles from downtown Anchorage, Nike Site Summit stood guard over the city for two decades from its mountaintop location on the far eastern edge of Fort Richardson. Decommissioned in 1979, it was listed on the NRHP in 1996. Efforts in the late 1990s to preserve the site had limited success, despite strong local and state support. Throughout the 2000s, the fate of Site Summit hung in the balance as the DoD first curtailed access to the site in the wake of 9/11, then began the process of documenting and preparing the site for demolition, completing HAER documentation and conducting an oral history project in 2002 to record the personal experiences of Nike Hercules missileers who served there (Hollinger 2004). In 2009, after consultations with the Advisory Council on Historic Preservation, the Alaska State Historic Preservation Office, and an Anchorage organization of veterans and citizens dedicated to the preservation and interpretation of the site known as Friends of Nike Site Summit (FONSS), the DoD ultimately agreed to preserve the site. DoD's decision to selectively retain structures critical to the historical understanding of Site Summit and demolish only unsalvageable and unused structures was a victory for all parties involved, as it not only helped address military training needs, human health and safety concerns, and issues of vandalism associated with trespassing at the site, but put the FONSS in the driver's seat for the stabilization, preservation, and restoration work. Creating Nike Site Summit Historic District on what is now Joint Base Elmendorf-Richardson, FONSS began restoration efforts in June 2010 and, in collaboration with the Air Force, continues to rehabilitate and preserve the site, one facility at a time, working toward its original Cold War condition (Figures 5.3 and 5.4).

The role of Cold War veterans in the process has been undeniable. Lewis (2011) notes that

> A number of *Nike* veterans have been involved in the [Site Summit] preservation efforts, including two that were stationed at the site in the 1970s and two that periodically worked at the site. Having individuals with first-hand knowledge of the site involved in its preservation is invaluable. Manuals from the 1950s and '60s explain the interrelationship and purpose of the buildings at a *Nike Hercules* Missile site; however the *Nike* veterans explain that things were not always done according to the manual. Some buildings were used quite differently from the way they were described in the manuals.

Within the larger population of Cold War veterans exists a group who have interest in Cold War heritage for profoundly personal reasons. Atomic veterans are former Cold War military personnel who identify themselves as such due to their participation in atmospheric nuclear testing. Assigned to a variety of nuclear testing duties, including nuclear warfare maneuvers, radioactive cloud sampling, aircraft and ship decontamination, post-shot retrieval of test equipment and instrumentation, test site

Figure 5.3. Nike Site Summit sentry building, near Anchorage, Alaska, before restoration work in June 2010. By permission of Darrell Lewis, National Park Service.

remediation, and other similar assignments, these men served in some of the most dangerous assignments of the Cold War. As a consequence of this service, they were more likely than most servicemen to experience radiation exposure and contamination, and many have suffered for decades from what strongly appear to be radiation-related illnesses. In what has become a prolonged and contentious struggle to understand the health effects of Cold War nuclear military service and to grant the service benefits owed atomic veterans, the DoD seems uninformed as to the precise nature of work atomic veterans performed. To substantiate their case, atomic veterans deserve strong, veridical archaeological interpretations of the Cold War sites where they served. The physical evidence gathered by archaeologies of the Cold War at former nuclear testing sites would not only help produce better, more humanistic interpretations of that historic

Figure 5.4. Nike Site Summit sentry building after restoration work in September 2010. By permission of Darrell Lewis, National Park Service.

past, but such studies might be instrumental in revealing the presence and nature of any latent radiological hazards at the sites that might yet require remediation. Increased knowledge and recognition of the dangers of Cold War service could lead, in turn, to greater consensus on radiation exposure–related illnesses, and perhaps bring about a more compassionate resolution regarding the legacy health issues related to Cold War nuclear testing military service.

Summary

This chapter has addressed some of the challenges facing the archaeological study and stewardship of America's Cold War cultural heritage, including issues of site access, researcher safety, and a daunting history of

Cold War secrecy. In overcoming these challenges and exposing Cold War truths there are rewards, most notably the appreciation of atomic tourists whose genuine and enduring interest in the sites of twentieth-century atomic science and technology is noteworthy. Finally, as the world looks to a future in which governments and the public will increasingly be called upon to understand and manage the pervasive and sometimes even hazardous remains of the Cold War, it will be ever more important to consider the critical information, service, and stewardship roles of America's Cold War veterans.

6

CONCLUSION

Humans have been reshaping the world's landscapes in ways both large and small for millennia. And yet, despite almost a century of work, archaeologists have only just begun to explore and interpret the enduring materiality of that history. One might rightly ask, with all of human history in some need of archaeological study, why should North American historical archaeology expend any of its increasingly limited resources on the study of a period with as much contemporaneity as the Cold War? The answer to that question is as multifaceted, complex, and paradoxical as the Cold War itself.

The need for earnest archaeological study of the Cold War is made most urgent by the fact that the material record of the period is rapidly disappearing from the global landscape for a number of different but sometimes interconnected reasons. One reason is that some of the real property upon which American Cold War structures were built and used has returned to private ownership. Many of these privately owned sites are in such a state of decay or ruin that they are not only unavailable for study but are hazardous to human health and safety. Most are at risk of being razed for various economic, environmental, or liability reasons. Unlike government-owned sites, which are subject to federal cultural resource preservation laws, and as a result have often been well studied and documented, these private sites can be razed or renovated without ever having been assessed for their historical significance. It would behoove the historical archaeology community to work with private landowners to help recover and record the material histories of the sites in order to help save and manage any Cold War heritage deemed worth saving.

Government-owned Cold War sites are also in pragmatic jeopardy, however. Those sites that are not currently in use, especially if they are in deep ruin or decay or are thought to contain hazardous wastes are increasingly placing significant maintenance burdens on their owners. While most federal agencies, including the DoD, have knowledgeable and experienced cultural resource management teams, their workloads are increasing at a time when economic and organizational pressures are building to decontaminate, decommission, and often raze Cold War sites that are ineligible for historic preservation under the NRHP criteria, but might still be worthy of study. As demolition increasingly becomes the choice for property management in prolonged periods of economic cutbacks, archaeologists are making difficult but seemingly judicious choices to record and study those sites that must be lost and to work to preserve the more important or valuable remaining sites. The same economic forces driving these demolitions are also causing organizations to reduce their workforces, forcing governmental cultural resource departments to do more with less.

Beyond these cases of loss or abandonment, it is equally apparent that other forces are also at work. Even those Cold War concrete fortresses constructed to withstand the mightiest explosions made by humankind are no match for nature and decades of willful neglect. In the Pacific, the steel-reinforced concrete bunkers left over from nuclear testing are slowly being toppled as tropical vines entwine; plant roots penetrate; and marine humidity corrodes, erodes, and crumbles the aging concrete (Figure 6.1). Across North America, the few ballistic missile launch sites not still in military use, converted to doomsday homes, or demolished under twentieth-century international nuclear disarmament treaties are increasingly falling victim to vandalism, graffiti, and the unrelenting forces of nature, which floods silos, rusts ironwork, and erodes concrete. The same environmental and social effects also work to erase other neglected bunkers, buildings, and airfields from the Cold War landscape.

Further complicating global Cold War study and preservation efforts is the fact that the era's ubiquitous gray concrete aesthetic provides little incentive for the average citizen to appreciate its sites, let alone be concerned about their study, protection, and preservation. Internationally, efforts to preserve the remains of the Cold War, perhaps predictably, pale in comparison to heritage conservation work on other more aesthetically pleasing sites (Wainwright 2009). Compared to the great monuments and

Figure 6.1. Former nuclear weapons testing station on Aerokoj Island at Bikini Atoll in 2009. Heavy beach erosion from rising tides have left the once-inland structure at the shoreline. By permission of Steve Brown.

landscapes of world history, the Cold War landscape presents itself as a dark and foreboding, even repugnant, sibling to which dread and disdain seem proper reactions. Indeed, it takes a special person to love a crumbling concrete bunker, and it will take many such people if the best of the North American Cold War landscape is to survive the twenty-first century.

Yet another incentive for studying the physical remains of the Cold War is because for many Americans it is a subject that is largely being forgotten. Wiener (2012) compellingly argues that despite an intense postwar tribute effort, in which the notion was sown that America won the Cold War, this conflict simply isn't being remembered the way other previous wars have been. While Wiener finds no incontrovertible cause of the forgetting, he suggests there may be several potential reasons. For one, Americans by and large have failed to intertwine their personal or family identities with official Cold War narratives, and traditional efforts at conflict mythmaking have not yet found popular appeal. This is unlike previous wars, in which Americans often either linked their personal identities to having fought in the war or built family heroism stories around foreign military service. Wiener asserts that the few memory activists (often historians) who are engaged with the Cold War have either focused their public interpretations on issues tangential to the conflict, or have placed greater emphasis on the postwar cleanup of the sites than on the sites' original missions during the Cold War. As an example, Wiener points to the former Weldon Spring Uranium Feed Materials Plant, where greater tourism emphasis is placed on the giant mound of entombed hazardous waste than on the Cold War history of the site.[9] Wiener asserts that Cold War memorials emphasizing reassurance that the dangers of the sites are being "managed" evoke very little enthusiasm among visitors looking for the Cold War past.

Wiener describes the fates of nearly 50 museums, monuments, and other sites of American memory in which neither conservative nor liberal interpretations of the Cold War have successfully found long-term representation. Despite powerful and sustained efforts by both political institutions and cultural groups to support and sometimes shape the public memory of the Cold War, these museums and sites have failed to represent accurately the material aspects of this important element of twentieth-century history. Looking at the ways in which Americans appear to have intentionally and inexplicably forgotten the Cold War, Wiener describes how Cold War artifacts, from Titan missiles to Elvis Presley's 1958 Army uniform, have been presented and represented in America's museums in order to shape public memory. Through the creation of displays dedicated to what Wiener describes as the "good war framework"—a hawkish interpretation of the Cold War as a great victory—the conflict is portrayed as a necessary battle between freedom and totalitarianism and between good and evil. Ultimately, the forgetting of the Cold War in America seems due to the fact that this "good war framework" has been met with public skepticism and even rejection. While Cold War strategists continue to insist that deterrence worked, the public seems to find that argument unconvincing and may even be left wondering if the Cold War might have been an enormous waste of time, money, and commitment (Wiener 2012).

Wiener's argument has powerful implications for the archaeology of the Cold War. In cases where these contrived efforts have failed to create convincing representations of the Cold War, archaeological efforts to explicate and investigate authentic sites of Cold War work might have far greater success. Archaeology has the potential not only to investigate and explicate the Cold War material past, but to more objectively and deeply represent the physical realities of everyday life and living.

Probably the strongest motivation for the archaeology of the Cold War lies in the fact that without such efforts the Cold War's secrets may cause it to be forever lost to the past. In ways that came to define the very nature of the Cold War, secrecy was implemented and employed during the era with great effect and consequence. Veiled in secrecy and protected by a collective silence, the nuclear weapons proliferation, political machinations, propaganda campaigns, acts of espionage, and proxy wars that characterized the era have left behind a vast and enigmatic built landscape abounding in untold stories. The practical details of the everyday work of Cold War nuclear weapons scientists, for example, are still mostly known only through oral histories and scant mentions in official reports,[10] while the number of men who actually experienced atmospheric nuclear weapons tests continues to dwindle. Those still alive hold fading memories of experiences more than a half-century old, making them inherently subject to inaccuracies.

Fortunately, historical archaeology possesses the ability to retrieve physical evidence of the past; cast new light on obscure historical referents, objects, and ruined spaces; and in the process rouse old men's memories. Therein lies the promise of the archaeology of the Cold War, the hope that even if the deepest secrets of Cold War are never made public, the materiality of the daily work lives and workplaces of millions who served in the conflict might be at least partially known through archaeological investigation. There is no better time to study the Cold War past than the present. Waiting until all the conflict's participants have passed, archival records have been lost, and sites have been buried under bulldozer blades will be an archaeological opportunity squandered.

Future Research Directions

While many areas in the archaeology of the Cold War offer potential for future study, three areas appear to me to hold the most significant promise. The first of these is potential studies of North American missile launch sites, which are some of the most abundant and accessible Cold War archaeological sites. While many of the more recently occupied (or still active) sites are confined to the Great Plains, equally plentiful and chiefly unstudied are the more than 265 former Nike missile battery sites that broadly dot the North American and international landscape. Not only are these sites more widespread than ICBM sites, but they appear to open particularly promising windows on the practices of everyday Cold War continental defense life, as anecdotal evidence suggests missile battery crews were also actively engaged in the social life of the communities surrounding their battery.

I am not alone in anticipating the Nike site's potential. Smoley (2008) calls Nike locations the "quintessential Cold War site[s]" for their potential ability to articulate the complexities of Cold War life within the broader, often contradictory global context of violence. Nike sites, for example, represent the underlying dread of Soviet nuclear air attacks juxtaposed against the defensive extremes to which Americans were willing to go in deploying immensely destructive weapons near metropolitan areas. To achieve its defensive mission, the Nike Hercules missile's nuclear warhead would have exploded over the heads of the very citizens it was meant to protect, raining down highly radioactive debris. Yet the potential dangers of a nuclear airburst were tacitly accepted by Americans as the price of protection against a Soviet nuclear attack capable of doing greater damage. Arguing that public memory and historic preservation of the missile system are limited due to its relative ubiquity, and that the Cold War significance of the Nike warrants greater public attention, Smoley advocates for crafting a rhetorical balance between public memory and the historic preservation of Nike sites in order to properly deal with all memories of our Cold War past. Nike sites, he argues, might help explicate the strangely liminal space between war and peace that the Cold War occupied in the absence of direct combat during a decades-long ideological standoff. This, Smoley argues, might explain how "hot" the Cold War might have actually become were it not for the Nike's strong contribution to the U.S. defensive posture.

Of particularly strong potential are studies of Nike sites using research designs incorporating excavations, which have been a widely neglected research practice in the archaeology of the Cold War. Because the abundant Nike sites are supported by strong archival and oral history resources, the political and operational aspects of the sites are fairly well known. Missing from the histories are the stories of ordinary, everyday life at the Nike sites, including moments like that shown in Figure 6.2. Excavation may help shed more light on these kinds of private, off-duty moments.

Figure 6.2. Nike life was not all radar and missiles. Army Lieutenant Colonel Lee James, commander of the 54th Anti-Aircraft Missile Battery, prepares to putt on the seventh hole of the chip-and-putt nine-hole golf course while his crew looks on at the Nike Missile Battalion site at Granite, Maryland, July 1955. The crew was part of the air defense protection for the Baltimore area. By permission of the Army Chemical Center, Maryland.

Perhaps less obvious yet still intrinsic to any substantive understanding of the Cold War are archaeological studies focused on aspects of science and technology. The artifacts, places, and spaces created in the pursuit of Cold War scientific discovery provide broad opportunities for archaeological and material culture studies of scientific advancements in aerospace engineering, computer science, communications, geoscience, material science, oceanography, physics, and space science, to name only a few fields. One promising area of investigation under the archaeology of science construct is the study of temporary encampments and research stations created specifically for Cold War scientific studies. From entire islands used for nuclear weapons tests in the Pacific to research stations and field camps in the Antarctic, the U.S. propensity to take science afield in during the Cold War left a wake of potential archaeological sites. Nuclear weapons testing, for example, spawned temporary scientific encampments and outposts on the islands of Parry, Christmas, Johnston,

Hermite (Montebello Islands), and Amchitka (Alaska), as well as in Algeria, at Mururoa Atoll (French Polynesia), and at Maralinga and Emu Field (Australia). The Cold War occupation of these sites left behind significant material evidence in the form of middens, buildings, airfields, and concrete bunkers. Anecdotal evidence suggests that much of the material remains of nuclear testing work at Enewetak Atoll in the Marshall Islands was disposed of in the lagoon. In this case, the use of remotely operated and autonomous underwater vehicles offers strong potential for collecting important artifacts, as well as bathymetric, photographic, and sonar data on submerged objects associated with the Cold War occupation.

Beyond these potential studies of men, machines, and science are opportunities for archaeological studies aimed at revealing the more human(e) aspects of the Cold War. These may, for example, include studies of civil defense sites, which are broadly represented in family fallout shelters, and studies of antinuclear protest sites, peace camps, and the places and spaces of opposition whose occupants sought to bring a peaceful end to the Cold War. While sites of former opposition and protest typically lack significant architectural features to study, site occupations generally leave substantial material remains for archaeologies of the contemporary past. Marginalized by the era's news media and mostly overlooked in hegemonic histories, the peace camps of the Cold War were essential elements of the late twentieth-century protest experience and as such are potent subjects for archaeological study. Because they were chiefly women's organizations, peace camps represent unique opportunities to explore the material experiences of women in antinuclear and antiwar protest.

Equally significant and yet unstudied by archaeologists are sites of environmental racism, where evidence of Cold War nuclear production and testing is found among profound and persistent effects of environmental contamination and pollution. Uranium mines and mining activities played a central role in Cold War nuclear weapons production while creating grave environmental and health consequences for the Native Americans from whose land much of the uranium ore was extracted and for whom the everyday work of uranium mining would prove perilous.

In these and many other areas, archaeologists, historians and others interested in studying the material culture of the Cold War should continue to apply and expand the analytical constructs and theoretical frameworks discussed in Chapter 2, but look as well for relevant new constructs that help inform an understanding of the era. Post-processual archaeological studies exploring the characteristics and properties of Cold War policies and politics are in short supply. Studies of the material aspects and effects of fear, xenophobia, paranoia, subjugation, and secrecy, for example, might be useful in revealing new stories about everyday Cold War life that could uniquely contribute to our understanding of contemporary American life and politics. Cold War archaeology has as much to teach us about the convoluted origins and manifestations of ideological discord and the complicated material natures of socialized paranoia and xenophobia as it does about the technical evolution of twentieth-century industrialized warfare. The potential of archaeology to contribute substantively to an understanding of Cold War life is immense, but it also needs a catalyzing interest from academia to propel the field to new heights.

Final Thoughts

The Cold War was unquestionably unlike any other conflict in American history. It was a war so lengthy and omnipresent that it became almost invisible in American life, yet it profoundly affected the lives of all those who lived through it. The weapons of mass destruction, and the notions of mutually assured destruction they spawned, would forever change the nature of warfare. Under the shadow of "the Bomb," a generation of American children grew up fearing the apocalyptic capacity of war while ducking and covering together under their school desks during what seemed to be an endless series of earnest yet essentially futile classroom drills. As fears of communism ran rampant in American society, government officials ripped open the personal lives of writers, musicians, and artists, some of whom never worked in their fields again. Some returned to work by inventing the lurid tales of alien invasion, foreign infiltration, subversion, and espionage that filled the comic books and movie screens of the era and forever changed the once-hopeful nature of American popular culture.

Despite its many misdeeds, the Cold War ushered in an era of unprecedented technological growth and economic prosperity across North America. Hundreds of world-changing advances in the fields of aviation, communications, computing, law enforcement, medicine, and manufacturing had their origins in Cold War military science and technology. Today, Americans travel on interstate highways originally constructed to facilitate the rapid cross-country movement of Cold War troops and supplies. We find our way around using a satellite-based GPS originally developed to provide Cold War Navy submarines with the precise navigational capabilities needed to accurately launch ballistic missiles while at sea. We are entertained, informed, and interconnected with the world by an Internet that is a direct descendent of ARPANET, a Cold War military communications network originally designed to facilitate the sharing of high-performance computer resources among government research institutions. Without the Cold War few if any of these and other technologies would likely exist, and modern life would be much different and certainly more difficult.

Above all, the Cold War left us with a vast built landscape unlike anything in the history of humanity. It is in many respects a secretive, dark, and foreboding landscape but is nonetheless monumentally powerful and impressive. And yet as deliberately durable as this landscape seems to be, it is proving to be neither permanent nor indestructible. Much of it decays even now under the relentless assault of nature and neglect. The world must decide, and decide fairly quickly, if it wants to preserve any of the most important material aspects of the Cold War. If we decide not to preserve our Cold War heritage, we do so at the risk of losing opportunities to study and preserve for the future those sites that were most relevant and evocative of the period. We risk losing sites that are capable of telling compelling stories of Cold War patriotism, courage, fortitude, and sacrifice—and of power, protest, and love—in ways that other places and spaces in human history cannot. And yet at the same time we must be aware of how we commemorate the Cold War and what we choose to celebrate. Recognizing that one person's meat is another's poison, commemorations of the Cold War must be mindful of the reality that the antithesis to stories of patriotism, courage, and sacrifice may be histories of subjugation, fear, and destruction.

My vision of the archaeology of the Cold War is not voyeuristic tourism, but neither do I think that its mission should be to produce dull narratives of architectural history, make endless mappings of vacant buildings, or fortify banal artifact collections. To achieve its powerful potential, the archaeology of the Cold War must dig deeply (sometimes literally) into not only the material aspects of the nationalism, violence, secrecy, and mendacity that inspired the conflict, but also into the physical expressions of imperialism, exclusion, racism, sexism, and xenophobia that accompanied it. Well practiced, such archaeology can be meaningful scholarly work aimed at understanding how the persistent accumulation of apocalyptic technologies and perverse manipulation of human lives during the Cold War managed to change the nature of warfare, reshape the landscapes of the world, and alter the course of human history.

Ultimately, archaeologies of the Cold War will help us tell stories that clarify, depoliticize, and humanize a conflict and era that was so deeply shrouded in mystery, so perversely dogmatic, and so implausibly nationalistic that it almost defies belief. As scholarly interest in the archaeological study of the Cold War grows, there seems little doubt that it will teach us more about those dark decades of twentieth-century American life than we could ever have imagined.

NOTES

1. There remains some debate among historians as to the exact starting and ending dates of the Cold War. For the start of the Cold War, I refer to George Orwell's October 19, 1945, essay in the British newspaper *Tribune* entitled "You and the Atomic Bomb" in which he coins "Cold War" in describing a polarized, unconquerable nation-state (as theorized by American philosopher James Burnham) that is engaged "in a permanent state of 'cold war' with its neighbors" (Orwell 1968), which is how one might see the United States under Pax Americana. I chose 1989 as the most suitable ending date, based on not only the fall of the Berlin Wall in November, but the removal of the border fence between Hungary and Austria in May, the numerous Eastern European revolutions of that spring and summer, and the public declaration that the Cold War was over by Chairman Mikhail Gorbachev and President George H. W. Bush at the Malta Summit in December of that year.

2. In the United States there are, as of 2015, no degree programs in conflict archaeology, archaeology of the contemporary past, or archaeology of the Cold War, and there are only limited course offerings in the archaeology of the contemporary past.

3. Two hundred megatons is equivalent to the explosive energy released by 200 million metric tons of Trinitrotoluene (TNT). If divided and used equally, this amount of TNT would easily be enough to destroy all the roughly 125 million houses in the United States today (figure from 2006 American Housing Survey of the United States, U.S. Department of Housing and Urban Development) allowing for a more than ample 1.6 tons of TNT per house.

4. This estimate is based on a roughly 2,400-mile round-trip between Loring AFB and Clarksville Base at Campbell AFB in Tennessee at the B-36 Peacemaker's average cruising speed of 275 miles per hour. The estimate does not include any bomb acquisition and loading time.

5. The archaeology of the contemporary past is clearly one of the Swedish research team's strengths. See Burström 2007, 2008; Burström and Karlsson 2008; and Burström et al. 2006.

6. Perforated steel planking was widely used around the world during and after World War Two by both the U.S. and Soviet militaries for construction of temporary airfield

runways and vehicle passage over soft or muddy ground (see Smith 1989). Because of the numerous twentieth-century wars and conflicts in which the United States was involved, it is now a ubiquitously reused conflict surplus material the world over that perhaps deserves further research.

7. The term "atomic age" was coined by *New York Times* reporter William Laurence in his news report about the Trinity test. This period is generally considered to have begun with the detonation of the first atomic bomb in 1945 and to have ended in 1980, when an accident at the Three Mile Island nuclear power plant served as what is widely considered to be the culminating landmark failure of the promise of atomic energy.

8. For more on this atomic tourism opportunity, see http://wikitravel.org/en/Chernobyl.

9. While Wiener visited and wrote about the mound at the former Weldon Spring Plant, he could just as easily have been talking about the former Cold War sites at Fernald, Portsmouth, Paducah, or Rocky Flats, all of which provide substantially more information about the site's cleanup in their visitor's centers than about the site's Cold War mission.

10. The exception here is the Nevada Test Site Oral History Project, a comprehensive oral history collection program at the University of Nevada, Las Vegas, dedicated to documenting, preserving, and sharing the remembered past of workers and others affiliated with and affected by the NTS during the Cold War nuclear testing era. For more, see http://digital.library.unlv.edu/ntsohp/.

REFERENCES CITED

Aaron, Jayne D., and Judy A. Berryman
1997 *Rocky Flats Plant, Bounded by Indiana St. & Rts. 93, 128 & 72, Golden Vicinity, Jefferson County, Colorado.* HAER No. CO-83. Historic American Engineering Record, National Park Service, U.S. Department of the Interior. Intermountain Support Office, Denver, Colorado.

Ackland, Len
1999 *Making a Real Killing: Rocky Flats and the Nuclear West.* University of New Mexico Press, Albuquerque.

Adams, George R.
1974 *Mare Island Naval Shipyard, National Register of Historic Places—Inventory Nomination Form.* National Park Service, Washington, D.C.

Arkush, Elizabeth, and Mark W. Allen
2006 *The Archaeology of Warfare: Prehistories of Raiding and Conquest.* University Press of Florida, Gainesville.

Assmann, Jan
2011 *Cultural Memory and Early Civilization: Writing, Remembrance, and Political Imagination.* Cambridge University Press, New York.

Bailey, Greg, Cassie Newland, Anna Nilsson, John Schofield, Stephen Davis, and Adrian Myers
2009 Transit, Transition: Excavating J641 VUJ. *Cambridge Archaeological Journal* 19(1):1–28.

Baldwin, William C.
1996 *Four Housing Privatization Programs: A History of the Wherry, Capehart, Section 801, and Section 802 Family Housing Programs in the Army.* U.S. Army Corps of Engineers Office of History, Alexandria, Virginia.

Bamford, James
2004 *A Pretext for War: 9/11, Iraq, and the Abuse of America's Intelligence Agencies.* Doubleday, New York.

Bass, George F.
1966 *Archaeology under Water.* Frederick A. Praeger, New York.

Beck, Colleen M.
2002   The Archaeology of Scientific Experiments as a Nuclear Testing Ground. In *Matériel Culture: The Archaeology of Twentieth-Century Conflict*, edited by John Schofield, William Johnson, and Colleen Beck, pp. 65–79. Routledge, London.

Beck, Colleen M., Harold Drollinger, and Nancy G. Goldenberg
2000   *An Historical Evaluation of the Test Cell A Facility for Characterization Activities Associated with Decontamination and Decommissioning, Area 25, Nevada Test Site, Nye County, Nevada*. Desert Research Institute, Las Vegas, Nevada.

Beck, Colleen M., Harold Drollinger, and John Schofield
2007   Archaeology of Dissent: Landscape and Symbolism at the Nevada Peace Camp. In *A Fearsome Heritage: Diverse Legacies of the Cold War*, edited by John Schofield and Wayne Cocroft, pp. 297–320. Left Coast Press, Walnut Creek, California.

Beck, Colleen M., Nancy G. Goldenberg, Harold Drollinger, Robert C. Jones, and Diane L. Winslow
1996   *A Historical Evaluation of the Engine Maintenance Assembly and Disassembly Facility, Area 25, Nevada Test Site, Nye County, Nevada*. Desert Research Institute, Las Vegas, Nevada.

Beck, Colleen M., John Schofield, and Harold Drollinger
2011   Archaeologists, Activists, and a Contemporary Peace Camp. In *Contemporary Archaeologies: Excavating Now*. 2nd ed., edited by Cornelius Holtorf and Angelia Piccini, pp. 95–111. Peter Lang, Frankfurt am Main.

Bickford, Anne, Franz Reidel, Tom Eley, and Julian Holland
2011   *Archaeological Investigation: Parramatta Observatory Site. Excavation Report*, Vols. 1–2. Archaeology and Heritage Pty., Parramatta, NSW, Australia.

Bonham, Kevin
2013   Cavalier County Still Has Eye on Missile Site. *Grand Forks Herald*, 13 June:A1. Grand Forks, North Dakota.

Broadwater, John D.
2012   *USS Monitor: A Historic Ship Completes Its Final Voyage*. Texas A&M University Press, College Station.

Brown, Steve
2010   Physical Traces of the Nuclear Test History of Bikini Atoll: A Preliminary Survey Report. Unpublished report to ICOMOS. On file at Kili-Bikini-Ejit Local Government and Historic Preservation Office, Republic of the Marshall Islands.

2013a   Archaeology of Brutal Encounter: Heritage and Bomb Testing on Bikini Atoll, Republic of the Marshall Islands. *Archaeology in Oceania* 48(1):26–39.

2013b   Poetics and Politics: Bikini Atoll and World Heritage Listing. In *Transcending the Culture-Nature Divide in Cultural Heritage: Views from the Asia-Pacific Region*, edited by Sally Brockwell, Sue O'Connor, and Denis Byrne, pp. 35–52. ANU Press, Canberra.

Brugge, Doug, Timothy Benally, and Esther Yazzie-Lewis
2006   *The Navajo People and Uranium Mining.* University of New Mexico Press, Albuquerque.
Buchanan, Melissa, and Elizabeth Auxier
2000   *Department of Energy, Mound Facility, One Mound Road, Miamisburg, Montgomery County, Ohio.* HABS No. OH-2470. Historic American Buildings Survey, National Park Service, U.S. Department of the Interior, Washington, D.C.
Buchinger, Maria-Luise, and Matthias Metzler
2006   The Soviet Murals in Forst Zinna near Juterborg (Germany), a Cycle of Paintings in the Barracks of the 57th Construction Battalion. In *Re-Mapping the Field: New Approaches in Conflict Archaeology*, edited by John Schofield, Axel Klausmeier, and Louise Purbrick, pp. 28–34. Westkreuz-Verlag, Berlin.
Buchli, Victor, and Gavin Lucas
2001   *The Archaeology of Alienation—A Late Twentieth-Century British Council House.* In *Archaeologies of the Contemporary Past*, edited by Victor Buchli and Gavin Lucas, pp. 158–168. Routledge, London.
Burström, Mats
2007   *Samtidsarkeologi—Introduktion till ett forskningsfält.* Studentlitteratur, Lund.
2008   Looking into the Recent Past: Extending and Exploring the Field of Archaeology. *Current Swedish Archaeology* 15–16:21–36.
2011   Creative Confusion: Modern Ruins and the Archaeology of the Present. In *Rethinking Time: Essays on History, Memory, and Representation*, edited by Hans Ruin and Andrus Ers, pp. 119–128. Södertörns högskola, Huddinge.
Burström, Mats, Tomás Diez Acosta, Estrella González Noriega, Anders Gustafsson, Ismael Hernández, Håkan Karlsson, Jesús M. Pajón, Jesús Rafael, Robaina Jaramillo, and Bengt Westergaard
2009   Memories of a World Crisis: The Archaeology of a Former Soviet Nuclear Missile Site in Cuba. *Journal of Social Archaeology* 9(3):295–318.
Burström, Mats, Anders Gustafsson, and Håkan Karlsson
2006   The Air Torpedo of Bäckebo: Local Incident and World History. *Current Swedish Archaeology* 14:7–24.
2013   From Nuclear Missile Hangar to Pigsty: An Archaeological Photo-Essay on the 1962 World Crisis. In *Counterpoint: Essays in Archaeology and Heritage Studies in Honour of Professor Kristian Kristiansen*, edited by Sophie Bergerbrant and Serena Sabatini, pp. 733–737. Archaeopress, Oxford.
Burström, Mats, and Håkan Karlsson
2008   Världskris i ruin. Samtidsarkeologiska undersökningar av sovjetiska kärnvapenbaser på Kuba. Samtidsarkeologi. Varför gräva i det förflutna. *Södertörn Archaeological Studies* 6:41–48.
Cagle, Mary
1973   *History of the Nike Hercules Weapon System.* Historical Monograph AMC 75M. U.S. Army Missile Command, Redstone Arsenal, Alabama.
Cameron, Rebecca
1994   Coming in from the Cold: Military Heritage in the Cold War. *Report on the*

Department of Defense Legacy Cold War Project. Office of Air Force History, Washington, D.C.

Cannan, Deborah K., J. Hampton Tucker, William T. Dod, and Katherine E. Grandine
1995 *Charleston Navy Yard Historic District, National Register of Historic Places Registration Form.* Christopher Goodwin & Associates, Frederick, Maryland.

Capelotti, P. J.
2010 *The Human Archaeology of Space: Lunar, Planetary, and Interstellar Relics of Exploration.* McFarland, Jefferson, North Carolina.

Carman, John
1997 *Material Harm: Archaeological Studies of War and Violence.* Cruithne Press, Glasgow, UK.

Center for Land Use Interpretation (CLUI)
2015 Kings Bay Submarine Base. Electronic document, http://clui.org/ludb/site/kings-bay-submarine-base, accessed November 15, 2014.

Cleary, Mark C.
1991 The 6555th's Role in the Development of Ballistic Missiles: The Eastern Test Range in the 1950s. Electronic document, http://afspacemuseum.org/library/histories/TheCape.pdf, accessed May 15, 2015.

Coates, James
1988 Protest Brings Back the '60s Antiwar Activists Rally at Nevada Nuclear Test Ground. *Chicago Tribune,* 20 March:A1, A5. Chicago.

Cocroft, Wayne, and Roger J. C. Thomas
2003 *Cold War: Building for Nuclear Confrontation, 1946–89.* London: English Heritage.

Cocroft, Wayne, and Louise K. Wilson
2006 Archaeology and Art at Spadeadam Rocket Establishment (Cumbria). In *Re-Mapping the Field: New Approaches in Conflict Archaeology,* edited by John Schofield, Axel Klausmeier, and Louise Purbrick, pp. 15–21. Westkreuz-Verlag, Berlin.

Collins, Lori, and Travis Doering
2013 Fort Matanzas National Monument Digital Documentation Project. Electronic document, Alliance for Integrated Spatial Technologies. University of South Florida, Alliance for Integrated Spatial Technologies. Tampa. http://www.academia.edu/4322481, accessed May 15, 2015.

Conlin, David L., and Matthew A. Russell
2006 Archaeology of a Naval Battlefield: H. L. Hunley and USS *Housatonic. International Journal of Nautical Archaeology* 35(1):20–40.

Corbett, Michael
1994 *Historic Evaluation of the Peacekeeper Rail Garrison Test Igloo and Rail Garrison Launch Site, Vandenberg Air Force Base, California.* Earth Tech, Colton, California; Dames and Moore, Austin, Texas.

Day, Samuel H.
1988 *Nuclear Heartland: A Guide to the 1,000 Missile Silos of the United States.* Progressive Foundation, Madison, Wisconsin.

Delgado, James P.
1996 *Ghost Fleet: The Sunken Ships of Bikini Atoll.* University of Hawaii Press, Honolulu.

Delgado, James P., Daniel J. Lenihan, Larry E. Murphy, Larry V. Nordby, and Jerry L. Livingston
1991 *The Archeology of the Atomic Bomb: A Submerged Cultural Resources Assessment of the Sunken Fleet of Operation Crossroads at Bikini and Kwajalein Atoll Lagoons.* National Park Service, Santa Fe, New Mexico.

Dewar, James A.
2004 *To the End of the Solar System: The Story of the Nuclear Rocket.* University Press of Kentucky, Lexington.

Diaz, Kevin
1984 Year-Long Sperry Vigil Ends in 17 Arrests. *Minneapolis Star and Tribune,* 1 October:113. Minneapolis, Minnesota.

Diez Acosta, Tomás
1991 Informe sobre las regiones de emplazamiento de las unidades coheteriles estratégicas Soviéticas desplegadas en el territorio de la República de Cuba en el periodo de la Crisis de Octubre. Unpublished report. Copies available from Cuban Institute of History, Havana, Cuba.

Donaldson, Milford W.
2015 The Preservation of California's Military Cold War and Space Exploration Era Cultural Resources. In *Archaeology and Heritage of the Human Movement into Space,* edited by Beth Laura O'Leary and P. J. Capelotti, pp. 91–110. Springer, Heidelberg.

Doretti, Mercedes, and Luis Fondebrider
2001 Science and Human Rights: Truth, Justice, Reparation and Reconciliation, a Long Way in Third World Countries. In *Archaeologies of the Contemporary Past,* edited by Victor Buchli and Gavin Lucas, pp. 138–144. Routledge, London.

Drollinger, Harold, Nancy G. Goldenberg, and Colleen M. Beck
2000 *An Historical Evaluation of the Test Cell C Facility for Characterization Activities Associated with Decontamination and Decommissioning, Area 25, Nevada Test Site, Nye County, Nevada.* Desert Research Institute, Las Vegas, Nevada.

Edwards, Susan
1997 Atomic Age Training Camp: The Historical Archaeology of Camp Desert Rock. Unpublished MA thesis, University of Nevada, Las Vegas.

Elliott, Robert H.
1953 Battery D, 18th AAA Gun Battalion. *Antiaircraft Journal* 94(4):31–33.

Fehner, Terrence R., and F. G. Gosling
2000 *Origins of the Nevada Test Site.* DOE/MA05183. U.S. Department of Energy, Washington, D.C.

2006 *Atmospheric Nuclear Weapons Testing, 1951–1963. Battlefield of the Cold War: The Nevada Test Site,* Vol. I. DOE/MA-0003. U.S. Department of Energy, Washington, D.C.

Feskov, Vitalii I., Konstantin A. Kalashnikov, and Valerii I. Golikov
2004   Советская Армия в годы холодной войны, 1945–1991. (*The Soviet Army during the Cold War, 1945–1991*). Tomskiĭ Gos. Universitet, Tomsk.

Fletcher, Roy
1989   Military Radar Defence Lines of Northern North America—An Historical Geography. *Polar Record* 26 (159):265–276.

Funk, Jeanette
1983   Women Pitch Tents for Peace. *Michigan Daily*, 12 October:1. University of Michigan, Ann Arbor.

Furman, Necah
1990   *Sandia National Laboratories: The Postwar Decade*. University of New Mexico Press, Albuquerque.

Gall, Michael J.
2004   Thomas A. Edison: Managing Menlo Park, 1876–1882. Unpublished MA thesis, Monmouth University, West Long Branch, New Jersey.

Gall, Michael J., Richard Veit, and Allison Savarese
2007   Keeping Edison's Secrets: Archaeological Documentation of Thomas A. Edison's Menlo Park Patent Vault. *Historical Archaeology* 41(4):20–31.

Geier, Clarence R., Lawrence E. Babits, Douglas D. Scott, and David G. Orr (editors)
2010   *The Historical Archaeology of Military Sites Method and Topic*. Texas A&M University Press, College Station.

Gerber, Michele Stenehjem
1992   *On the Home Front: The Cold War Legacy of the Hanford Nuclear Site*. University of Nebraska Press, Lincoln.

Gerson, Joseph
2007   *Empire and the Bomb: How the U.S. Uses Nuclear Weapons to Dominate the World*. Pluto Press, Ann Arbor, Michigan.

Gillett, Terri, Mary Beth Reed, Mark T. Swanson, and Steven Gaither
2007   *Savannah River Site Cold War Historic Property Documentation Narrative and Photography, 700/A Area—Site Administration, Safety, Security, and Support*. New South Associates, Stone Mountain, Georgia.

Gold, Robert
2009   Spacecraft and Objects Left on Planetary Surfaces. In *Handbook of Space Engineering, Archaeology, and Heritage*, edited by Ann Garrison Darrin and Beth L. O'Leary, pp. 399–420. CRC Press, Boca Raton, Florida.

Gorman, Alice
2005   The Cultural Landscape of Interplanetary Space. *Journal of Social Archaeology* 5(1):85–107.
2009   Heritage of Earth Orbit: Orbital Debris—Its Mitigation and Cultural Heritage. In *Handbook of Space Engineering, Archaeology, and Heritage*, edited by Ann Garrison Darrin and Beth L. O'Leary, pp. 381–397. CRC Press, Boca Raton.
2015   Robot Avatars: The Material Culture of Human Activity in Earth Orbit. In

Archaeology and Heritage of the Human Movement into Space, edited by Beth L. O'Leary and P. J. Capelotti, pp. 29–47. Springer, Heidelberg.

Gorman, Alice, and Beth L. O'Leary
2007   An Ideological Vacuum: The Cold War in Outer Space. In *A Fearsome Heritage: Diverse Legacies of the Cold War*, edited by John Schofield and Wayne Cocroft, pp. 73–92. Left Coast Press, Walnut Creek, California.

Grant, Clement L.
1954   *The Development of Continental Air Defense to 1 September 1954*. USAF Historical Division, Maxwell Air Force Base, Montgomery, Alabama.

Graves-Brown, Paul
2007   Avtomat Kalashnikova. *Journal of Material Culture* 12(3):285–307.

Gregory, Carrie J., and Martyn D. Tagg
2008   *Recording the Cold War: Identifying and Collecting Cold War Resource Data on Military Installations*. Technical Report 08-41. Statistical Research, Tucson. Submitted to Department of Defense Legacy Resource Management Program, Washington, D.C.

Grguric, Nicolas K.
2008   Fortified Homesteads: The Architecture of Fear in Frontier South Australia and the Northern Territory, ca. 1847–1885. *Journal of Conflict Archaeology* 4(1–2):59–85.

Gusterson, Hugh
1992   Coming of Age in a Weapons Lab: Culture, Tradition and Change in the House of the Bomb. *Sciences* May–June:16–22.
1996   *Nuclear Rites: A Weapons Laboratory at the End of the Cold War*. University of California Press, Berkeley.
2004   Nuclear Tourism. *Journal for Cultural Research* 8(1):23–31.

Haber, Barbara
1984   I Was There . . . Livermore Women's Peace Camp. Originally published as It's about Times. *Abalone Alliance* February–March 1984. San Francisco. http://foundsf.org/index.php?title=Livermore_Women%27s_Peace_Camp, accessed February 1, 2015.

Hampton, Roy
2012   *Historic Context for Evaluating Mid-Century Modern Military Buildings*. Report 11-448. Hardlines Design Company, Columbus, Ohio.

Hansen, Peer, Thomas Pedersen, and Morten Stenak (editors)
2013   *Den Kolde Krigs anlæg*. Kulturministeriet, Kulturstyrelsen, Copenhagen.

Hanson, Todd A.
2009   Exploding the Strangelove Myth—Cold War Nuclear Weapons Work and the Testing Times of William Ogle. In *The Atomic Bomb and American Society—New Perspectives*, edited by G. Kurt Piehler and Rosemary Mariner, pp. 261–284. University of Tennessee Press, Knoxville.
2010   Uncovering the Arsenals of Armageddon—A Historical Archaeology of Cold War Ballistic Missile Launch Sites in North America. *Archaeological Review from Cambridge* 25(1):157–172.

Harrison Rodney, and John Schofield
2010   *After Modernity: Archaeological Approaches to the Contemporary Past.* Oxford University Press, New York.

Hawthorne-Tagg, Lori S.
2001   *Shooting the Sky: Cold War Archaeology of Air Defense Training on McGregor Range.* Report No. 521. Lone Mountain Archaeological Service, Albuquerque, New Mexico.

Heefner, Gretchen
2012   *The Missile Next Door: The Minuteman in the American Heartland.* Harvard University Press, Cambridge, Massachusetts.

Hess, Bill
1983   Why the Big Fuss about Cruise Missiles? *Courier,* 23 October:3. Prescott, Arizona.

Hess, Jeffery A.
1984   *Rocky Mountain Arsenal, Commerce City, Adams County Colorado.* HAER No. CO-021. Historic American Engineering Record, U.S. Department of the Interior, National Park Service, Washington, D.C.

History Associates
1987   *History of the Production Complex: The Methods of Site Selection.* History Associates, Rockville, Maryland.

Hollinger, Kristy
2004   *Nike Hercules Operations in Alaska: 1959–1979.* Conservation Branch, U.S. Army Garrison Alaska, Anchorage.

Hubbs, Mark E.
1992   *Stanley R. Mickelsen Safeguard Complex, Nekoma, Cavalier County, ND.* HAER ND-9. Historic American Engineering Record, U.S. Department of the Interior, National Park Service, Washington, D.C.

Jacobson, Michael
2009   The Landscapes of Hope and Fear: A Study of Space in the Ludlow Strikers' Colony. In *The Archaeology of Class War: The Colorado Coalfield Strike of 1913–14,* edited by Randall McGuire and Karin Larkin, pp. 187–218. University Press of Colorado, Boulder.

Johnson, Leland
1997   *Sandia National Laboratories: A History of Exceptional Service in the National Interest.* Sandia National Laboratories, Albuquerque, New Mexico.

Johnson, William, Barbara Holz, and Robert Jones
2000   *A Cold War Battlefield: Frenchman Flat Historic District, Nevada Test Site, Nye County, Nevada.* Desert Research Institute, Las Vegas, Nevada.

Kiddey, Rachel, and John Schofield
2011   Embrace the Margins: Adventures in Archaeology and Homelessness. *Public Archaeology* 10(1):4–22.

Kirk, Gwen
1985   Addresses for Women's Peace Camps in the U.S. *Heresies: A Feminist Publication on Art & Politics* 5(20):64. http://heresiesfilmproject.org/wp-content/uploads/2011/10/heresies20.pdf, accessed February 1, 2015.

Krasniewicz, Louise
1992   *Nuclear Summer: The Clash of Communities at the Seneca Women's Peace Encampment.* Cornell University Press, Ithaca, New York.

Kuranda, Kathryn M.
2003   *Housing an Army: The Wherry and Capehart Era Solutions to the Postwar Family Housing Shortage (1949–1962).* U.S. Army Environmental Center, Frederick, Maryland.

Lambert, Patricia
2002   The Archaeology of War: A North American Perspective. *Journal of Archaeological Research* 10(3):207–241.

Lavin, Mary K.
1998   *Thematic Study and Guidelines: Identification and Evaluation of U.S. Army Cold War Era Military-Industrial Historic Properties.* Report SFIM-AEC-EQ-TR-98035. U.S. Army Environmental Center, Aberdeen Proving Ground, Maryland.

Lederman, Rachel
1989   Looking Back: The Women's Peace Camps in Perspective. In *Exposing Nuclear Phallacies*, edited by Diana E. H. Russell, pp. 244–256. Pergamon Press, New York.

Lennon, John J., and Malcolm Foley
2000   *Dark Tourism: The Attraction of Death and Disaster.* Continuum, London.

Lewis, Darrell
2011   Partnership Breathes New Life into Historic Nike Hercules Missile Site. *RPPN (Recent Past Preservation Network) Bulletin* 2(2):13–20.

Lonnquest, John C., and David F. Winkler
1996   *To Defend and Deter: The Legacy of the United States Cold War Missile Program.* U.S. Army Construction Engineering Research Laboratory, Champaign, Illinois.

Lowry, Christopher, and Mary Henry
1997   *Historical Background for McGregor Range. McGregor Guided Missile Range Survey Project, New Mexico.* Vol. I, *The Archaeology of Landscape—General Survey.* U.S. Army Air Defense Artillery Center, Fort Bliss. El Paso, Texas.

Lucas, Gavin
2004   Modern Disturbances: On the Ambiguities of Archaeology. *Modernism/Modernity* 11(1):109–120.

MacBride, Laurie
1985   Nanoose Peace Camp Opens Again. *Peace Magazine*, 6 May. http://peacemagazine.org/archive/v01n3p06b.htm, accessed February 1, 2015.
1986   Momentum Builds at Nanoose. *Peace Magazine* 8(February–March). http://peacemagazine.org/archive/v02n1p08.htm, accessed February 1, 2015.

Makhijani, Arjun, Howard Hu, and Katherine Yih
1995   *Nuclear Wastelands: A Global Guide to Nuclear Weapons Production and Its Health and Environmental Effects.* MIT Press, Cambridge, Massachusetts.

Maroncelli, James M., and Timothy L. Karpin
2002   *The Traveler's Guide to Nuclear Weapons: A Journey through America's Cold War Battlefields.* Historical Odysseys, Lacey, Washington.

Marshall, Yvonne, Sasha Roseneil, and Kayt Armstrong
2009   Situating the Greenham Archaeology: An Autoethnography of a Feminist Project. *Public Archaeology* 8(2–3):225–245.

Massie, Jeannie, Carl Maag, Stephen Rohrer, and Robert Shepanek
1982   *Shots Encore to Climax: The Final Four Tests of the Upshot-Knothole Series, 8 May–4 June 1953.* Report DNA 6018F. Defense Nuclear Agency, Washington, D.C.

McWilliams, Anna
2013   *An Archaeology of the Iron Curtain: Material and Metaphor.* Stockholm Studies in Archaeology 59. Stockholm University, Stockholm.

Monteyne, David
2011   *Fallout Shelter: Designing for Civil Defense in the Cold War.* University of Minnesota Press, Minneapolis.

Moshenka, Gabriel
2010   Working with Memory in the Archaeology of Modern Conflict. *Cambridge Archaeological Journal* 20(1):33–48.

Myers, Adrian T.
2008   Between Memory and Materiality: An Archaeological Approach to Studying the Nazi Concentration Camps. *Journal of Conflict Archaeology* 4(1–2):59–85.

National Research Council
1993   *Assessment of the Possible Health Effects of Ground Wave Emergency Network.* National Academies Press, Washington, D.C.

Neufeld, Jacob
1990   *The Development of Ballistic Missiles in the United States Air Force, 1945–1960.* Office of Air Force History, Washington, D.C.

Nichols, Kenneth D.
1987   *The Road to Trinity.* Morrow, New York.

Norris, Robert S.
1992   Nuclear Notebook: Pantex Lays Nukes to Rest. *Bulletin of the Atomic Scientists* 48(8):48–49.

Nowlan, Patrick
1999   *Identification and Evaluation of Cold War Properties at Fort Bliss, Texas.* U.S. Army Construction Engineering Research Laboratory, Champaign, Illinois.

Nowlan, Patrick, Sheila Ellsworth, Roy McCullough, Mira Metzinger, Jim Gorski, and Andy Bonhert
1996   *Cold War Properties Evaluation. Phase I: Inventory and Evaluation of Launch Complexes and Related Facilities at Vandenberg Air Force Base, California.* U.S. Army Construction Engineering Research Laboratory, Champaign, Illinois.

Orange, Hilary
2012 Cornish Mining Landscapes: Public Perceptions of Industrial Archaeology in a Post-Industrial Society. Unpublished Ph.D. diss., University College, London.
Orwell, George
1968 *The Collected Essays, Journalism and Letters of George Orwell.* Vol. IV: *In Front of Your Nose, 1945–1950.* Harcourt, Brace & World, New York.
Pajón, Jesús M., Ismael Hernández, Rafael Robiana, Estrella González, Burström, Mats, Tomás Diez, Håkan Karlsson, and Anders Gustafsson
2006 *Reconocimiento geodinámico y arquehistórico preliminar del área de emplazamiento de las unidades coheteriles Soviéticas grupo R-12 Santa Cruz de los Pinos, Pinar del Río, Cuba, durante la crisis de octubre de 1962.* Centro de Antropología de Cuba, Havana.
Parchami, Ali
2009 *Hegemonic Peace and Empire: The Pax Romana, Britannica and Americana.* War, History and Politics. Routledge, London.
Pasternak, Judith Mahoney
2002 A Journey to Pacifism. *Nonviolent Activist* January–February:7. http://www.warresisters.org/nva/nva0102-2.htm, accessed November 30, 2014.
Pearson, Marlys, and Paul R. Mullins
1999 Domesticating Barbie: An Archaeology of Barbie Material Culture and Domestic Ideology. *International Journal of Historical Archaeology* 3(4):225–259.
Penders, Thomas
2012 Aerospace Archaeology and the Study of Missile Crash Sites: An Example from the Jupiter Missile Crash Site (8BR2087), Cape Canaveral Air Force Station, Brevard County, Florida. *Florida Anthropologist* 65(4):227–243.
Penders, Thomas, Lori D. Collins, and Travis F. Doering
2009 High Definition Laser Scanning of the Beehive Blockhouses, Launch Complex 31/32, Cape Canaveral Air Force Station (CCAFS), Brevard County, Florida. Poster presented at the 74th Annual Conference of the Society for American Archaeology, Atlanta, Georgia.
Penson, Chuck
2008 *The Titan II Handbook: A Civilian's Guide to the Most Powerful ICBM America Ever Built.* Chuck Penson, Tucson, Arizona.
Petrauskas, Gediminas
2011 The Investigation of the Daugėliškiai Forest Staff Bunker of the Union of Lithuanian Freedom Fighters. *Archaeological Studies Lithuania* 2(1):515–522
Podvig, Pavel (editor)
2001 *Russian Strategic Nuclear Forces.* MIT Press, Cambridge, Massachusetts.
Polmar, Norman, and Kenneth J. Moore
2003 *Cold War Submarines: The Design and Construction of U.S. and Soviet Submarines, 1945–2001.* Potomac Books, Dulles, Virginia.
Ponton, Jean, Carl Maag, Martha Wilkinson, and Stephen Rohrer
1981 *Shots ESS through MET and Shot Zucchini: The Final Teapot Tests 23 March–15 May 1955.* Defense Nuclear Agency, Washington, D.C.

Ponton, Jean, Stephen Rohrer, Carl Maag, Robert Shepanek, and Jean Massie
1983   *Operation Dominic II, Shots Little Feller II, Johnnie Boy, Small Boy, and Little Feller I, 7 July–17 July 1962*. Defense Nuclear Agency, Washington, D.C.

Poole, Charles R., and K. C. Harrison
1954   *Project History of Line 1 Operations at Iowa Ordnance Plant, January 1, 1947, through July 1, 1954*. Silas Mason Company, Burlington, Iowa.

Potter, James M., and Jason P. Chuipka
2010   Perimortem Mutilation of Human Remains in an Early Village in the American Southwest: A Case for Ethnic Violence. *Journal of Anthropological Archaeology* 29(4):507–523.

Quinn, Michael
1986   *White Sands Missile Range, V-2 Rocket Facilities*. HAER NM-1B. Historic American Engineering Record, U.S. Department of the Interior. National Park Service, Washington, D.C.

Ray, Thomas W.
1965   *A History of Texas Towers in Air Defense, 1952–1964*. ADC Historical Study Number 29. Air Defense Command, Colorado Springs, Colorado.

Reed, Craig W.
2010   *Red November: Inside the Secret U.S.-Soviet Submarine War*. HarperCollins, New York.

Reed, Mary Beth, Mark T. Swanson, Steven Gaither, J. W. Joseph, and William R. Henry
2003   *Savannah River Site at Fifty*. U.S. Department of Energy, Washington, D.C.

Renshaw, Layla
2010   The Scientific and Affective Identification of Republican Civilian Victims from the Spanish Civil War. *Journal of Material Culture* 15(4):449–463.

Rice, Glenn E., and Steven A. LeBlanc
2001   *Deadly Landscapes: Case Studies in Prehistoric Southwestern Warfare*. University of Utah Press, Salt Lake City.

Rose, Kenneth D.
2001   *One Nation Underground: The Fallout Shelter in American Culture*. New York University Press, New York.

Roy, Susan
2011   *Bomboozled: How the U.S. Government Misled Itself and Its People into Believing They Could Survive a Nuclear Attack*. Pointed Leaf Press, New York.

Saitta, Dean J.
2007   *The Archaeology of Collective Action*. University Press of Florida, Gainesville.

Saitta, Dean J., Mark Walker, and Paul Reckner
2005   Battlefields of Class Conflict: Ludlow Then and Now. *Journal of Conflict Archaeology* 1:197–214.

Salmon, John S.
2011   *Protecting America: Cold War Defensive Sites. A National Historic Landmark Theme Study*. National Historic Landmarks Program, National Park Service, U.S. Department of the Interior, Washington, D.C.

Saunders, Nicholas (editor)
2004   *Matters of Conflict: Material Culture, Memory and the First World War*. Routledge, London.
2012   *Beyond the Dead Horizon: Studies in Modern Conflict Archaeology*. Oxbow Books, Oxford.

Schaffel, Kenneth
1991   *Emerging Shield: The Air Force and the Evolution of Continental Air Defense, 1945–1960*. Office of Air Force History, Washington, D.C.

Schiffer, Michael
2013   *The Archaeology of Science: Studying the Creation of Useful Knowledge*. Springer International, Cham, Switzerland.

Schofield, John
2005   *Combat Archaeology: Material Culture and Modern Conflict*. Duckworth, London.
2009   *Aftermath: Readings in the Archaeology of Recent Conflict*. Springer, New York.

Schofield, John, and Mike Anderton
2000   The Queer Archaeology of Green Gate: Interpreting Contested Space at Greenham Common Airbase. *World Archeology* 32(2):236–251.

Schofield, John, Colleen Beck, and Harold Drollinger
2006   Alternative Archaeologies of the Cold War: The Preliminary Results of Fieldwork at the Greenham and Nevada Peace Camps. In *Landscapes under Pressure: Theory and Practice of Cultural Heritage Research and Preservation*, edited by Ludomir R. Lozny, pp. 149–162. Springer, New York.

Schofield, John, and Wayne Cocroft (editors)
2007   *A Fearsome Heritage: Diverse Legacies of the Cold War*. Left Coast Press, Walnut Creek, California.

Schofield, John, William Johnson, and Colleen Beck (editors)
2002   *Matériel Culture: The Archaeology of Twentieth-Century Conflict*. Routledge, London.

Schofield, John, Axel Klausmeier, and Louise Purbrick (editors)
2006   *Re-mapping the Field: New Approaches in Conflict Archaeology*. Westkreuz-Verlag, Berlin.

Schwartz, Stephen I. (editor)
1998   *Atomic Audit: The Costs and Consequences of U.S. Nuclear Weapons since 1940*. Brookings Institution Press, Washington, D.C.

Scott, Douglas D.
2010   *Uncovering History: The Legacy of Archaeological Investigations at the Little Bighorn Battlefield National Monument, Montana*. National Park Service, Midwest Archaeological Center, Lincoln, Nebraska.
2013   *Uncovering History: Archaeological Investigations at the Little Bighorn*. University of Oklahoma Press, Norman.

Scott, Elizabeth
1994   *Those of Little Note: Gender, Race, and Class in Historical Archaeology*. University of Arizona Press, Tucson.

Shackel, Paul A., and Barbara J. Little
1992   Post-Processual Approaches to Meanings and Uses of Material Culture in Historical Archaeology. *Historical Archaeology* 26(3):5–11.

Sharpley, Richard, and Philip R. Stone
2009   *The Darker Side of Travel: The Theory and Practice of Dark Tourism.* Aspects of Tourism. Channel View Publications, Bristol, UK.

Shiman, Phillip
1997   *Forging the Sword: Defense Production during the Cold War.* U.S. Army Construction Engineering Research Laboratory, Champaign, Illinois.

Smith, Richard K.
1989   Marston Mat. *Air Force Magazine.* April:84–88.

Smoley, John K.
2008   Seizing Victory from the Jaws of Deterrence: Preservation and Public Memory of America's Nike Air Defense Missile System. Unpublished Ph.D. diss., University of California–Santa Barbara.

Spargo, Peter
2005   Investigating the Site of Newton's Laboratory at Trinity College, Cambridge. *South African Journal of Science* 101:315–321.

Spires, David N.
2012   *On Alert—An Operational History of the United States Air Force Intercontinental Ballistic Missile Program, 1945–2011.* Air Force Space Command, Colorado Springs, Colorado.

Starbuck, David R.
2011   *The Archaeology of Forts and Battlefields.* University Press of Florida, Gainesville.

Stenak, Morten, Thomas Pedersen, Peer Hansen, and Martin Jespersen
2014   *Kold Krig: 33 Fortællinger Om Den Kolde Krigs Bygninger og Anlæg i Danmark, Færøerne Og Grønland.* Kulturministeriet, Kulturstyrelsen, Copenhagen.

Stone, Philip R.
2012   Dark Tourism and Significant Other Death: Towards a Model of Mortality Mediation. *Annals of Tourism Research* 39(3):1565–1587.

Stone, Philip R., and Richard Sharpley
2008   Dark Tourism: A Thanatological Perspective. *Annals of Tourism Research* 35(2):574–595.

Sullivan, Daniel
2006   Materials in Use in U.S. Interstate Highways. Fact Sheet 2006-3127. United States Geological Survey, Washington, D.C.

Sutton, George P.
2003   History of Liquid Propellant Rocket Engines in the United States. *Journal of Propulsion and Power* 19(6):978–1007.

Temme, Virge Jenkins
1998   For Want of a Home: A Study of Wherry and Capehart Military Family Housing. Unpublished M.A. thesis. University of Illinois, Urbana-Champaign.

Terp, Holger
2005 *Greenham Common Peace Camp Songbook*. Working Paper 2. Copenhagen: Danish Peace Academy. Electronic document, http://www.fredsakademiet.dk/abase/sange/greenham.htm, accessed January 31, 2015.

Thompson, Erwin N.
1990 *Navy Yard Puget Sound, National Register of Historic Places Registration Form*. National Park Service, Washington, D.C.

Titus, Costandina
1986 *Bombs in the Backyard: Atomic Testing and American Politics*. University of Nevada Press, Reno.

Trigg, Jonathan
2007 Memory and Memorial: A Study of Official and Military Commemoration of the Dead, and Family and Community Memory in Essex and East London. *Journal of Conflict Archaeology* 3(1):295–315.

Tucker, Jonathan B.
2007 *War of Nerves—Chemical Warfare from World War I to Al-Qaeda*. Anchor Books, New York.

Twiss, Pamela, and James Martin
1998 *Quality of Life and Shelter: A History of Military Housing Policy and Initiatives since the Adoption of the All-Volunteer Force Concept (1973–1996)*. Military Family Institute of Marywood University, Scranton, Pennsylvania.

Ulrich, Rebecca
1998 *Tech Area II: A History*. Report SAND98-1617. Sandia National Laboratories, Albuquerque, New Mexico.

U.S. Congress, U.S. Senate
1963 *Nevada Test Site Community: Hearings before the Subcommittee on Legislation and Subcommittee on Communities of the Joint Committee on Atomic Energy*. Vol. 1: *September 12–October 16, 1963*. H.R. 8003 and S. 2030, 88th Cong., 1st sess., Government Printing Office, Washington, D.C.

1990 Department of Defense Appropriations Act for 1991. S.3189, 101st Cong., 2d sess., *Congressional Record* 137, pt. 36: S15232. Government Printing Office, Washington, D.C.

U.S. Environmental Protection Agency, Radiation Protection Division
2008 *Technical Report on Technologically Enhanced Naturally Occurring Radioactive Materials from Uranium Mining*. Vol. 1: *Mining and Reclamation Background*. Government Printing Office, Washington, D.C.

Van Citters, Karen
2003 *Documentation of the TRESTLE at Kirtland Air Force Base, New Mexico*. Van Citters: Historic Preservation, Albuquerque, New Mexico.

Van Citters, Karen, and Kristen Bisson
2003 *National Register of Historic Places Historic Context and Evaluation for Kirtland Air Force Base, Albuquerque, New Mexico*. Van Citters: Historic Preservation, Albuquerque, New Mexico.

Vanderbilt, Tom
2002 *Survival City: Adventures among the Ruins of Atomic America.* Princeton Architectural Press, Princeton, New Jersey.

Viscuso, Mary Jo, Steven Geller, Martha Wilkinson, James Striegel, and Burt Collins
1981 *Shot Priscilla: A Test of the Plumbbob Series, 24 June 1957.* Defense Nuclear Agency, Washington, D.C.

Wainwright, Angus
2009 Orford Ness—A Landscape in Conflict? In *Europe's Deadly Century: Perspectives on Twentieth-Century Conflict Heritage*, edited by Neil Forbes, Robin Page, and Guillermo Pérez, pp. 134–142. English Heritage, Swindon, UK.

Weinberger, Sharon, and Nathan Hodge
2008 *A Nuclear Family Vacation: Travels in the World of Atomic Weaponry.* Bloomsbury USA, New York.

Weitze, Karen J.
1999 *Cold War Infrastructure for Strategic Air Command: The Bomber Mission.* U.S. Army Corps of Engineers, Fort Worth, Texas.

Whitman, Edward C.
2005 SOSUS: The "Secret Weapon" of Undersea Surveillance. *Undersea Warfare* 7(2). http://www.navy.mil/navydata/cno/n87/usw/issue_25/sosus.htm, accessed May 1, 2015.

Wiener, Jon
2012 *How We Forgot the Cold War: A Historical Journey across America.* University of California Press, Berkeley.

Wilson, Ross
2011 Archaeology on the Battlefields: An Ethnography of the Western Front. *Assemblage* 11(1):1–14.

Winkler, David F., and Julie L. Webster
1997 *Searching the Skies: The Legacy of the United States Cold War Defense Radar Program.* U.S. Army Construction Engineering Research Laboratory, Champaign, Illinois.

Witt, Lisa
2004 *TRESTLE: The Landmark of the Cold War.* Avista Video Histories, Albuquerque, New Mexico.

Wolf, Richard
1987 *United States Air Force Basic Documentation, Roles and Missions.* Office of the Air Force Historian, Washington, D.C.

INDEX

Page numbers in *italics* refer to illustrations.

ADC. *See* Air Defense Command
AEC. *See* Atomic Energy Commission
AFB. *See* Vandenberg Air Force Base
Africa, 35
AFWL. *See* Air Force Weapons Laboratory
Aircraft response, 81–84
Air Defense Command (ADC), 30, 41–42, *42*, 44
Air defense training, 111, 115
Air Force Weapons Laboratory (AFWL), 81
Air-launched cruise missiles (ALCMs), 64
AK-47. *See* Avtomat Kalashnikova
Alabama, 42, 45
Alaska, 43, 138–40, 150
ALCMs. *See* Air-launched cruise missiles
Alternate Joint Communications Center, 56–57
American memory, 146
America's Space Race, NTS, NRDS and, 106–10
Antennae, intelligence-gathering (Wullenwebers), 6
Antiaircraft weapon systems, 114
Antinuclear protests, 6, 100–105, 134–35
ARAACOM. *See* Army Antiaircraft Artillery Command
Archaeology: access, 126–27, 130–33; atomic tourism, 132–37; of Cold War, 9, 11, 24–27, 146–47; Cold War conflict and era humanized by, 153; contemporary past, 17–19; as form of material witness, 18–19; frameworks for, xvi–xvii, 9, 11–27; Frenchman Flat at Nevada Test Site, 93–99; implications for Cold War, 146–47; literature, 68–124; at McGregor Range, 111–15; research and studies, 137–41; research and studies at Cape Canaveral, 115–22; scholarship, 7–10; scientific encampments and, 149–50; sites, 68–124; studies of NTS and Peace Camp, 100–105; submarines and wreckages, 127; surveys, 88–92, 101–5; US secrecy policies and, 130–32. *See also* Cold War archaeology
Archaeology of contemporary past, 9, 11, 16–20. *See also* Contemporary archaeology
Archaeology of science, 149–50; in Cold War study frameworks, 9, 11, 20–24; definition and characteristics of, 21–22; evolution of, 22; nuclear weapons testing and, 23–24, 85–110; overview and characteristics of, 20–24; scientists' considerations for, 21; Trestle study, 84–85
Archival documents, discrepancies in, 91–92
Arizona, 66
Arkansas, 63
Arkansas, USS battleship, 70–71, *71*

"Arms race," 4
Army Antiaircraft Artillery Command (ARAACOM), 45–46, *46*
Artificial forest, 99
ATLAS. *See* Transmission Line Aircraft Simulator
Atlas ICBMs, 51, *53*, 53–54
"Atomic age," 156n7
Atomic bomb, 133, 156n7; as discrete project, 21; Hiroshima and, 29–30; Manhattan Project to build, xv–xvi; Nagasaki and, 29–30; SRP and production of, 37; testing, 36, 133, *134*, 136; themed events and, 133; USSR's successful test of, 36; of World War Two, 35
Atomic Energy Act, 30
Atomic Energy Commission (AEC), 30, 37, 89–90
Atomic testing sites, 32–34, 69–71, *71*, 87
Atomic tourism, 72, 132–37
Atomic training operations, 89–90
Atomic veterans, 139–41
Atomic weapons, 30–41, 70–71, *71*, 93
Avtomat Kalashnikova (AK-47), USSR assault rifle, 14–15

B-36 Peacemaker, 48, 155n4
BAECP. *See* Burlington Atomic Energy Commission Plant
Baker atomic weapons test, 70–71, *71*
Ballistic Missile Early Warning System (BMEWS), 6, 43, *43*, 67
Barbie dolls, 17
Battle readiness, 110–15
"Beehive" blockhouses, 121–22, *122*
Bikini Atoll, 23, 32; atomic tourism and, 71–72; background and history of, 68–71; bunker conditions at, 72–73, *73*; inundation possibilities of, 73–74; landscape modifications and, 72–73; post-survey research, 73–74; Republic of Marshall Islands, 68–74, *71*; residual radiation hazards and, 71; UNESCO World Heritage site, 123–24

Blockhouses, "beehive," 121–22, *122*
BMEWS. *See* Ballistic Missile Early Warning System
Bombers, 27, 29–30, 48, 53–54, 155–54
Bombs, Iowa Ordnance Plant and World War Two, 38–39. *See also* Atomic bomb
Bomb shelters, 59, 59–60
B Reactor facility (Hanford), 35
Brutalist aesthetic architecture, xvi, *8*, 8–9
Buildings. *See specific buildings*
Bunkers, 56–57, *58*, 67, 72–73, *73*, 144, *145*
Burke, Edmund, 136
Burlington Atomic Energy Commission Plant (BAECP), 38–39, 60–61

California, 3, 32–33, 40, 48, 54, 56, 66
Camera stations, 97
Camp David, 56
Camp Desert Rock (CDR), 87–92
Camp Mercury, 88
Canada, 6, 28, 42–43, 50, 57, 66–67, 135–36
Canadian Forces Station Carp, 57
Cape Canaveral AFS: archaeological studies at Florida's, 115–22; Cape Kennedy at, 116; Cold War Space Race represented at, 115–16; islands occupying launch complexes of, 116; Jupiter Missile Crash Site and, 117–18; laser scanning survey, 122, *123*; Launch Complex 39 at, 116; missiles tested at, 116; as point of origin for EMTR, 116–*17*; surveys, 118–19
Capehart, Homer E., 45, 67
Cape Kennedy, 116
Capsule storage buildings, 48, *49*
CDR. *See* Camp Desert Rock
CETO. *See* Civil Effects Test Operations
Charleston Naval Shipyard (CNSY), 55–56
Charlie test of Operation Tumbler-Snapper, 133, *134*
Chemical weapons, 39
Chernobyl nuclear power plant, 136
Cheyenne Mountain, 57, *58*, 67
Circularly Disposed Antenna Arrays, 6
Civil defense sites, 59–60

Civil Effects Test Operations (CETO), 97–98
Classified information, 131–32
Clinton Engineer Works, 34–35
CNSY. *See* Charleston Naval Shipyard
COC. *See* Combat Operations Center
Cold War, 85, 148; American memory and artifacts of, 146; archaeological scholarship roots of, 7–10; atomic weapon production sites, 30–41; beginnings as Manhattan Project wartime effort, x–xviii; being forgotten, 145–47; bunkers, 56–57, *58*, 67, 72–73, *73*; humanized by archaeology of, 153; cultural heritage and stewardship issues of, 9–10, 125–42; debates on dates of, 155n1; direction for future research of, 10, 16, 143–53; economy, 3, *3*; evaluations for properties of, 26–27; frameworks for studies of, xvi–xvii, 9, 11–27; H3D for landmark preservation of, 120–22; landscape historical periods of, 28–67; North American landscape and creation of, 28–67, 152; North American peace camps of, 65, *66*; research challenges of, 125–26; Science and technology, 3–6, 11–12, 151–52; secrecy and, 11, 59–60; stakeholders as atomic tourists of, xviii; studying material culture of, 149–51; UK's studies of, 25–26; veterans, 137–41
Cold War archaeology, 24–27; conflict and, xvii; implications for, 146–47; perspectives and intersections of, xvii; physical hazards, 127–30; studies from archaeological literature, 68–124. *See also* Archaeology of science
Cold War Installations Project, 26
Cold War periods, 3–6, 11–12, 151–52. *See also* Early Cold War (1945–1957); Late Cold War (1976–1989); Middle Cold War (1958–1975)
Cold War sites, xvii–xviii; atomic testing, 32–34, 69–71, *71*, 87; atomic tourism, 132–37; Bikini atoll as UNESCO World Heritage, 74; Cape Canaveral, 117–18; context and backgrounds of archaeological, 68–124; GWEN, 63; historic, 13, 127; importance of preserving, 144–45; International, 6; Jupiter Missile Crash Site, 117–20, *119*; launches and, 47, 50, 53–55, 63–65, 75–76, 95, 106, 110–15, 123, 126, 135, 147, 152; National Stockpile weapons, 47–48; New Mexico, McGregor Range, 110–15; Nike Hercules missile, 6, 29, 138–39; Nike Launch, 112–13; OSS, 48; safety and physical hazards of, 127–30; underground bunkers as command and control, 56–58, *58*, 67. *See also* Early Cold War (1945–1957); Late Cold War (1976–1989); Middle Cold War (1958–1975); Missile sites; Nevada Test Site; Nike Site Summit; Production sites; Soviet missile sites; Trinity Site
Colorado, 35, 37–40, 54, 57–58, 63
Combat Operations Center (COC), 57
Coming in from the Cold—Military Heritage in the Cold War, 25
Command and control sites, 56–58, *58*
Communism, 2–3, 151
Concrete pillboxes, 48, *49*
Conflict. *See* Modern conflict archaeology
Conflict archaeology, xvii; in Cold War study frameworks, 9, 11–14; Cold War viewed as, 11–14; definition and development of, 12–14; LBBNM investigations advancing, 13–14; North America's material culture and, 12–14. *See also* Modern conflict archaeology
Connecticut, 40, 55
Contemporary archaeology, 11, 16–20
Continental defense sites, 41–55, 61–63
Control sites. *See* Command and control sites
Crisis de Octubre, 75, 123
Cruise missiles, 64
Cuba, 9, 74–81, *76*, 123
Cuban Missile Crisis, 6, 55, 118
CV-3 (*Saratoga*, USS), 70

Danish Agency for Culture (DAC), 26
Dark tourism, 136–37
Day, Samuel, 135
Defense: ADC and, 30; ARAACOM network for, 45–46, *46*; civil sites for, 59–60; continental sites for, 41–55, 61–63; DoD and, xvii, 25–26, 30, 138–40, 144; infrastructures for, 50; late Cold War continental sites for, 61–63; McGregor Range training for air, 111, 115; middle Cold War sites for, 51–55, 59–60; national, 3; NORAD system and, *42*, 57; OCD and, 60; training for air, 111, 115
Democratic Republic of the Congo, 35
Denmark, 6, 26, 29
Department of Defense (DoD), xvii, 25–26, 30, 138–40, 144
Department of Defense Appropriations Act, 25
Deployments, 41, 43–47, 51; of Atlas F ICBM, 53–54; B-36 bomber, 48; Cuba and Soviet R-12 Dvina MRBM, 74–75; of missiles, 6, 29, 54; nuclear-armed bomber, 27, 29–30, 53–54; of submarines, 55
Desert Research Institute (DRI), 86–87, 95–99, 103, 106–10
Desert Rock Exercises, 89–90, 93–95, *94*
Detention structures, 105
DEW. *See* Distant Early warning
Diefenbunker. *See* Canadian Forces Station Carp
Discrepancies, in archival documents, 91–92
Disenfranchised groups, xvi, 150
Distant Early warning (DEW), 42–43
DoD. *See* Department of Defense
DRI. *See* Desert Research Institute

Early Cold War (1945–1957): continental defense sites, 41–50; evolution of, 29–50; first period as, 9, 28–50; research and development sites of, 30–34
Eastern Middle Test Range (EMTR), 116, *117*

East Germany, 135–36
Edison, Thomas, 22–23
8BR2087. *See* Jupiter Missile Crash Site
Eisenhower, Dwight D., 50, 51
Electromagnetic pulse (EMP), 62, 63, 81–84
ELF. *See* Extremely low frequency
El Purio (Cuba), 76, *77*
E-Mad. *See* Engine Maintenance and Disassembly
EMP. *See* Electromagnetic pulse
EMP testing, 81–84
EMTR. *See* Eastern Middle Test Range
Encampments, 149–50
Enewetak Atoll, 32, 150
Engine Maintenance and Disassembly (E-Mad), 108–9
English Heritage, 25, 101
Environmental racism, xvi, 150
EOD. *See* Explosive Ordnance Demolition
Exercises: Desert Rock atomic training, 89–90; Snezhok, 92
Explosions, nuclear, xvi, 82–83, 98
Explosive Ordnance Demolition (EOD), 69
Extremely low frequency (ELF), 62–63

Fairchild AFB, *53*, 53–54
Fallout shelters, *59*, 59–60
Federal-Aid Highway Act of 1944, 50
Fernald Feed Materials Production Plant, 36–37
Florida, 33, 115–22
Florida, archaeological studies at Cape Canaveral, 115–22
FONSS. *See* Friends of Nike Site Summit
Forest, artificial, 99
Fort Bliss, 111, 114
Frenchman Flat: archaeology, 93–99; artificial forest for testing at, 99; biological effects experiments, 99; camera stations, 97; Kay Blockhouse, 96–97; operation shots held at, 93–95, *94*; viewing area bleachers for VIPs at, 97, *98*
Friends of Nike Site Summit (FONSS), 139

GAMA. *See* Ground-launched cruise missile alert and maintenance area
George Washington, USS, 55
Georgia, 55
"Ghost fleet," 69–70
GIUK. *See* Greenland, Iceland, United Kingdom
GLCM. *See* Ground-launched cruise missile
Global Positioning System (GPS), 120–22, 152
Global superpower, 1–2
Glory trips, 33, 110
Gloveboxes, 37, *38*
GPS. *See* Global Positioning System
Graffiti, 103, *103*
Gravel gerties, 39
Greenbriar, 57
Greenland, Iceland, United Kingdom (GIUK) gap, 44
Groton Naval Shipyard, 40, 55
Ground-launched cruise missile alert and maintenance area (GAMA), 64
Ground-launched cruise missiles (GLCM), 64
Ground Wave Emergency Network (GWEN), 63
GWEN. *See* Ground Wave Emergency Network

H3D. *See* High definition digital documentation
HAER. *See* Historic American Engineering Record
Hanford Engineer Works (HEW), 35
Hawaii, 82
H-bombs (thermonuclear fusion devices), 4
Heritage stewardship, xvii, 9–10, 25–27, 72–74, 125–42, 144, 152
HEW. *See* Hanford Engineer Works
High definition digital documentation (H3D), 120–22
Hiroshima, 29–30
Historic American Engineering Record (HAER), 81, 110, 128, *129*, 139
History, xvi, 13, 127; Bikini Atoll background and, 68–71; oral, 131; periods of Cold War landscape, 28–67; secrecy and gaps of information in, 19; Swedish and Cuban institutions and, 75; veterans' efforts for preserving, 138–41

ICBM. *See* Intercontinental ballistic missile
Idaho, 54
IFC. *See* Integrated Fire Control
Industrialized warfare, 15
Integrated Fire Control (IFC), 46, 112–13
Intercontinental ballistic missile (ICBM), 5, 50, 64, 110–11, 121–22, *122*, 148; arrival of Atlas, *53*, 53–54
Iowa Ordnance Plant, 38–39
Iron Curtain, 2

Jackass Flats, 106
Japan, xvi, 69
Joint Long Range Proving Grounds, 116
Jupiter Missile Crash Site (8BR2087), 117–20, *119*

Kansas, 53–54, 63
Kay Blockhouse, 96–97
Kennedy, John F., 116
Kentucky, 36, 47–48
Kiwi reactors, 106–7, *107*
Kwajalein Atoll, 33, 69

Landscape modifications, 72–73
Laser scanning, 121–22, *123*
Lashup radar systems, 41
LASL. *See* Los Alamos Scientific Laboratory
Late Cold War (1976–1989): continental defense sites of, 61–63; cruise missile production sites of, 64–65; production sites, 64–65; protest sites, 64–65; resolution, 60–67; third period as, 9, 29, 60–67
Laurence, William, 156n7
LBBNM. *See* Little Bighorn Battlefield National Monument
Legacy Resource Management Program, 25

178 · Index

Little Bighorn Battlefield National Monument (LBBNM), 13–14
Living memory, 16–17, 19
Los Alamos, 133
Los Alamos Scientific Laboratory (LASL), 30–31, *31*, 106
Louisiana, 48
LSM-60, USS, 70

MAD. *See* Mutual assured destruction
Magnetic resonance imaging (MRI), 5
Maine, 41, 48, *49*
Mallinckrodt Chemical Works, 36–37
Manhattan Project, x–xviii
Mare Island Naval shipyard, 40–41, 55–56
Maryland, 149
Massachusetts, 44, 48
Mass production, 15
Material culture, 16–20, 149–51
Material witness, 18–19
McGregor Range, 110–15, 123
Medium-range ballistic missile (MRBM), 74–75
Menlo Park Laboratory, 22–23
MET. *See* Military Effects Test
Metal detection, 13–14
Michigan, 41, 59, 63, 66
Middle Cold War (1958–1975): civil defense sites, 51–55, 59–60; command and control sites of, 56–58; continental defense sites, 51–55; production sites and, 55–56; revolution, 51–60
Military, 36; housing, 44–45, 67, 90; technology, 1, 6; wooden structures, 30–32, *31*
Military Effects Test (MET), 95
Mining, uranium, xvi, 34–37, 150
Minnesota, 65–66
Minuteman missiles, 51, 54, 121–22, *122*, 135
MIRV. *See* Multiple independently targetable reentry vehicle
Missiles, 3, 61; ALCM and GLCM and, 64; Cape Canaveral's tested, 116; deployments of, 6, 29, 54; determining flight orientations of, 120; minuteman, 51, 54, 121–22, *122*, 135; SLBM, 54–55; Titan, 51; training for system and force, 111–12, 115; USSR and threat of, 51. *See also* Nike Ajax missiles; Nike Hercules missiles
Missile Site Control Building, *8*
Missile sites, 138–39; Crisis de Octubre, 75; international, 6, 29; Nike Ajax, 29; Nike Hercules international, 6, 29; Nike SAM batteries and Nike Ajax, 46–47, *47*; Soviet, 74–81
Missouri, 36, 52, 54
Modern conflict archaeology: in Cold War study frameworks, 9, 11, 14–16; definition and development of, 14–16; focus of industrialized warfare in, 15; postmodern/post-processual theory in, 15
Moleholes, 52, *52*
Montana, 54, 66
Mound Laboratory, 34
Mount Pony, 57
Mount Weather, 57
MRBM. *See* Medium-range ballistic missile
MRI. *See* Magnetic resonance imaging
Multiple independently targetable reentry vehicle (MIRV), 55
Mushroom cloud, 70–71, *71*
Mutual assured destruction (MAD), 60

Nagasaki, 29–30
NARA. *See* National Archives and Records Administration
NASA. *See* National Aeronautics and Space Administration
National Aeronautics and Space Administration (NASA), 116
National Archives and Records Administration (NARA), 131
National Fallout Shelter Survey, 60
National Historical Landmarks: B Reactor facility, 35; Mare Island Naval shipyard as, 40–41; Naval service craft as, 41; PSNS granted status as, 56; Trinity Site as, 136; USS Nautilus as, 41
National Park Service (NPS), 26

National Register of Historic Places (NRHP), 26–27, 144; Desert Range, 114; Nike Site Summit, 138; Peace Camp 105
National Security Act, 30
National Stockpile Sites, 47–48
Nautilus, USS, 39–40
Navajo sovereign lands, 35–36
Naval shipyards, 40
Nebraska, 51, 53–54, 63
Nerve gas (sarin gas), 39, *40*
Nevada Proving Grounds, 85, 88
Nevada Test Site (NTS), 32; America's Space Race and NRDS at, 106–10; atomic bomb testing at, 133, *134*; map of principal areas at, *86, 87*; Nevada Proving Grounds known as, 85, 88; nuclear weapons testing at, 23–24, 85–110; Peace Camp archaeology, 100–105
New Hampshire, 40, 44
New Jersey, 41
New London Naval Submarine Base, 39–40
New Mexico, 30, *31*, 35, 41, 47, 54, 81–85, 110–15, 133, 136
New York, 41, 44, 48, 54, 65–66
Newport News Shipbuilding, 56
Nike Ajax missiles, *3*, 29, 46–47, *47*
Nike Hercules missiles: deployments of, 29; HAER and oral reports of, 139; sites, 6, 29, 138–39; U.S. defensive posture and, 148.
Nike Missile Battalion site, *149*
Nike SAM batteries, 46–47, *47*, 123
Nike Site Summit, 138–39, *140–41*
NORAD. *See* North American Aerospace Defense Command system
North American Aerospace Defense Command (NORAD) system, *42*, 57
North American landscape, 6; Cold War creation and, 28–67, 152; nuclear warhead missiles and, 48, 50, 54–55, 60, 64; periods of development in, 9, 28–67
North Bay (NORAD), 57
North Dakota, 8, 61, *62*
NPS. *See* National Park Service

NRDS. *See* Nuclear Rocket Development Station
NRHP. *See* National Register of Historic Places
NTS. *See* Nevada Test Site
Nuclear explosions, xvi, 82–83, 98
Nuclear reactors, *109*, 109–10
Nuclear Rocket Development Station (NRDS), *86, 87*; America's Space Race and NTS, 106–10; DRI archaeological investigations at, 106–10; HAER and radiological protection methods at, 128, *129*; Phoebus engines and rail transport for, 108–9, *109*; Project Rover and development of, 106–8, *107*
Nuclear weapons, 23–24, 47–48, 85–110; testing, 93

Oak Ridge National Laboratory (ORNL), 34–35
Office of Civil Defense (OCD), 60
Ohio, 34, 36
Oklahoma, 54, 63
Operational Storage Site (OSS), 48
Operation Big Shot, 133, *134*
Operation Crossroads, 32
Operation Dominic, 81–82
Operation Plumbbob, 89–90, 95, 97–98
Operation Ranger, 93–94, 96–97
Operation Teapot, 89, 93–95, *94*
Oral history, 131
Oregon, 41
ORNL. *See* Oak Ridge National Laboratory
OSS. *See* Operational Storage Site

Pacific Proving Grounds (PPG), 32, 96
Paducah Gaseous Diffusion Plant, 36–37
Pagoda Hill, 104–5, *105*
Pantex Plant, 39, 61, 65, *66*
PAR. *See* Perimeter Acquisition Radar
PARCS. *See* Perimeter Acquisition Radar Attack Characterization System
Past. *See* Contemporary past; Material past
Pax Americana, 2–3

Peace Camp, 150; antinuclear protest areas in, 101–5; archaeological survey site findings, 101–5; archaeology studies at NTS, 100–105; cattle guard trespassing enforcements at, 103–5; detention structures, 105; graffiti at Tunnel of Love, 103, *103*; groups holding antinuclear protests at, 100–102; landscape of NTS, 100; as meeting criteria for NRHP, 105; North American Cold War, 65, 66; Pagoda Hill as ceremonial area for, 105, *105*; Red Lady sculpture, *104*, 105; Shadow Children sculpture at, 102, *102*
Pennsylvania, 56
Perforated steel (Marston matting) planking, 79, 155n6
Perimeter Acquisition Radar (PAR), 61, *62*
Perimeter Acquisition Radar Attack Characterization System (PARCS), 61–62
Permanent System radar stations, 41–42, *42*
Phoebus engines, 108–9, *109*
Physical hazards, 127–30
Plutonium, 35, 37, *38*
Polonium, 34
Portsmouth Gaseous Diffusion Plant, 36
Portsmouth Naval shipyard, 40
PPG. *See* Pacific Proving Grounds
Prinz Eugen, 69
Priscilla shot, 95, 97–98
Production sites: early Cold War atomic weapon, 30–41; late Cold War cruise missile, 64–65; submarine, 55–56
Project ELF, 62–63
Project Rover, 106–8, *107*, 110
Protests, 6, 100–102
Proving grounds, 31–33, 85, 88, 96, 111, 116
Puget Sound Naval Shipyard (PSNS), 56

Q Areas, 48

Racism, environmental, xvi, 150
Radar stations, 41–43, *42–43*, 67, 127
Radiation hazards, 71, 92, 127–29, 140

Radio-controlled aerial target (RCAT), 111, 115
RAF. *See* Royal Air Force Station Flyingdales
Raven Rock Mountain Complex, 56–57
RCAT. *See* Radio-controlled aerial target
Reactor Maintenance and Disassembly (R-MAD), 108, *108*
Readiness Crew Buildings, moleholes of, 52, *52*
Red Lady sculpture (Nevada Test Site Peace Camp), *104*, 105
"Red Menace," 2–3
Republic of Marshall Islands, 9, 68–74, *71*, 127–28
Research and development sites, 30–34
Resolution, Late Cold War, 60–67
RMA. *See* Rocky Mountain Arsenal
R-MAD. *See* Reactor Maintenance and Disassembly
Rocky Flats Nuclear Weapons Plant, 35, 37, *38*, 65–66
Rocky Mountain Arsenal (RMA), 39
Royal Air Force Station Flyingdales, 6
Royal Commission on Historical Monuments of England (English Heritage), 26–27

SAC. *See* Strategic Air Command
Safety, 127–30
Sagua La Grande, 76, *77*
SAM. *See* Surface-to-air missile
San Cristobal, Cuba, 77–79, *78*, *80*
Sandia Laboratory, 31–32
Santa Cruz de los Pinos (San Cristobal, Cuba), 77–79, *78*, *80*
Saratoga, USS (CV-3), 70; wreckage, 23
Sarin gas (nerve gas), 39, *40*
Savannah River Plant (SRP), 37
Scorpion, USS, 127
SCRU. *See* Submerged Cultural Resource Unit
Sculptures, 102, *102*, *104*, 105

Secrecy, 19, 142; archaeological access and, 130–33; Cold War and, 11, 59–60
Sentry building (Nike Site Summit), 139, *140–41*
Shadow Children sculpture (Nevada Test Site Peace Camp), 102, *102*
Ships, 23, 40–41, 55–56, 69–71, *71*, 127
Sites. *See* Cold War sites
Sitiecito (Cuba), 75–76
Skate, USS, 40
Skipjack, USS, 56
Skysweeper, 45–46, *46*, 111, 114–15
SLBM. *See* Submarine-launched ballistic missile
Snezhok exercises, 92
Sound Surveillance System (SOSUS), 43–44
South Carolina, 37, 55, 66
South Dakota, 48, 54, 63
Soviet missile sites, Cuba, 74–81
Soviet Union, 28. *See also* Union of Soviet Socialist Republics
Space Race, 115–16
Sputnik, 50
SRMSC. *See* Stanley R. Mickelsen Safeguard Complex
SRP. *See* Savannah River Plant
Stanley R. Mickelsen Safeguard Complex (SRMSC), 8, 61–62
Stations. *See* Camera stations; Radar stations
Strategic Air Command (SAC), 30, 48
Submarine-launched ballistic missile (SLBM), 54–55
Submarines: archaeology of, 127; deployments of, 55; naval shipyards building, 40; production sites of, 55–56; project ELF for communication with, 62–63; USS *George Washington*, 55; USS *Nautilus* as first nuclear, 39–40; USS *Scorpion*, 127; USS *Skate*, 40; USS *Skipjack*, 56; USS *Thresher*, 127
Submerged Cultural Resource Unit (SCRU), 69–70, 72

Surface-to-air missile (SAM), 46–47, *47*, 64, 110–11, 123
Surveys, 60; archaeological, 88–92, 101–5, 113–14; Bikini Atoll research of post-, 73–74; Cape Canaveral, 118–19, 122, *123*; Santa Cruz de los Pinos metal detector, 78–79

Tactical Air Command (TAC), 30
Technoscience, 4
TEL. *See* Transporter erector launcher
Tennessee, 34–35
Texas, 39, 47, 54, 65–66
Texas Towers radar systems, 44
Thermonuclear fusion devices. *See* H-bombs
The Traveler's Guide to Nuclear Weapons: A Journey through America's Cold War Battlefields, 135
Thresher, USS, 127
Titan missiles, 51
TNT. *See* Trinitrotoluene
Tourism, xviii, 71–72, 142; antinuclear activism and, 134–35; archaeology and, 132–37; dark, 136–37; as international phenomenon, 135–36; Trinity Site, 133, 136
Training: AEC atomic operations, 89–90; force missiles and system, 111–12, 115; McGregor Range air defense, 111, 115; nuclear warfare, 87–92
Training camps, 92
Trans-Canada Highway Act of 1949, 50
Transmission Line Aircraft Simulator (ATLAS), 81–85
Transporter erector launcher (TEL), 64
Trespassing (Nevada Test Site), 103–5
Trestle: aerial view of, 81–82; aircraft response and EMP testing at, 81–84; as archaeology of science study, 84–85; EMP testing at, 81–84; wooden bolt system, 83, *84*
TRESTLE: The Landmark of the Cold War (documentary), 85

Trinitrotoluene (TNT), 155n3
Trinity Site, 133, 136
Truman, Harry, 36, 56
Tunnel of Love (Nevada Test Site Peace Camp), 103, *103*

U.K. *See* United Kingdom
UNESCO World Heritage site, 74
Union of Soviet Socialist Republics (USSR): AK-47 assault rifle as symbol for, 14–15; arms race, 4; concerns over military strength of, 36; Cuba and deployment of R-12 Dvina MRBM by, 74–75; missile threat of, 51; race for space, 4–5; radiation exposure at Exercise Snezhok of, 92; Sputnik satellite and, 50; successful test of atomic bomb and, 36;
United Kingdom (U.K.), 6, 18, 25–26, 135–36
United States (U.S.): arms race competition between USSR and, 4; emergence as global superpower, 1–2; military technology and, 1, 6; Nike Hercules missiles and defensive posture of, 148; policies of secrecy in, 130–32; race for space between USSR and, 4–5; tension between Russia and, xv; USSR and fearsome heritage of, xvi–xvii; weapons of mass destruction determent and, xv–xvi
University of California Radiation Laboratory, 32
Uranium, 36–37, 67
Uranium mining, xvi, 34–37, 150
US. *See* United States
USSR. *See* Union of Soviet Socialist Republics

Vandenberg Air Force Base (AFB), 33–34, 53, 110
Veterans, 137–41
Virginia, 44, *47*, 56

Warsaw Pact, 2–3
Washington, 35, 41, 44, *46*, 48, *53*, 54–56, 65–66
Weapons of mass destruction, 151; political and economic instability leading to, xvi–xvii; Third World country involvement with, xvi, 2; US and determent for, xv–xvi; USSR and, 2
Weldon Spring Uranium Feed Materials Plant, 36–37
West Germany, 6, 29, 92
Wherry, Kenneth S., 45, 67
White Sands Proving Ground, 33, 111
Wisconsin, 62–63, 66
World War Two, 1–2, 35, 38–39
Wullenwebers (Circularly Disposed Antenna Arrays), 6
Wyoming, 36, 53

Yakima (Washington) Firing Center, *46*
Yucca Flat, 88, 133

Todd A. Hanson is an anthropologist at Los Alamos National Laboratory in New Mexico. He is the author of numerous articles and book chapters on the archaeology, ethnohistory, and material culture of the Cold War.

THE AMERICAN EXPERIENCE IN ARCHAEOLOGICAL PERSPECTIVE

Edited by Michael S. Nassaney

The Archaeology of Collective Action, by Dean J. Saitta (2007)
The Archaeology of Institutional Confinement, by Eleanor Conlin Casella (2007)
The Archaeology of Race and Racialization in Historic America, by Charles E. Orser Jr. (2007)
The Archaeology of North American Farmsteads, by Mark D. Groover (2008)
The Archaeology of Alcohol and Drinking, by Frederick H. Smith (2008)
The Archaeology of American Labor and Working-Class Life, by Paul A. Shackel (2009; first paperback edition, 2011)
The Archaeology of Clothing and Bodily Adornment in Colonial America, by Diana DiPaolo Loren (2010; first paperback edition, 2011)
The Archaeology of American Capitalism, by Christopher N. Matthews (2010; first paperback edition, 2012)
The Archaeology of Forts and Battlefields, by David R. Starbuck (2011; first paperback edition, 2012)
The Archaeology of Consumer Culture, by Paul R. Mullins (2011; first paperback edition, 2012)
The Archaeology of Antislavery Resistance, by Terrance M. Weik (2012; first paperback edition, 2013)
The Archaeology of Citizenship, by Stacey Lynn Camp (2013; first paperback edition, 2019)
The Archaeology of American Cities, by Nan A. Rothschild and Diana diZerega Wall (2014; first paperback edition, 2015)
The Archaeology of American Cemeteries and Gravemarkers, by Sherene Baugher and Richard F. Veit (2014; first paperback edition, 2015)
The Archaeology of Smoking and Tobacco, by Georgia L. Fox (2015; first paperback edition, 2016)
The Archaeology of Gender in Historic America, by Deborah L. Rotman (2015; first paperback edition, 2018)
The Archaeology of the North American Fur Trade, by Michael S. Nassaney (2015; first paperback edition, 2017)
The Archaeology of the Cold War, by Todd A. Hanson (2016; first paperback edition, 2019)
The Archaeology of American Mining, by Paul J. White (2017)
The Archaeology of Utopian and Intentional Communities, by Stacy C. Kozakavich (2017)
The Archaeology of American Childhood and Adolescence, by Jane Eva Baxter (2019)
The Archaeology of Northern Slavery and Freedom, by James A. Delle (2019)

The Archaeology of Prostitution and Clandestine Pursuits, by Rebecca Yamin and
    Donna J. Seifert (2019)
The Archaeology of Southeastern Native American Landscapes of the Colonial Era,
    by Charles R. Cobb (2019)

www.ingramcontent.com/pod-product-compliance
Lightning Source LLC
Chambersburg PA
CBHW031437160426
43195CB00010BB/763